FAMILY MATTERS
Perspectives on the Family and Social Policy

Other Pergamon Titles of Interest

Troubled Children/Troubled Systems
Steven J. Apter

Social Learning Practice in Residential Child Care
Barrie J. Brown & Marilyn Christie

Health, Behavior and the Community: An Ecological Perspective
Ralph Catalano

Evaluation Strategies in Criminal Justice
William S. Davidson, *et al.*

Sexually Abused Children and their Families
Patricia Beezley Mrazek & C. Henry Kempe

Behavioral Research and Government Policy
David Meister

The Cry for Help: and the Professional Response
Jack Kahn & Elspeth Earle

A Related Pergamon Journal

CHILD ABUSE & NEGLECT*
THE INTERNATIONAL JOURNAL

The Official Journal of the International Society
for Prevention of Child Abuse and Neglect

Editor-in-Chief
C. Henry Kempe, University of Colorado Medical Center, Denver, USA

Child Abuse & Neglect provides an international, multi-disciplinary forum on
the prevention and treatment of child abuse and neglect, including sexual abuse.
The scope also extends further to all those aspects of life which either favour or
hinder optimal family bonding.

Contributors are from the fields of social work, nursing, medicine, psychology
and psychiatry, law, police, legislators, educators, and anthropologists as well
as concerned lay individuals and child oriented organizations.

*Free specimen copy gladly supplied on request.

FAMILY MATTERS
Perspectives on the Family and Social Policy

PROCEEDINGS OF THE SYMPOSIUM ON PRIORITY FOR THE FAMILY
HELD AT THE ROYAL SOCIETY OF MEDICINE, LONDON, NOVEMBER 3-5, 1981

Edited by

ALFRED WHITE FRANKLIN

PUBLISHED ON BEHALF OF THE ROYAL SOCIETY OF MEDICINE

PERGAMON PRESS
OXFORD · NEW YORK · TORONTO · SYDNEY · PARIS · FRANKFURT

U.K.	Pergamon Press Ltd., Headington Hill Hall, Oxford OX3 0BW, England
U.S.A.	Pergamon Press Inc., Maxwell House, Fairview Park, Elmsford, New York 10523, U.S.A.
CANADA	Pergamon Press Canada Ltd., Suite 104, 150 Consumers Rd., Willowdale, Ontario M2J 1P9, Canada
AUSTRALIA	Pergamon Press (Aust.) Pty. Ltd., P.O. Box 544, Potts Point, N.S.W. 2011, Australia
FRANCE	Pergamon Press SARL, 24 rue des Ecoles, 75240 Paris, Cedex 05, France
FEDERAL REPUBLIC OF GERMANY	Pergamon Press GmbH, Hammerweg 6, D-6242 Kronberg-Taunus, Federal Republic of Germany

First edition 1983

Library of Congress Cataloging in Publication Data
Symposium on Priority for the Family (1981: London, England)
Family matters.
1. Family—Great Britain—Congresses. 2. Family policy—Great Britain—Congresses. I. Franklin, Alfred White, 1905-. II. Royal Society of Medicine (Great Britain) III. Title.
HQ614.S9   1981   306.8'5'0941   82-15011

British Library Cataloguing in Publication Data
Symposium on Priority for the Family *(1981: London)*
Family matters.
1. Family—Great Britain
I Title II. Franklin, Alfred White
III. Royal Society of Medicine
306.8'0941   HQ614
ISBN 0-08-028928-2

In order to make this volume available as economically and as rapidly as possible the typescript has been reproduced in its original form. This method unfortunately has its typographical limitations but it is hoped that they in no way distract the reader.

Printed in Great Britain by A. Wheaton & Co. Ltd., Exeter

Acknowledgements

Discussion meetings must be based on careful planning and on the wise selection of congenial members. During 1980 a small steering committee was formed to define the objective and to select possible participants. This committee consisted of Joan Cooper, Joan Court, Alfred White Franklin, Moyna Gilbertson, Mia Kellmer Pringle and Malcolm Wicks. The influence and the support of the Study Commission on the Family will be apparent to all. Finally the Symposium on Priority for the Family was held at The Royal Society of Medicine, London, from Tuesday November 3 to Thursday November 5, 1981 through the kindness of the Officers and Council of the Open Section. Without this backing the meetings could not have taken place. But we enjoyed much more than the business arrangements. Sir John Stallworthy, the President of the Society, Dame Anne Bryans, the President of the Open Section and Mr R. T. Hewitt, the Executive Director of the Society gave us their enthusiastic support. Miss Muriel Mitchell, the Conference Secretary was as generous with her time as we have all learned to expect. Judge Helge Rostad of the Supreme Court of Oslo has kindly provided a copy of the Ombud Bill presented to the Norwegian Parliament which is reproduced in English in the Appendix.

As Editor I wish to record my gratitude to the Participants and Discussants who tolerated my authoritarian manner with exemplary patience. Finally I thank Pergamon Press for their technical help in producing this book and Sheila Holland for typing the text.

AWF

Contents

List of Contributors

Hugh Bevan, LL.M., Barrister, Professor of Law (specializing in Child Law), University of Hull.

Peter Bottomley, Member of Parliament for Greenwich, Woolwich West (Conservative). MA (Cambridge). Chairman, Family Forum. Peter Bottomley founded Family Forum to bring together voluntary organisations concerned with family policy. During his seven years (since 1975) in Parliament he has been promoting the family perspective on social and economic policy in addition to emphasising the importance of the family life cycle as the main contribution of family policy.

Jonathan Bradshaw, BSS., M.A., D.Phil., Professor and Director of the Social Policy Research Unit, University of York.

Muriel Mitcheson Brown, Ph.D., B.A., D.S.A., Lecturer in Social Administration at the London School of Economics and Political Science and Member of the DHSS/SSRC Joint Working Party on Transmitted Deprivation.

Madeleine Colvin, Barrister, employed at the Children's Legal Centre, an organis-ation concerned with the laws affecting children and young people.

Joan D. Cooper, C.B., B.A., Hon. Research Fellow, University of Sussex. Formerly Chief Inspector, Home Office Children's Department and later Director, Social Work Service, D.H.S.S.

Joan Court B.A. Hons (Cantab) M.S.W., S.R.N., S.C.M. Independent Social Worker (Tria

Elsa Dicks, J.P., M.A., Co-ordinator of the Voluntary Organisations Liaison Council for the under fives (VOLCUF).

Sue Dowling, M.B., B.S., M.Sc. (Social Medicine), M.F.C.M., Lecturer in Community Medicine, University of Bristol. Director of the C.P.A.G./D.H.S.S. Study — 'Reaching the Consumer in the antenatal and Pre-school Child Health Services'. Formerly Senior Medical Research Officer to 'Child Health and Education in the seventies' (the national 5 year follow-up of the 1970 British Birth Cohort).

The Rev. Canon G. R. Dunstan, M.A., D.D. (Hon.), F.S.A., F. D. Maurice Professor of Moral & Social Theology, King's College, London. A Director of the King's College Centre of Law, Medicine & Ethics.

Alfred White Franklin, M.A., M.B., F.R.C.P, Consulting Paediatrician to Saint Bartholomew's Hospital, President, International Society for the Prevention of Child Abuse and Neglect (ISPCAN).

Michael D. A. Freeman, LL.D., Reader in English Law, University College, London.

Moyna P. Gilbertson, M.S.C.P., Chief Executive Officer, Association for Spina Bifida and Hydrocephalus (a national charity). Hon. Sec. the Open Section, Royal Society of Medicine.

Esther N. Goody, Ph. D. Camb. (Social Anthropology). Lecturer in Social Anthropology University of Cambridge, Member of the D.H.S.S./S.S.R.C. Joint Working Party on Transmitted Deprivation. Research in West African family systems, especially marriage, divorce and fostering led to comparative research into how ethnic groups adapt to living in/with other cultures and to interest in the ability of statutory services to respond appropriately to ethnic and sub-cultural differences.

Charles Douglas Grieve, General Secretary, Tobacco Workers' Union, Member of the T.U.C. General Council.

Fae Hall, M.A., D. Phil. (Oxon.), Research Fellow, Family Research Unit, The London Hospital Medical College.

Clyte Hampton, B.Sc., Advisory Teacher (Health Education) I.L.E.A. Part Author of Schools Council Health Education Project (5-13).

Jeff Henderson, Lecturer in Sociology and Fellow of the Centre of Urban Studies and Urban Planning, University of Hong Kong.

Pam Hutchence, Housing Officer, Harding Housing Association.

Valerie Karn, B.A. (Oxon.), Ph.D. (Birmingham), Senior Lecturer in Social Policy, Centre for Urban and Regional Studies, University of Birmingham.

Sue Kruk, B.A., Dip. Social Administration, Research Worker, Family Research Unit, The London Hospital Medical College.

Sir Edmund Leach, B.A. (Cantab.) Ph.D. (Lond., L.S.E.), F.B.A., Professor Emeritus of Social Anthropology, University of Cambridge, Fellow (Former Provost) of King's College, Cambridge. Reith Lectures 1967 (published as 'A Runaway World') commented on the role of the family in contemporary Britain.

Tom Luce, Local Authority Social Services Division, D.H.S.S.

Peter Moss, M.A., B.Phil., Research Officer, Thomas Coram Research Unit.

John Park, B.A., M.I.H., Director of Housing, London Borough of Greenwich. Sometime member of the Housing Services Advisory Group.

Mia Kellmer Pringle, Ph.D., D.Sc., C.B.E., Consultant to U.N.I.C.E.F. (Europe). Founder-Director, National Children's Bureau; and First Co-director, National Child Development Study (1958).

Lesley Rimmer, Research Officer, Study Commission on the Family.

Clifton Robinson, O.B.E., J.P., B.A., Dip. Ed., M.Brit.Psy.Soc., Deputy Chairman, Commission for Racial Equality.

Lionel Swift, Q.C.

Sir John Stallworthy, F.R.C.S., F.R.C.O.G., President, Royal Society of Medicine.

Don Venvell, B.A., Assistant Education Officer (Support Services), I.L.E.A. health welfare and supplementary education needs of Inner London school children.

Malcolm Wicks, Research Director and Secretary of the Study Commission on the Family.

Stephen Wolkind, M.D., F.R.C. Psych., Senior Lecturer in Child Psychiatry, The London Hospital Medical College.

Introduction

ALFRED WHITE FRANKLIN

One assumption and two questions provided the basis for this symposium. They were put to the participants in the following words: If we agree that the family is the essential unit of society, is sufficient priority given to its needs and how can the several statutory and voluntary provisions for the family be better co-ordinated.

DEFINITION

For the limited purposes of the symposium discussions, families are defined as being made up of one or more adults caring within a household for one or more children from birth to the tenth birthday.

The needs and the importance of the aged, the adolescent, those handicapped in body and in mind, and the demands which their presence makes on family life are recognised and accepted without reservation. Nevertheless for the short-term three day period of discussion to be useful, the range had to be limited. The thinking behind the choice of this particular age group was that the care needed for the optimal growth and development of that new member of our society, the dependent child, is best given, perhaps can only be given, within a family. Love and commitment are hard to find outside. The need for care begins at the time of conception. Furthermore the most sensitive periods for development seem to be fetal life, infancy and early childhood. While these ideas apply to our Western society, no claim is made that they are either universal or permanent for *Homo sapiens*.

GLOBAL THINKING

Society makes many statutory provisions to assist families but they are offered in fragmented and unco-ordinated ways, account being seldom taken of the needs of the family as a whole. Indeed, the best interests of one member can sometimes be diametrically opposed to the best interests of another or of the family itself. Global thinking and planning are necessary because although a child can be conceived of as a unit of population, an economic unit, an educational unit or a legal unit, a dependent child can never actually be a biological unit either in body or mind. Nor can the family operate as an isolated unit.

THE NETWORK

Sir Edmund Leach elaborates this point in Chapter 1, stressing the essential
nature of the supporting network. The main purpose of the symposium was to
examine how the network might be strengthened and how any stresses which, albeit
inadvertently, society imposes on the family might be lightened. These themes were
followed into the various problems of health, housing, education, fiscal policy,
the law and the unforeseen impact of legislation on family life. If anything has
gone wrong, how can it be put right? What positive efforts can be encouraged to
counter and overcome the obstacles that both bureaucracy and human nature place in
the way of co-operation between Government Departments, Agencies statutory and
voluntary, differently labelled professionals and the man and woman in the street.

THE 'ORDINARY' FAMILY

We accomplish much by concentrating on families with recognised difficulties for
example by caring for handicapped children, but we still think and act as if
'ordinary' families can survive undamaged without any special consideration in our
highly complicated society with its mixture of cultures. The toll of family breakdown measured by divorce and single parent families and of abused and neglected
children suggests that this is far from the truth. The plan to hold this symposium
and to spread its deliberations beyond the necessarily few participants to the
public at large stemmed in my mind from my belief as a paediatrician that the plight
of abusing and neglecting families might be thereby improved. Environmental
factors and especially socio-economic stress, bad housing conditions, poverty, unemployment, the frustrations of having no power to choose, all contribute to this
form of family breakdown, although it cuts across all social divisions and
boundaries. There are no simple explanations nor easy remedies. We do have an
elaborate country-wide system which seeks to prevent vulnerability and to support
the vulnerable. Excellent as this is in intention and valuable as it is in
execution, those with the responsibility for carrying it out find themselves wanting solutions which they cannot directly influence. For example, the social
worker's request for adequate housing for a young single girl when sent home from
the maternity hospital with her new baby may or may not be regarded as important by
the housing officer. His supply of housing stock in its turn depends on the
application of housing policy over which he has no control. Collaboration at local
level in which families play their part, now often missing, needs encouragement at
central and governmental level. Greater sensitivity to family stress must be
combined with awarding priority to the family through which the welfare of the next
generation can be safeguarded.

We recognise the enemies of family life. The extent to which they may be disarmed
is the true measure of our concern as a society. What follows in this book explores
the problems. The reader may discern in our discussions the seeds of some
solutions.

CHAPTER 1

Are there Alternatives to the Family?

EDMUND LEACH

Two propositions were suggested as a basis for the discussion and I shall look at both with some scepticisim.

1. 'The family is still the essential unit of our society'

2. 'Families, for this Symposium, are defined as consisting of one or more adults caring for one or more children from birth to the tenth birthday'

In the first of these propositions the word 'our' suggests that perhaps there might be some other kind of society where this was not the case. The second seems highly contrived to say the least; formally it would include institutions such as Dr Barnardo's Homes as 'families', though I dare say that this is not what was intended.

THE CONCEPT OF FAMILY

The anthropologists of the late nineteenth century, who were all recruited from the affluent classes, were quite satisfied that, despite the suffering which they could see all around them, if they cared to look, they lived in the best of all possible societies which represented the ultimate peak of human progress. They did not know very much about any other kind of society but they imagined a variety of hypothetical, and therefore inferior, alternative social systems by inventing models contrasted with that which they knew from direct experience.

The Christian capitalist society into which they had been born was constructed around monogamous marriage and strict sexual restraint, at any rate for women, together with the dogma that the husband was the patriarchal, authoritarian head of the family. This 'perfected' domestic system was supposed to be the culmination of a progression through a sequence of more primitive, more barbaric, stages of social organisation.

First there had been a state of sexual promiscuity in which children were reared by their mothers simply because their fathers could not be identified.

After that notions of incest began to operate (for no obvious reasons) and the savage bands of promiscuous males formed themselves into exogamous groups which obtained their sexual mates by capture from other like groups.

3

The next stage was a fantasy Land of the Amazons. The roles of the sexes were
reversed. Women came to dominate men both sexually and politically. The domestic
family was now a polyandrous institution in which authority lay in the hands of
women ('matriarchy') and political office was transmitted from mother to daughter
('matrilineal descent': misinterpreted!).

With the development of ideas of property male dominance asserted itself.
Patriarchy and patrilineal inheritance replaced matriarchy and matriliny. Polygyny
replaced polyandry.

Finally, under the influence of Christian morality, the virtues of the monogamous
male dominated, family were fully recognised.

Marx and Engels (1940) read this stuff and were suitably impressed. But whereas
the original authors of these theories, McLennan (1970) in Britain and Morgan
(1964) in the United States in particular, believed that their model represented
social progress, Marx and Engels read it as a parable of decline from a Golden Age
of Primitive Communism in which there was no private property and no exploitation
either of women by men or of children by parents.

Marx and Engels were interested in these problems only as matters of theory.
They themselves lived a comfortable bourgeois existence employing domestic servants
and exploiting their wives and children without compunction, but the zealots who
later tried to put Marxist ideas into practice took their theories quite literally.

It is for this reason, as the indirect heritage of Morgan, Marx and Engels, that,
for a while, Israeli Kibbutzim and Maoist Chinese communes denied the existence of
any 'natural' dependency of children on parents and endeavoured to create arti-
ficial institutions in which children were raised in bisexual collectives not
wholly unlike the Dr Barnardo's Homes to which I referred earlier.

These experiments do not seem to have worked very well. This is not surprising
since the model of primitive communist society from which they derive is quite
unlike any society which anthropologists have ever encountered outside the world
of fantasy. On the other hand anthropological research over the past 80 years has
demonstrated very clearly that real human societies are extremely varied. Since
children are always dependent on adults, 'families', in the very loose sense of my
opening formula, are always present in one form or another but their characteristics are often radically different from the norms which are likely to be taken
for granted by most people.

This does not imply that forms of the family which appear strange should be
objects for emulation though it might be useful if those who play a professional
role in our child care and family welfare services had some awareness of the range
of human variability in this area. Otherwise the 'unusual' is liable to be
interpreted as 'abnormal' in a pathological sense. But it would be absurd to
expect that non-anthropologists should know very much about these matters.

So let it suffice that we now know that human children can be reared successfully
in a great variety of domestic 'family' situations. If we consider the whole
human species then the type of 'family' which most people would consider to be
normal is rather unusual. And even here in Britain the empirical facts are very
much more varied than many people imagine.

Some of these variations have a long history and it is to these historical
materials that I shall be devoting most of my attention. I do not intend to give
you a kind of Cook's Tour of World Ethnography.

HISTORY

  Etymology does not, as a rule, throw much light on social facts but in this case
it is not without interest. Our word 'family' comes direct from Latin *familia*.
The original Roman *familia* was a domestic group rather than a simple kin-group. It
included all members of the household, many of whom were in the status of slave.
Indeed the basic Roman idea was not one of kinship at all. *Familia* derives from
familus meaning 'servant'. The male head of the *familia* had absolute authority
over all its members of the household but although, in this role, he was called the
pater familias, 'the father of the family', those who were related to him by blood
or marriage were usually a minority of the total group.

  The word family in sixteenth century English had a similar extensive meaning. In
the Bible, for example, it is used for a large corporation as an alternative for
the words 'house' and 'tribe'. In some of these contexts anthropologists would now
write 'lineage' but Biblical 'families' may include non-kinsmen. Thus a man's
'house' 'might consist of his mother, his wives and the wives' children, his con-
cubines and their children, sons-in-law and daughters-in-law and their offspring,
illegitimate sons, dependants and aliens, and slaves of both sexes' (Hastings 1909).

  In nineteenth century England the 'families' of estate owning country gentlemen
were rather similar. The household consisted of a small army of domestic servants,
who received board and lodging but negligible pay, plus the wife and children of
the male head of the family. In many situations this minor potentate would blandly
declare that his domestic servants were all 'part of the family'.

  The 'families' of less affluent persons were, of course, much smaller. But the
households of even quite modest craftsmen might include apprentices who were
treated very like adopted sons and often ended up as sons-in-law.

  The position in the labouring class, which formed the largest section of the
population, was rather different but even there the family structure was not of the
simple Pa, Ma and the Baby type which seems to have become the happy family model
for much contemporary thinking.

  Prior to the late nineteenth century most labourers worked on the land. They
lived in hovels owned by the local squire; they received near starvation wages.
Several important generalisations follow:

1. The fact that many of the unmarried girls of the labouring class were employed
   as domestic servants in the households of the squire and the vicar was of
   great economic importance for the labourers concerned.

2. There was a continuous drift away from the country villages into the cities.
   This came about partly by young men joining the army and partly by their just
   going off as individuals to take a chance. Although some such individuals
   later came back home there was no general movement from the cities to the
   countryside. This was because:

   a) village labourer living standards were so low;

   b) the squire owned all the available housing. (The only villagers with their
      own freeholds were the pub keepers and the craftsmen such as wheelwrights
      and blacksmiths).

3. Because ordinary village labourers moved around so little they mostly married
   girls nearby either from the same or a next door village.

4. This set of circumstances meant that most of the labourers living in a
village at any one time were quite closely related to one another as biological kin.

This was an important fact. Note that I am not saying that in English villages
of 150 years ago all relationships were perceived as kinship relationships — as
often happens in situations observed by anthropologists. On the contrary, in the
English system the recognition of kinship is optional. Immediate neighbours who
are biological first cousins or even siblings are quite often not on speaking
terms. But the situation in the traditional British village, which still prevails
to a quite surprising extent, was that almost every individual had a number of
known kin living nearby and that some of those kin would be recognised. This
meant that everyone had close neighbours who could be called in to help in times
of special hardship.

This was a matter of especial importance for married women with young children.
Although the general conditions of life were quite terrible, most women had a
sister or a sister-in-law or an aunt or a cousin living within a few hundred yards
who could be relied upon to help with the children in times of real crisis.

Except in a few worn out slum areas this pattern is very seldom encountered in
modern urban society. We all have neighbours but very often they do not rate
among our acquaintances. In any case the obligations of a neighbour are seldom
felt to be anything like as strong as the obligations of a recognised kinsman.

Village life in England has many material disadvantages, and this has been the
case for centuries. But few villagers with children have any need to feel lonely.
And that is a very important fact. By contrast, life in a modern conurbation can
be very lonely indeed.

There are some internal contradictions in what I have just said which deserve
our closest attention. British middle class culture sets high value on individual
privacy. The sort of people who write to the newspapers are constantly making a
fuss because their privacy has been infringed by the media or in some other way.
And this is something deeply felt. Anthropologists mostly have middle class backgrounds and when they engage in fieldwork for the first time they often report
that this is one of the things that strikes them most forcibly: the lack of privacy
and the lack of any feeling among their informants that privacy is something that
ought to be respected. But privacy and loneliness go together. And modern parents
who need support from kin and near neighbours must be prepared to forego their
claims to privacy.

But I am running on too fast. Besides the use of 'family' to mean domestic
group in the Roman sense there are two other meanings of considerable antiquity.

Even in late mediaeval times the word could be used as an equivalent to the older
English term 'kindred' — the general collectivity of persons linked to the speaker
by descent from a common ancestor by either male or female links. This meaning
still survives. When kinsfolk assemble for a wedding or a funeral they are often
spoken of collectively as 'the family' even when the biological relationship is
quite remote.

The significance of such a grouping is very much tied in with property. People
who share a common, even if tenuous, interest in an ancestral estate or family
business, form large 'families' of this kind but where there is no hereditable
property the extended family dwindles in size. In most parts of our present
social system these 'kinship network' families are unimportant.

Finally of course there is the use of the word 'family' to denote the nuclear

family of parents and children. Although it is popularly supposed that this is
the 'basic' meaning of the term — what the word 'really means' — history shows
otherwise. The sense of 'family' as 'the group consisting of parents and their
children, whether living together or not' first appears in the literature only
towards the end of the seventeenth century. And the reasons for this seems very
plain. As communications improved and the growth of trade and industry led to
increasing mobility of labour, domestic groups tended to break up. Brothers and
sisters found themselves living in different counties instead of just down the
road or in the next village. 'Family' then came to denote the residual bond between parents and children. But where families of .this kind were split up
spatially the individual members could no longer support one another in the way
that had been possible when they were all close neighbours.

In more recent times, general literacy, an efficient postal service, and the
telephone have helped to maintain the cohesion of married siblings and their
parents even when the individuals concerned live far apart and even when they all
live in cities; but a sister or a mother who is living fifty miles away cannot
just drop in for five minutes to mind the baby.

FAMILIES AND DOMESTIC GROUPS

All along I have been putting stress on two themes. First the importance of
recognising the role of the 'family' as a domestic group rather than as a kinship
group and second on the need to appreciate that what matters is not whether all
members of this domestic family live together under one roof but whether they are
sufficiently close neighbours to be of practical help in times of domestic crisis.
Or, to put the general issue differently, you will be led into error if you
consistently think of the domestic family of parents and children as an isolated
'thing in itself', which needs care and support as a 'thing in itself'. The social
reality that needs our attention is the network of relationships which link together these micro-scale domestic families into larger groupings which are involved
in reciprocal obligations of mutual help.

If there is an adequate network of relationships with neighbours who are also
recognised kin then it is not so important whether the individual domestic unit is
a two parent family or a one parent family or simply, in terms of our rubric, 'one
or more adults looking after one or more children'.

Trouble starts when such networks are inadequate and the same individual parents
have to look after the same individual children without let up hour after hour, day
after day, week after week. The adults can't stand it and neither can the children.
My somewhat heretical view is that what is important about primary school for at
least 80 per cent of the children is not what they learn in matters of reading,
writing and arithmetic and so on, but that for a few hours each day, during term,
they get away from their parents.

FAMILIES OR NETWORKS?

But what can we do about it? The industrial conurbation has come to stay. Modern
technology makes it possible for an industrial society to consist of a mesh of
small villages rather than of lumps of massive conurbation but that is not how
things are ever going to be during my lifetime or yours.

Moreover industrial capitalism of the American sort, which we are expected to
emulate, sets great store by a high rate of labour mobility. So the pattern which
anthropologists encounter throughout the world (and which was the normal pattern
in Britain also until only a short while back) in which many close neighbours are
recognised kin is likely to become increasingly rare.

Are there any alternatives to such kin-neighbour networks? I must confess that I am highly sceptical about the effectiveness of social engineering exercises in which conurbations are broken up into small scale local communities (or neighbourhoods) on the assumption that, with adequate encouragement, the fact of being a neighbour can be made to carry the same sense of obligation as that which has traditionally been seen as the 'natural' concomitant of close kinship.

The difficulty arises because whereas kinship is thought of as a permanent 'fact of nature' which can be reinvoked after long intervals of dormancy, neighbourliness is a temporary accident. Moreover because our society is so drastically fragmented by barriers of social class, ethnic difference, differences of educational background, differences of religious sect, and so on, a sense of neighbourly responsibility seldom comes at all easily. The people next door cannot be treated 'as if they were kin' unless we genuinely feel that they are 'people like us' and, as a rule, we do not!

I also consider it a waste of time to attempt a frontal attack on the divisiveness of social class and race and religion. Caste is outlawed in the Indian constitution; the Soviet Union proclaims from time to time that it is a classless society. The evidence of detached observers indicates that in both these cases the divisions of society, though different from those encountered in this country, are just as marked and socially disjunctive as those which we know.

As a social anthropologist I do not find this at all strange. The mutually supportive 'we-groups' of human society seldom contain more than a few hundred individuals; usually they are much smaller than that. One way or another we always find ways of cutting up the population at large into small sub-sections of this scale. Perhaps this is regrettable but we might as well put up with it.

If ever the political reformers did succeed in devising a 'classless society' they would only find that the community had sorted itself out into 'we-groups' of some other kind. My advice to would-be reformers is 'Go along with what you have. Do not attempt to destroy the various facets of we-group solidarity, but exploit them and make them serve as a form of fictive kinship'.

In this context an institution which deserves attention is one which is found in Roman Catholic and Eastern Orthodox societies but is especially prominent in the countries which were formerly Spanish or Portuguese colonial territories. This is *compadrazgo* or 'coparenthood'. In detail it takes various forms but what is common to these variations is that when a child is given godparents a network of pseudo-kinship resembling that of affinity is set up, not only between the child and its own individual godparents but also between the real parents and the several godparents, and sometimes between all the children of the real parents and all the children of the godparents. These ties often involve lasting obligations on both sides and may, on occasion, be of great economic and political importance.

What needs to be noticed here is firstly that:

1. it is assumed that the bonds of 'kinship' are stronger and more enduring than the bonds of ordinary friendship or neighbourliness;

2. the model for the bond of pseudo-kinship is that of the social relationship established by marriage rather than the biological relationship established by procreation and birth;

3. although pseudo-kinship relationships may be set up in many different circumstances the strongest and most enduring bonds are those established in a church in the context of a baptism.

It also needs to be understood that pseudo-kinship of the *compadrazgo* type, which binds together individuals living in quite different households, is quite a different phenomenon from either 'adoption' or 'fostering' where a child is brought into a household other than that of its natural parents on a permanent or temporary basis.

I am not suggesting that we can reinvent a form of *compadrazgo* which will fit in with the circumstances of our very secular society. My point rather is to draw attention to what institutions of this kind actually do. In contrast to adoption and fostering they are not forms of 'child care'. They are systems whereby the mutual support network of adults is increased to provide a network of pseudo-'affinal kin'.

If you live in a contemporary, fairly rural, English village as I do and keep your eyes and ears open you will observe that the people who most often work together and are called in to help with minding the children or repairing the garden fence are, 'affines':- 'my sister-in-law' or 'my brother-in-law'. What is needed in the lonely deserts of industrial conurbations is that near neighbours should feel themselves to be related in this sort of way. I do not know how such a state of affairs might be brought about.

But I do seriously suggest to you that the problems of family life are not really concentred within the 'family' as now commonly understood — that is to say within the nuclear family of husband, wife and children. The structural weaknesses of our social system at the micro-level of domestic affairs are not inside the family but outside it. It is because the parents, as individuals, do not have supportive kin (or pseudo-kin) close at hand to ease the strain that they so often behave like caged animals. They then turn inwards and rend one another and their children. But the problem in these circumstances is not:- 'How shall we save the children from the savagery of their parents?' but rather 'How can we remove the bars from the cages in which the parents feel themselves entrapped?'.

Years ago in my 1967 Reith Lectures I achieved notoriety with the following quotation:

'Far from being the basis of the good society, the family, with its narrow privacy and tawdry secrets, is the source of all our discontents.'

I was using 'family' in the restricted sense of the isolated domestic nuclear family of parents and children. If 'family' is given that narrow meaning then I would in no way wish to qualify my formula and I am in complete disagreement with the proposition which I cited in my opening sentence that 'the family is the essential unit of our society'.

What is essential of course is that children shall be reared and it is obvious enough that the natural parents of a child are, in the great majority of cases, the obvious persons to be principally reponsible for that rearing. But it is entirely impractical, and directly in conflict with human experience in general, that the natural parents should be wholly responsible for the upbringing of their children.

It is a major weakness of our social system that, for various reasons of an economic and fiscal kind, the law has developed in such a way that the nuclear family has come to be treated as the standard unit in social statistics. Because it is so treated it is regarded as an isolate, and because it is so regarded it tends to become isolated.

From a sociological point of view the nuclear family is no more that an entirely transient segment in the developmental cycle of a cluster of domestic groups. As an entity it begins with a wedding which links two previously existing

segments and begins to break up again with another wedding which repeats the same
process over again. The family, in this popular sense, can never be, and should
never be, regarded as an isolate 'unit' of any kind whatsoever.

I am not asking that social workers, doctors and psychiatrists should be socio-
logically or anthropologically sophisticated but unless they can understand the
quite fundamental point that nuclear families are not individuals writ large but
transient entities meshed in with other such entities all of which are progressing
through independent developmental cycles towards early extinction, then this
symposium on priority for the family will be a complete waste of time.

I have not of course answered the question posed in my title but that is because
the question is itself misleading. There is no single entity 'the family' to
which other conceivable institutions might provide 'alternatives'. The point of
my whole argument has been that whenever we have a situation where 'families' are
perceived as isolated entities, like matches in a matchbox, they have already
ceased to provide a plausible context for the rearing of children. It is not
'families' that call for your attention but the networks of relationship which
link families together.

DISCUSSION

By objecting to the first proposition that 'the family is still the essential
unit of our society' Sir Edmund did, in fact, illustrate the main object of the
discussions. This was to review those external circumstances that put a breaking
stress on the adults trying to care in isolation for dependent children, and to
examine the support systems provided in our society. No-one expected the parent/
child relationship to carry the whole load. The network of support which all
recognised as essential came best from neighbourliness. Modern industrial society
by breaking down family structure had led to family isolation. In return the state
had taken over much that was previously done to help the family by neighbours and
friends. Kindred has become geographically less available, although posts and
telephones were now countering physical distances, and relationships are harder
to build with neighbours than with kin. On the other hand, kinship was often
limiting and restrictive while neighbours could be adopted as courtesy uncles and
aunts, as and when family circumstances demanded. Two fresh points raised were
the need for town planning to enlarge its concepts from two to three generation
living. And the thought that primary school did much more than relieve parents
from the continuous care of their children. It also provides new contacts for the
whole family. The first proposition could be improved with no loss to its meaning
by rephrasing it as 'the family is essential to our Society' and for this reason
can claim priority.

CHAPTER 2

Changing Family Patterns: Some Implications for Policy*

LESLEY RIMMER

INTRODUCTION

Many aspects of family patterns and family formation have changed significantly over the last 50 or so years. And more recently there have been important changes in the number and timing of births within marriage, the extent of cohabitation and illegitimacy, and in patterns of divorce and remarriage. A number of these changes have been described elsewhere (Rimmer 1981). This paper focuses on a restricted range of issues — notably trends in divorce, in the number and characteristics of one parent families, and in remarriage and reconstituted families.

FAMILY PATTERNS

MARRIAGE AND DIVORCE

There is a certain paradox in saying that in some ways marriage has never been more popular, while at the same time noting the substantial increases in divorce in recent years. First marriage rates which were around 60 per thousand in the early years of this century, rose to around 80 per thousand for bachelors and over 90 per thousand for spinsters in the late 1960s and early 1970s (OPCS 1980a), and peaked in 1970. Since then they have fallen back somewhat to around 60 per thousand for bachelors and 75 per thousand for spinsters. This reflects both the increasing proportions of couples who cohabit prior to marriage, and the consequent changes in the age at first marriage. Whether it will dramatically affect the proportions of those who will ever marry is another matter. The average age at first marriage in the mid 1970s, at around just under 24 for bachelors and $21\frac{1}{2}$ for spinsters, is some two and three years lower, repectively than at the turn of the century. At the other end of the life cycle, the chances of surviving into old age have increased. A boy born in 1977 could expect to live to nearly 70 and a girl to 76. In 1901 the figures would have been 48 and 52 years respectively. When these two facts are combined the potential for longer marriages of a full half century has increased.

But at the same time we have seen a dramatic increase in divorce. The number of divorces has risen from 46,000 in 1968 to 143,000 in 1978 and 148,000 in 1980, having dropped back to 138,000 in 1979. Divorce rates have risen from around 3 per thousand of the married population in the mid 1960s to 12 per thousand in 1980 (OPCS 1980b and 1981a).

---

*All figures relate to England and Wales except where specified.

Undoubtedly such statistics should be treated with caution. The divorce Reform
Act of 1969 gave a sharp, and some would suggest temporary, upward shift to the
number of divorces, and allowed the formal dissolution of many marriages which had
de facto already ended. The recent rise in the number of divorces, especially
those of short duration, may reflect the short term impact of the Family Law
Reform Act. The Act reduced the age of marriage without parental consent and
allowed an increased number of early marriages. Such teenage marriages are
particularly likely to break down and part of the current high level of divorce
can be 'explained' in this way.

On the other hand there is evidence to suggest that divorce statistics,
especially in the 1960s, underestimated the number of marriages which had broken
down and until recently the extent of informal separation arrangements was not
known (Dunnell 1979). In some ways then, divorce statistics can be seen both to
understate and overstate the risk of marriage breakdown, and predicting future
trends on the basis of current experience is full of hazards. Yet if we are to
plan services and systems of income support, we need some estimate of how many
children and families are at risk.

On the basis of current trends more than one in every four 'new' marriages is
likely to end in divorce. Some 60 per cent of divorces currently involve dependent
children, of whom, 24 per cent are under five, and 45 per cent between five and ten
(OPCS 1981b).

Figure 1 shows the number of children by age group involved in their parents'
divorce. In 1970 4.7 children of every thousand children under five years were
involved in their parents' divorce. By 1976 this had risen to 10.5 and by 1979 it
had reached 12.6. For the 5-10 year age group, the figures are respectively 7.3,
15.2 and 15.9.

The number of children involved in divorce has been growing, but the average
number of children of each divorcing couple has stayed remarkably constant. In
the short term, the trend for a higher proportion of divorces to occur in the
early years of marriage, and the trend to delayed first births in some social
groups, may mean that in future fewer divorces will involve children, but this is
a particularly tentative conclusion.

As yet there are no reliable estimates of how many children could expect,
during their childhood, to experience their parents' divorce. But we can combine
the available data and suggest an approximation. With one in four marriages ending
in divorce, 60 per cent of these involving dependent children, and about 12 or 13
children in every thousand involved in divorce each year, we might expect between
one in five and one in six children born today to witness their parents' divorce
before they reach 16 years. Added to this should be an unknown number who will
see their parents separate but not divorce. Nearly a quarter of the families who
are currently 'one parent families' is headed by a separated (but married) woman,
so substantially more children will experience the temporary separation of their
parents, even if it does not eventually lead to divorce.

ONE PARENT FAMILIES

In many ways the term 'one parent family' is a convenient but misleading short-
hand for a complex variety of family situations. We should remember that all
children in fact have two parents, and that it is the respective rights and
obligations of each of these which is the subject of much current debate. Recently
the concept of the bi-nuclear family has been introduced into sociological
literature, and this may act as a welcome counterweight to the under emphasis on
the role of the 'missing' parent (Ahrons 1981).

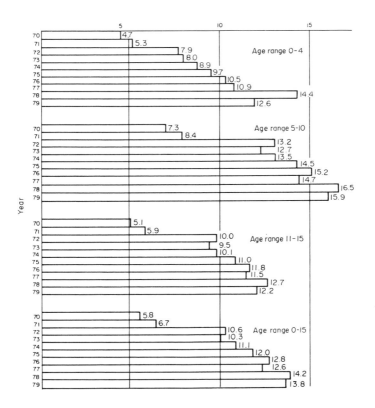

Fig. 1. Children of divorced couples per 1000 children
Source: R. Leete, Changing Patterns of Family Formation
and Dissolution, Table 4.2. Updated from OPCS Monitor
FM2 81/2.

In 1980, the National Council for One Parent Families (1980) estimated that there
were some 920,000 one parent families in Britain, with the care of about one and a
half million children. On this basis, one in eight families is headed by a lone
parent. This proportion is higher amongst some ethnic minority groups (Community
Relations Commission 1978; Ghodsian and Essen 1980). The number of one parent
families, the majority of them headed by women, has been increasing at about 6 per
cent a year throughout the 1970s, and there has been a disproportionate increase
in the number of divorced mothers within the lone parent group.

While there has been growing recognition of the increased numbers of one parent
families, the implications of current trends are often underestimated, because
much of the data is cross-sectional: that is, it shows the situation at one point
in time. Such estimates appreciably understate the cumulative number of parents
(and children) in the population who have ever lived or will live in a one parent
family at some time.

Some evidence on a longitudinal basis is now becoming available. The National

Child Development Study of a cohort of children born in 1958 showed that at age 7 years 3 per cent of the sample were living in a one parent family. By age 11 this had risen to 5 per cent and by age 16 it was as high as 9 per cent (Davie *et al* 1972; Lambert and Streather 1980; Ferri 1976b; Lambert 1978). But there was evidence of considerable movement in and out of one parent family situations, and over 12 per cent of the children in the study had been living in a one parent family on one of these three occasions. Given that there are others who will have been in one parent families between the interview dates, even the 12 per cent figure is an underestimate (Lambert 1978).

More recently, the Child Health and Education Study at the University of Bristol has shown that just under 5 per cent of the sample of children were born to un-supported women. Five years later in 1975, just under 6 per cent of the children were living in a one parent family. At some time during their first five years, however, a much larger proportion, nearly 11 per cent of all children, had experienced an epidsode of living in a one parent family (Burnell and Wadsworth 1981).

Although the definition of what constitutes 'one parent' status differs in these studies it would seem that children born in 1970 are more likely to experience family changes at an earlier age than children born in 1958 (Burnell and Wadsworth 1981).

From the point of view of policy we need to know not just how many children will be in a one parent family, but how long this situation will last. For some children the period in a one parent family may be relatively short, but we still know too little about the duration of one parent status. Evidence from the National Children's Bureau showed that three-quarters of children at age 7 years being cared for by their mothers alone were still in this situation at 11 years of age, and that only one mother in five was remarried or cohabiting (Ferri 1976b). Over a third of the children who had been born to unsupported mothers in the Child Health Education Study were still members of a one parent family at age 5 years. (Burnell and Wadsworth 1981). Whereas these figures suggest that for some children living with one parent is a long term experience, on the other hand, although more than 12 per cent of the 1958 cohort experienced a one parent state at one inter-view date, only 0.3 per cent were with their mothers alone at all four ages (Lambert 1978).

REMARRIAGE AND 'BLENDED' FAMILIES

Today over a third of 'new' marriages involves remarriage for one or other spouse. Of these, the vast majority involve divorces, and about one in nine 'new' marriages involves both spouses who have been divorced (OPCS 1980c). Remarriage rates are particularly high at ages under 30, where more than a third of divorced persons remarry each year. This suggests that 80 per cent of such divorcees will remarry within five years, and in 1978 some 36 per cent of women and 27 per cent of men who divorced were under 30 (OPCS 1980d). The potential for remarriage is there-fore high, and given that over half of all divorces involve children an increasing number of 'reconstituted' or blended families is being created.

For some children the period as a member of a one parent family will be a short, transitional period between membership to one two-parent family and of a new family with a new 'parent' figure and new brothers and sisters. The proportion of children who no longer live with both their natural parents increases as children grow older. The National Child Development Study showed that by age 7, 8 per cent of children were not living with both their natural parents (Davie *et al* 1972). And the likelihood that children will live in families without one or other of their natural parents seems to be increasing. The 1946 National Survey of Health

and Development showed that by age 15, 11 per cent of children were no longer in
the care of both natural parents, whereas for the 1958 cohort the figure was 16
per cent, that is 50 per cent higher when they were one year older (Ferri 1976a;
Douglas 1970).

In the Child Health and Education Study, almost 3 per cent of the children were
living in step families at age 5 years in addition to the 6 per cent who at that
time were in a one parent family. This suggests that some 8 per cent or more of
the children were no longer living with both natural parents (Burnell and Wadsworth
1981).

In the majority of cases where marriages end in divorce, mothers are given the
custody of their children. For most children, therefore, the new parent figure
will be a new father, but the balance between children not living with their
natural morther or father changes with the age of the child. In the National Child
Development Study, for example, six and a half times as many children at age 7
years had 'lost' their natural fathers as had 'lost' their natural mothers (5 per
cent). At 11 years there were only four and a half times as many (Ferri 1976a).
Nonetheless, at 16 years there were still 13 per cent substantially more children,
who had 'lost' their natural fathers (13 per cent) than the 5 per cent who had
'lost' their natural mothers (Fogelman 1976). But for a number of children there
will be no regular father or mother figure. We can only guess at the uncertainties
and difficulties that this creates for young children.

THE 'MODEL' FAMILY

All the evidence presented so far has in essence focussed on children in 'non-
standard' families, either with only one parent living at home or with step-
parents. But what of parents and children in unbroken, two (natural) parent
families? Whereas it is important to stress the implications and risks of marriage
breakdown for children, we should not forget that the majority of children are
still and will continue to be brought up by their two natural parents. For such
children the major contrast with their predecessors is that families are smaller,
with fewer siblings and brothers and sisters more closely 'spaced'. Equally they
are more likely to have mothers in paid employment and to have grandparents or
even great-grandparents, alive during their childhood.

IMPLICATIONS FOR POLICY

One of the major issues raised by the foregoing description of changing family
patterns is the extent to which the needs of children in different types of
families differ. Do children in one parent families have distinct needs from those
in two parent families? I wish to focus on one aspect, the finanical situation of
children in one parent families. In many ways, the social security system is
failing to cope adequately with increasing marriage breakdown. As a group, lone
parents are less well off than their two-parent counterparts and rely far more
heavily on state benefits and particularly on supplementary benefit and family
income supplement. Some 55 per cent of all one parent families are 'in poverty'
and 60 per cent of all children in families in receipt of supplementary benefit
come from one parent families (CSO 1979). An appreciation of the strains which such
low levels of income impose on lone parents and their children is an important part
of understanding the reality of life for them. The Supplementary Benefits
Commission, in evidence to the Royal Commission on the Distribution of Income and
Wealth suggested that ' ... the supplementary benefits scheme provides, particularly for families with children, incomes that are barely adequate to meet their
needs at a level that is consistent with normal participation in the life of the
relatively wealthy society in which they live' (Supplementary Benefits Commission

1978). The Finer Committee had previously noted that the supplementary benefit
system was never intended as a long term support measure. Yet some 23 per cent of
all one parent families in receipt of supplementary benefit have been on benefit
for over five years (DHSS 1981a), a length of time spent on benefit that is probabl
increasing.

Divorcees frequently remarry and take on obligations to new families, but very
few men's earnings are sufficient to support two families. A man's legal liability
to maintain his former wife either may not be possible or may impose hardships on
his new family. In any event, the woman with whom he is currently living has no
independent right to supplementary benefit. 'When a man is put in such a dilemma
the solution he will lean towards is tolerably clear. He will feed, clothe and
house those with whom he is living, knowing that the State will provide for the
others. It is the almost inescapable consequence of the principle on which the
supplementary benefit scheme is founded that wherever there is not enough money
for the husband to support two women it is the one with whom he is not living who
has to resort to the Supplementary Benefits Commission' (Finer 1974).

It is important, too, to consider the strains which the cohabitation regulations
in supplementary benefits may impose on developing relationships. Such relationships may be hampered by the knowledge that women forfeit benefit in their own
right if they begin to cohabit. Changes were introduced into the legislation to
allow a period of adjustment before a new 'father' was expected to take on responsibility for children who were not his own. But since cohabitation is more likely
to precede second and subsequent unions rather than first unions, this issue is
bound to remain important and a source of much concern when insensitively handled.

Most discussion of the policy implications of marriage breakdown, remarriage and
fertility patterns focusses on rates of divorce rather than on simple numbers. But
there are also important public policy implications of changing numbers of births,
for example, in a given period, whether these are caused by changing levels of
fertility, or the changed timing of births. Such changes have particular implications for the maternity services and the education system. Currently a whole
range of educational issues is dominated by the impact of falling school rolls.
The number of children of school age in England and Wales was a little under 9
million in 1979. It is expected to fall to 8 million by 1983, and possibly to 7½
million before the end of the decade (DES 1981). Such falling rolls have a number
of important implications, not least of which is their effect on parental choice.
The scale of the falling rolls problem has meant that some schools will actually
close, and there may be a conflict between parental choice and the Local Education
Authority's policy on contraction. 'The issue may be simply stated: are parents
to choose schools they prefer or is contraction to be planned, controlled and
managed at the expense of parents' freedom of choice?'(Briault and Smith 1980).
The issue has been particularly acute in the case of the closure of small rural
schools, and it was claimed recently that in one area of Dorset all but four of
twenty-two village schools will have been closed by September 1982 (Rodgers 1981).
But choice is not limited only to choice of school: within schools, pupils increasingly have a choice of optional subjects, and the consequences of such choices
may be significant later in the educational system or for career possibilities.
But, again, the patterns of options available and the range of the school curriculum are linked to the number of teachers. School staffing has normally been
determined by pupil-teacher ratios and as rolls fall schools are being forced to
shed staff. Redeployment of teachers is often unpopular with the teachers themselves and the schools to which they are redeployed. Thus much of the rearrange-
ment of staffing resulting from falling rolls is coming about through natural
wastage, that is, not replacing teachers who leave. In some instances, this can
have a distorting effect on the school curriculum. When specialist subject
teachers are not replaced, the teaching load in that subject may have to be reduced,
the subject dropped or non-specialist teachers co-opted to teach it. And again

this may be particularly acute in small schools. A 1981 DES Circular notes ' ...
small schools face the dilemma of a choice between excluding some subjects entirely
or devoting much of the time of a few specialist teachers to a small minority of
pupils in small groups. Moreover, staffing limitations can cause many subjects
including English and Mathematics, to be taught by teachers who lack specialist
training or experience in them: such expedients can reduce the quality of the
education provided'. Whereas the falling rolls problem for the first half of the
1980s is a problem for secondary schools, in the latter half it is a problem both
of secondary schools and of sixth forms, in which the range of options available
becomes a crucial question. Some authorities are already anticipating falling
sixth form numbers by amalgamating sixth forms into sixth form colleges.

At the national level such demographic swings are problematic, but we should also
be aware that movements of population can present problems for local education and
health authorities. And we must be increasingly sensitive to the spatial dimension
of family patterns. The situation regarding one parent families especially in
inner city areas, important in itself, can be used as an illustration. Whereas
nationally just over 12 per cent of families is headed by one parent, in many inner
area Authorities it is significantly higher, in 1978 29 per cent in Hackney, 24
per cent in Islington, 29 per cent in Lambeth and 24 per cent in Manchester. Even
within inner areas the proportions vary, 19 per cent within the Manchester and
Salford inner area, rising as high as 31 per cent in Regent-Ordsall and 30 per cent
in Moss Side (Wicks 1981). A further aspect of diversity is provided by family
patterns in the ethnic minorities. Today just over 3 per cent of the total population are of New Commonwealth and Pakistani origin, and whereas a number of the
problems faced by adults in these groups can be thought of as problems of their
'immigration', it is worth emphasising that 90 per cent of the children in ethnic
minority groups were born in Britain (CPRS 1980).

CONCLUSIONS

The above discussion merely illustrates the range of policy issues that are
affected by changing family patterns. Irrespective of whether or not Britain
needs an overall 'family policy' there is certainly a need to develop a family
perspective in policy making. This requires the careful monitoring of demographic
trends and a critical evaluation both of current policies and of policy proposals
in the light of changing family patterns. The Study Commission is currently
working on the development of such a family perspective and hopes to produce a
pilot 'Family Policy Review' within the next year.

DISCUSSION

Society has not yet appreciated the extent of the altered prevalence of marriage,
divorce, remarriage, one-parent families and reconstituted and blended marriages,
nor have these changes been taken into account in planning. The reasons for
marriage breakdown, the number of marriages that have broken down with only the
legal tie remaining and above all the effect on the children all need thorough
study. In fact the majority of children do remain in the nuclear family, but a
rising number have had experience of broken marriage, either separation or divorce,
and of living in a new family. Often when the mother goes out to work, grandparents have an increasing responsibility, while the trend for the man to have
custody of the children has remained constant during the 70s. The man who has two
families to support finds it difficult to keep them both above the poverty level.
When both natural parents have had a number of divorces the child may become
'lost' and a new problem is arising in the United States when neither natural
parent wishes the custody of the child.

The one-parent family, to which marriage breakdown now makes the largest contribution, is not yet accepted as a social norm and shame still attaches to the child of a broken marriage. The risk of poverty is great although widows and widowers have a higher status and regard in society and tend to be better off. Being a one-parent family is a transitional stage so that the prevalence figures at any one time can be misleading and conceal the greater proportion of children, perhaps 1 in 8, who have had the experience of living in one. Little is known about AID families.

The short-term bad effect of family breakdown on a child's education is well-known as is the high proportion of children with emotional disturbances who face these family difficulties. The long-term question is what kind of parents these children will make in their turn.

The needs of the children in all of these diverse family situations must be carefully studied and the wishes of the children ascertained and given greater importance. A child may actually prefer to remain in a home which seems too grotty to the observer.

The counselling resources would be best employed in prevention of a breakdown if enough were understood about when and how to intervene. Two methods can be discussed, altering the pressures which cause the breakdown or helping those concerned to cope with the *status quo*. Education could help through major projects at both primary and secondary level to create awareness of family life and the effects of family breakdown. The state which by its policies, fiscal and others, encourages divorce must accept responsibility for picking up the pieces.

CHAPTER 3

The Needs of Children and their Implications for Parental and Professional Care

MIA KELLMER PRINGLE

THE BASIC EMOTIONAL NEEDS OF CHILDREN

There are four basic emotional needs which have to be met from the very beginning of life to enable a child to grow from helpless infancy to mature adulthood. These are: the needs for love and security; for new experiences; for praise and recognition; and for responsibility. Their relative importance changes, of course, during the different stages of growth as do the ways in which they are met.

Probably the need for love and security is the most important because it provides the basis for all later relationships, not only within the family, but with friends, colleagues and eventually one's own family. On it depend the healthy development of the personality, the ability to care and respond to affection and, in time to becoming a loving, caring parent. This need is met by the child experiencing from birth onwards a continuous, reliable, loving relationship, first, with his mother, then father and then an ever-widening circle of adults and contemporaries. The security of a familiar place and a known routine make for continuity and predictability in a world in which the child has to come to terms with so much that is new and changing. A stable family life provides him with a sense of personal continuity, of having a past as well as a future, and of a coherent and enduring identity.

Only if the need for new experiences is adequately met throughout childhood and adolescence will a child's intelligence develop satisfactorily. Just as the body requires food for physical development and just as an appropriate balanced diet is essential for normal growth, so new experiences are needed for the mind. The most vital ingredients of this diet in early childhood are play and language. Through them the child explores the world and learns to cope with it. This is as true for the objective outside world of reality as it is for the subjective internal world of thoughts and feelings.

New experiences facilitate the learning of one of the most important lessons of early life, learning how to learn and learning that mastery brings joy and a sense of achievement. Educability depends not only on inborn capacity, but at least as much on environmental opportunity and encouragement. The emotional and cultural climate of the home, as well as parental involvement and aspirations, can foster, limit or impair mental growth.

Praise and recognition provide the most effective incentives for a helpless infant to grow into a self-reliant, self-accepting adult which requires an immense

amount of emotional, social and intellectual learning. It is accomplished by the
child's modelling himself on the adults who are caring for him, something which
requires a continuous effort, sustained throughout the years of growing up.
Eventually, a job well done becomes its own reward but that is a very mature stage.
Even the most mature adult responds, and indeed blossoms, when given occasionally
some praise or other forms of recognition.

Because growing up is inevitably beset by difficulties, conflicts and setbacks,
a strong incentive is needed. This is provided by the pleasure shown at success
and the praise given to achievement by the adults who love the child and whom he
in turn loves and wants to please. Encouragement and reasonable demands act as a
spur to perseverance. The level of expectation is optimal when success is possible
but not without effort. It cannot be the same for all children nor for all time.
Rather, it must be geared to the individual child's capabilities at a given point
in time and to the particular stage of his growth.

The need for responsibility is met by allowing the child to gain personal independence, at first through learning to look after himself in matters of his every
day care, such as feeding, dressing and washing himself. It is met too by his
having possessions, however small and inexpensive, over which he is allowed to
exercise absolute ownership. As he gets older, responsibility has to be extended
to more important areas, ultimately allowing him freedom over his own actions.
Eventually, in full maturity, he should be able to accept responsibility for others

Granting increasing independence does not mean withholding one's views' tastes
and choices, or the reasons for them; nor does it mean opting out from partici-
pating and guiding the lives of children; nor, indeed, condoning everything they
do. On the contrary, children need a framework of guidance and of limits. They
are helped by knowing what is expected or permitted, what the rules are, together
with the reasons for them, and whether these are in their interests or in the interests of others.

FAILURE TO MEET CHILDREN'S NEEDS

If one of the basic needs remains unmet, or is inadequately met, then development
may become stunted or distorted. The consequences can be disastrous (and costly)
later on, both for the individual and for society. Symptoms of maladjustment are,
like pain, danger signals, indicating intolerable tension between the personality
and the environment. The range of possible symptoms is wide but basically they
fall into two broad categories: fight or flight, attack or withdrawal. Aggressive-
ness calls forth much stronger adult reactions whereas the timid, over-conforming
child tends to be overlooked. Yet both types of behaviour are equally significant
calls for help, indicating that emotional, social or intellectual needs are not
being adequately met.

If the need for new experiences is not adequately met throughout childhood and
adolescence, intellectual ability will remain stunted. Also, the more unstimu-
lating, uneventful and dull life is, the more readily frustration, apathy, or
restlessness set in. This is shown clearly by the contrast between the eagerness,
alertness and vitality of normal toddlers whose life is filled with new experiences
and challenges and the aimlessness and boredom of adolescents with nothing to do
and nowhere to go.

The urban environment is hostile to the young. There is little freedom or
safety to explore or experiment, particularly without adult supervision. In
seeking legitimately for the excitement of new experiences, where few are to be
found or are attainable, the forbidden, risky or dangerous are liable to acquire
an aura of daring and excitement. What may start as a lark, giving vent to high

spirits and the desire for adventure, can all too easily turn into vandalism and mindless destruction.

Next, praise and recognition are almost invariably given for achievement rather than effort. In consequence, this need is most readily and often satisfied in the case of intelligent, healthy, adjusted and attractive children. In contrast, the intellectually slow, culturally disadvantaged, emotionally neglected or maladjusted get far less, if any, praise and recognition. Yet their need is immeasurably greater. Whatever small successes they achieve inevitably demand far more effort and perseverance: yet they receive less reward because they achieve less.

Therefore we should act as if all children were equal and then respect, as well as accept and cater for, their differences. Within such a framework, it is legitimate both to provide a democracy of opportunity while at the same time to strive for excellence so as to ensure an aristocracy of achievement.

When the fourth basic emotional need, namely to exercise responsibility, is denied opportunities for fulfilment, the child will fail to develop a sense of responsibility for himself, for others or for material objects. When such denial has gone hand in hand with lack of training in self-control and in planning ahead, such youngsters will tend to be impulsive, unwilling to wait and work for what they want, contemptuous of the rights of others, in short, irresponsible.

IMPLICATIONS FOR PARENTAL AND PROFESSIONAL CARE

PARENTAL CARE

There are, as I see it, at least six major styles of child-rearing:

1. One partner to undertake parenting on a full-time basis until the end of each child's compulsory schooling.

2. One partner to undertake parenting on a full-time basis until each child is at least five years old.

3. Truly shared parenting between the couple.

4. Both partners working part or full-time, delegating part of their children's care to other people or to institutions.

5. Single-handed parenthood by choice.

6. Creating settings quite different from conventional family life, such as communes.

In view of prevailing conditions and the needs of young children, only the first two patterns are likely to lead to optimal, emotional, social and intellectual care and stimulation. More choice will only become available when society's (and employers') attitudes change to accept the practice of shared parenting, and if a number of radical changes and modifications are made to substitute day-care facilities.

All types of pre-school provision would then have to be available free of charge according to the child's needs and parental wishes. If for the time being the economic situation makes this impracticable, would it not be fairer to provide free services for those in need and charge the others according to ability to pay? Equally important, all the advantages seem to lie in setting up integrated multi-purpose, pre-school centres on a neighbourhood basis, to provide both care and

education. Such centres would offer much greater flexibility and thus be able to
take account of changes in family circumstances, whether these are planned or unforeseen. The most suitable programme for any one child at any particular time
could be worked out on the basis of careful initial observation and assessment.
The appropriate balance between physical care, mothering, stimulation, adult guided
learning activities and child-initiated exploration could be determined and re-
adjusted in the light of progress made; so could the frequency and length of time
the child attends.

The degree and nature of the mother's (and father's) participation in the
centre's activities could similarly be flexible but would always be actively
encouraged. In this way, comprehensive pre-school centres would combine the best
features of day nurseries, nursery schools and playgroups. They could also be
available for use by childminders.

Adequate financial reward is required so that no mother of under-fives has to go
out to work for financial reasons. Husbands should have to acknowledge the value
of looking after young families by sharing their income with their wives as of
right. The state should pay realistic responsibility allowances to the parent,
whether married or single, who undertakes the child's full-time care.

In France and Hungary this is already done, the amount being related to the pay
of trained teachers and being highest for infants under three years. In Sweden,
either parent may take seven months leave on full pay after the birth of a child
and about 6 per cent of fathers do so now. The longer-term aim is that children
should be able to spend the first three years at home with one or other parent.

It has been argued that the view that very young children require full-time
mothers is merely an ideological basis for the discouragement of day-care services.
Might it not make more sense to turn this thesis on its head and ask: what are the
ideological reasons prompting those who argue for vastly increased group care for
the very young when countries such as Russia and Hungary, who introduced such care,
are now reversing this very policy? Given the high cost of good quality group care,
'upgrading' both the status of and the financial support for parenting may well
turn out to be the most cost-effective alternative in more senses than one.

IMPLICATIONS FOR PROFESSIONAL CARE

The rise of professionalism in the field of child development has inadvertently
undermined the confidence of many parents in their own ability to know and to cope.
The fact that the different professional workers do not speak with one voice and
may even give conflicting advice, has further contributed to parental uncertainty,
as has the general climate of a fading faith in religious and moral imperatives.
In a world so uncertain not only where it is going but where it wants or ought to
go, the bringing up of children has become an ever more difficult task.

Professional workers all too often underestimate parental knowledge and insight,
a failing shared by many a doctor, psychologist, teacher, social worker and
therapist. This is inevitably communicated to parents when they are seeking advice
and help, and contibutes to their inability to explain the reasons for their
concern.

Additional reasons are that laymen tend to be somewhat in awe of professional
experts; that in unfamiliar surroundings most people are liable to have difficulty
in marshalling their thoughts; and that special interviews and examinations are
likely to engender stress and anxiety, which then make the client appear less
competent. These reactions in turn serve to confirm the professional workers'
attitudes, leading them to underestimate parental understanding even further. So

both sides are locked in a mutually reinforcing circle of misapprehension, to the detriment of the child's well-being.

If parents are to be accepted as full partners, the role as well as the attitude of the 'expert' must change. The latter will have to translate into practical recognition the fact that it is parents who play by far the most important part in the care, health and education of their children, particularly during the vital early years; that most are deeply concerned for their well-being and development; but because child-rearing is a complex and challenging task, many parents become anxious at times about the significance of a problem and doubt whether their handling of it is appropriate. Consequently the first change required is that parental anxiety must always be taken seriously, even if it turns out to be a reflection of inexperience, self-doubt or exhaustion. A willingness to listen, to offer reassurance and guidance may be all that is required. Often rather than 'prescribing' what is to be done, the 'expert' could promote and support more confident parenting.

Parents are potentially the best 'detectors' of handicap. More attention should be paid to that rather maligned sixth sense 'maternal instinct', because it is often the mother who has the first suspicion that all is not well with her child. To be told either 'not to worry' or that the child will 'grow out of it' is a disservice, since such advice is unlikely to allay her anxiety which itself may have an adverse effect on the child's emotional development.

THE COST OF PREVENTION

How costly could it be to ensure that children's needs are met, so as to promote and ensure their optimal emotional, social, intellectual and educational development? No one really knows because no serious consideration has been given to this question. How much would it cost to have supportive services available to the family, sufficient in quality and quantity to prevent children who are 'vulnerable' or 'at risk' growing up emotionally disturbed, socially deviant, intellectually stunted and educationally backward? Again, no one can say because the question has not been asked.

A willingness to devote adequate resources to the care of children is the hall-mark of a civilised society as well as an investment in our future. Some argue that we do not know enough to provide positive care and creative education for all children. Others object that child-rearing is essentially a personal, private matter, while yet others retort that we cannot afford to spend more. So A. E. Houseman's despairing appeal 'When will I be dead and rid of the wrong my father did?' continues to be a reproach to our relatively affluent society.

DISCUSSION

Today's tendency with regard to the care of young babies is for parents to want to get parenthood over. With small families there is little opportunity for the older siblings to gain any practical experience of young babies. This may contribute to the denigratory attitude that caring for people is an unworthy job and certainly less worthy of time and attention than employment in a job. The myth that the young infant may be left, until with age it becomes a person, is dying, but for the professional woman the need to keep her feet on the ladder still outweighs every other concern. For the non-professional it is financial need that requires mothers to go out to work.

In policy planning the time has come for government to decide whether or not the mother's place is regarded as being in the home. If so, services as well as money should be made available and the single mother should be given an adequate allowance to make this possible. If not, full time day care must be provided and employers and Trade Unions must change their ideas and practices to allow for truly shared parenthood. Part-time employment for the married worker should be positively encouraged with appropriate arrangement of time-tables.

Education for parenthood should stress the importance of practical experience. In East African families the old children take responsibility for younger ones, one result being that boys take a real interest in family life.

However, with micro-processor development many jobs will simply disappear and many will become unisex and home based. Social results which will follow will be earlier retirement and with increased longevity a greater use of grandparents. Attitudes change more slowly than technology.

CHAPTER 4

The Family as the Patient

ALFRED WHITE FRANKLIN

The paediatrician is only one of the professionals concerned with child health.
Yet his attitude towards his patient and his explanations of what goes wrong with
the child greatly influence his co-workers and in many aspects of child care,
rightly or wrongly, he is found giving the lead.

THE FAMILY AND THE PAEDIATRICIAN

Originally his speciality of paediatrics confined itself to the study and treatment of children's diseases. But even when the chief problems were those of acute
and chronic infections and their aftermath the child had to be viewed and treated
as a member of a family group. Father's infected sinuses could produce his child's
acute nephritis and grandfather's coughed-up tubercle bacilli tuberculous meningitis
and the death of his grandson. The paediatrician's load was heavy. The development
of preventive immunisations, better standards of housing and hygiene and then the
discovery and manufacture of curative antibiotics rapidly altered the pattern and
relieved children's hospitals and their paediatricians of their main job.

Before this time it had been established that a sick child, still emotionally
dependent, progressed less well in hospital when separated from parents and better
when the ties of affection were not frayed nor broken. The concept of the patient
as a bundle of symptoms and signs in a bed had to be enlarged to include a place
for parents, one of whom might be admitted with the child. Hospital visiting was
liberalized, encouraged, sometimes even demanded by the doctor. That parents formed
part of the treatment was accepted even in bacterial disease, but they themselves
needed to know what was wrong, what was being done, what was likely to happen and to
be relieved of anxiety before they could give effective help. The family was involved in the treatment as well as the cause. So even in this limited sense, child
and parents, the family, is the patient. Recognising this need for parent counselling was stage one of paediatric enlightenment.

The second stage came from studies of congenital defects and of children with
chronic handicaps for whom there was now more time. Because at first little or no
medical or surgical treatment had been available, the paediatrician's role had been
to reach a diagnosis and give parents some prospect of what would become of the
child. What used to be said was that 'there is no treatment'. It soon became
apparent that while this was true in the strictly limited sense of no drugs and no
operations, there was a very great deal to be done. We could not ignore the

25

devastating effects which the birth and subsequent presence of a disabled child
sometimes had on parents and siblings. It became possible to separate the dis-
abilities directly due to the handicap and those which were not essential and could
be prevented. For example, unrecognised deafness led to failure of speech which a
hearing aid could prevent. The joints of children with cerebral palsy could be
prevented by expert physiotherapy from becoming fixed and deformed. The paediatrician's responsibility had enlarged from the treatment of children's diseases
to the active promotion of child health, including the encouraging of maximum self-
care and independence for the child and the attainment of maximum potential. The
important lesson was how much of the management depended on the parents. For these
measures to be effective the parents have to accept their problem and learn to live
with it. Their feeling of responsibility for what has happened (guilt feeling)
must be transformed into fuel for the constructive work of habilitation.

Treatment and management plans include filling in the gaps in experience resulting from the motor and sensory deficits. If you can't sit up when you are eight or
nine months old, you have no chance to take the required vertical view of the world
about you; you need, therefore, to be sat up with enough support. But there are
equally important dangers to emotional development which parents can avoid. The
child needs confidence that he has a future and this depends on the parents' belief
that this is so and that success and the attainment of the best possible future,
albeit limited, depend on their optimism and on their commitment to give continuing
loving care. Such parents enter a new world where progress comes in small slow
steps. It is a world full of dangers which have to be surmounted: of marital discord, of mutual recrimination, of isolation from neighbours and relatives. There
is too the danger of over-protection, dependence perpetuated and self-care denied,
formidable challenges which need not only understanding sympathy but also practical
help from our other world. The disintegration of his family is, for the handicapped child, a major disaster. The formation of groups of parents, first of
spastic children, launched a new and caring movement which continues to grow and
spread to other handicaps.

Technical surgical advances had begun to improve the lot of children with spina
bifida, in this case preventing complications like hydrocephalus and renal failure,
when the thalidomide accident drew public attention dramatically to the plight of
the handicapped. Public sympathy, mobilised at that time, continues to be a
potent force.

THE FAMILY AND THE HANDICAPPED CHILD

The strain on the family of the physically handicapped is great, yet the demands
made on the family of the severely mentally handicapped are even greater. Severe
mental handicap affects 3.7 per thousand under the age of 15 years, about a quarter
being the worst Mongol children. Fetal screening and termination of pregnancy are
expected to alter these figures, which were estimated by Kushlick in 1968. Actual
disease or abnormality of the brain is usually present and there is no class
difference.

A study by Butler and his colleagues (1978) showed that 'two-thirds of severely
handicapped Bristol children were dependent on their families for at least one
aspect of self-care, such as dressing or toileting'. A third needed night attention, 40 per cent were incontinent, a third could never be left unattended.
Despite the physical and mental strain and fatigue imposed on the family, from the
child's point of view the security and the constancy of loving care within the
family and help from siblings creates a better person than care in any institution
however well run with its diluted affection from a changing staff, although for the
older severely handicapped person institutional living may be unavoidable. The
basic personality will by then have been formed.

With mild mental handicap with its increased prevalence in the lower social
classes the importance of the environment and of standard of parenting is even
greater. Kushlick has defined mild mental handicap as 'a temporary incapacity
related largely to educational difficulties experienced in school' with a prevalence of 17.5 per thousand. Brain defect is less common and in the United Kingdom
the majority are found in the lower social classes, being five times as high in
the children of manual as compared with non-manual workers. The needs appear to
be cultural and social rather than medical (Kushlick 1968). In a recent study
among Swedish school children (Hagberg *et al* 1981), all brought up in good socio-
economic conditions, while a proportion had chromosomal abnormalities, 60 per cent
of the mildly mentally handicapped had no recognised cause. Explanations suggested
for class differences include better obstetric care in the higher social classes
and earlier language stimulation in infancy. Even in Mongol children stimulation
and love within the family can improve the child's performance. What the family
can give and what it withholds profoundly influences the dependent child. Lack of
love and of stimulation, reflecting cultural as well as individual practices, are
seen as causative factors, in theory at least reversible.

THE FAMILY AND THE COMMUNITY

COUNTERING SOCIO-ECONOMIC STRESS

The improvement of the family's socio-economic conditions, which is the subject
of this symposium, is even more complicated. For if the child depends on his
family for love and stimulation, for improvement in the socio-economic sphere the
family must depend largely on society. Cravioto (1972) searching for the cause of
mild mental handicap and the timing of its impact on the child wrote: 'When one
has a chain of events that goes all the way from the society to the individual,
such as is the case in mental functioning, it is difficult to know what is an
intervening variable and what is the actual etiologic agent'. Whatever the cause
and whenever it operates, alleviation has been attempted especially in the United
States by Head Start programmes to counter the bad effects of poverty on learning.
A list was compiled by Robert Cooke (1980) in 1965 as follows:

1. Improving the child's physical health and physical abilities.

2. Helping the emotional and social development of the child by encouraging self-
   confidence, spontaneity, curiosity and self-discipline.

3. Improving the child's mental processes and skills with particular attention
   to conceptual and verbal skills.

4. Establishing patterns and expectations of success for the child which will
   create a climate of confidence for his future learning efforts.

5. Increasing the child's capacity to relate positively to family members and
   others while at the same time strengthening the family's ability to relate
   positively to the child and his problems.

6. Developing in the child and his family a responsible attitude toward society,
   and fostering constructive opportunities for society to work together with
   the poor in solving their problems.

7. Increasing the sense of dignity and self-worth within the child and his
   family.

The success of the Head Start operations remains a source of controversy which
is unlikely to be resolved. Possibly intervention comes too late to produce
indisputable results.

The number of children with severe mental, like those with severe physical handicap, should fall with better take-up of services, improved antenatal and obstetric
care, the eradication of rhesus sensitisation now possible and proper treatment of
haemolytic disease of the newborn. The identification of abnormal fetuses by
amniocentesis followed by termination of pregnancy can make some contribution.
The full effect of this on either family life and relationships or on social policy
cannot be said to have as yet been adequately revealed.

REPRODUCTIVE COMPETENCE

Baird (1980) has recently discussed 'the effects of environmental factors on
reproduction'. Using the stillbirth and neonatal mortality rates to measure reproductive competence, he relates it to the mother's socio-economic circumstances
at the period when she herself was born and reared. Optimal conditions then are
the necessary precursor to a real improvement in results. Such an improvement
would be expected to lower the rates of prematurity and immaturity with their
dangers for the newborn, especially important because neonatal intensive care may
now be adding to the handicapped population.

Among the differentiating maternal features, height may provide the clue.
Illsley (1955) in Aberdeen conducted a socio-medical investigation into the
relations between class differences, stillbirths and infant mortality among over
4000 primiparous women bearing children between 1931 and 1951. Part of the study
concerned movement up and down the social class scale, the occupation of the
woman's father being compared with that of her husband. During the twenty years
the proportions in the five classes had changed, rising by 80 per cent in Class 1,
by less in Classes 11 to 1V, while Class V fell by 25 per cent. Certain features
of the woman characterised her selection of a mate in a higher class of which
tallness was one. Those who moved up tended to be tall, in good health with a
higher IQ, better nutrition and coming from smaller families. The opposites held
true for those who moved down. The gaps between the classes remained. The re-
cruitment into the lower classes of the less competent from the higher classes
could provide one reason for the higher infant mortality rates and the persistance
of the social class gradient.

The significance of height deserves a closer look in the light of the studies by
Dobbing and his colleagues (1973) on brain growth, first in animals and latterly
in the human. Dobbing concludes that higher mental functions have a considerable
basis in the brain, the development of which can be significantly spoiled by poor
environmental conditions during the growth spurts which occur at predetermined
chronological ages. In the human fetal brain, cell numbers are being established
in the second trimester (10-18 weeks). Myelination and then dendritic complexity
follow, the veolocity of brain growth increasing to its fastest around the time of
birth and continuing although more slowly for about eighteen months. Adverse
factors having limited the quantity of growth at this period, there can be no
catch-up and development is distorted. 'The brain appears to have a once-only
opportunity to grow properly'. At this time children should have the best environmental conditions among which nutrition is central to proper growth. 'Restriction
may well have lasting behavioural consequences.' Genetic elements cannot be excluded, but, if Dobbing be correct, here is surely an area for preventive socio-
medical effort depending for success on the health, the coping ability and the
integrity of the family. What is at issue is not only intelligence but also
behaviour.

EMOTIONAL FACTORS

Inadequate nutrition is not the sole cause for growth failure. Inadequate family care also plays a part. The functions of the family were spelled out by Spence (1946). 'The family exists, he wrote, first to ensure growth and physical health; secondly, to give the right scope for emotional experience; thirdly, to preserve the art of motherhood (nowadays parenthood); and fourthly, to teach behaviour'. Studies of families who abuse and neglect their children by Kempe and his Denver colleagues (Kempe and Kempe 1978) and inspired by him have shown that such families fail in all four functions. Growth failure in length (height) as well as in weight in infancy is characteristic. Deprivation dwarfism is recognised. Non-organic failure to thrive is now included in the tragic evidences of child abuse. Removal from the adverse environment leads to catch-up bodily growth, return home once more slows it down. If catch-up brain growth is impossible, the effect on the future intelligence and behaviour of the child can easily be surmised. A preset programme of growth within selected areas of brain and no catch-up if the moment is missed provide the basis for a 'distortion pathology' (Dobbing and Smart 1973) of the brain. The inescapable biological needs of the baby for nurturing during the stage of dependency include not only warmth, food, protection from accidents and environmental dangers, but also a sufficient emotional pabulum. Modern fashion would add stimulating educational techniques.

WHAT THE BABY NEEDS FROM ITS FAMILY

REACTION AND INTERACTION

A traditional fallacy has been that in the early months of life the baby is a passive object whose care may be safely delegated to any competent person. Mother plans a quick return to work for a year or two and then back to her child when he has become more of a person. Recent close, continuous and detailed observations of neonatal behaviour have revealed some surprises, especially in the sensory system and suggest that to satisfy his real needs her policy should be the exact opposite. What capacities and needs has the newborn baby?

The ability to expand the lungs, breathe, suck and swallow, all required for survival, have long been studied as has the development of control of bodily movement. More recently the sensory system and emotional responses have been tested. Can the newborn baby pay attention? Wolff (1965) has demonstrated attentive behaviour for spells of five minutes in the first week and thirty minutes at a month. Response to external stimuli is best during these periods. The baby also responds to inner needs such as hunger or pain. The language of communication is expressed in crying, then touching and in approaching and withdrawing. Much depends on the mother's skill in interpretation. The signal must be accepted, understood and given a positive answer. This beginning of human relationships for the baby is believed to be the model for such relationships for the rest of life. Is the mother available and does she give satisfying responses or not? On this depends the reaction of the baby which in turn determines the mother's next response. The relationship between newborn and mother is an interaction with a mutual exchange of responses of equal value to them both. What each does and feels determines and modifies the response of the other. The baby plays a vital part.

Eye-to-eye contact and the *'en face'* position have special value. A mother's first look deep into her baby's eyes may provide the first intimation of love between them. On the first day the baby can fix its gaze and follow a moving object, its first intentional act under its own control. If mother wears a mask, baby may withdraw. His eyes follow the drawing of a face and this more consistently than a drawing of facial features misplaced à *la Picasso*.

The newborn baby responds non-verbally to the speaking voice, especially his mother's and turns preferentially at two days to mother's breastpad. To these

evidences of selection and choice may be added appreciation of experience and
adaptability to the environment. 'The legitimate conclusions from these studies
seem to be that the newborn baby has not only its own individuality but also a
complex system of responses to sensory as well as motor stimuli, that it does
discriminate and that it can adapt to experience ... the details of care and
management of the neonate must be perceived as influencing development and as being
either advantageous or detrimental' (Franklin 1982). It is hardly necessary to
stress the importance, second only to proper obstetric conduct, of a secure and
supportive family situation in which the mother can give her new baby its optimal
mothering.

That the baby has much sensitivity and many skills has been amply demonstrated.
The bonding of affection between mother and newborn is promoted by bodily contact
and impeded by separation. Bonding failure has profound short and long term
effects, contributing greatly to rejection and child abuse. Language delay, with
its limiting effect on intellectural development, is a product both of malnutrition
and emotional maladjustment.

For a baby's optimal development satisfying maternal responses are necessary
from the time of birth. The baby deprived of its early emotional satisfaction is
a person spoiled with a personality at risk of distortion. Here lies the origin
of the vulnerability that predisposes the person to failure in coping, when the
time comes, with the problems of family life

MATERNAL SUPPORT

Birth, however, is not the beginning. The mother's responses appear to reflect
the emotional interaction between herself and her mother at the time of her own
birth. They also reflect her emotional state at the time of conception and during
her pregnancy. She needs a feeling of security to give her confidence, confidence
breeds happiness and happiness high self-esteem, the belief in herself which is
essential to successful motherhood. She needs the support of her consort and the
rest of her family. When we speak of family, however we define it, we mean that
group on which the mother knows that she can rely for support. Where else besides
from the family can the love and the commitment be found? It is for society to
identify and relieve as fully as possible the stresses on the early stages of
family life and to provide the necessary network of support.

DISCUSSION

The vulnerability of some parents puts them, when stressed, at risk of failing
to cope with family problems in general and in particular with adequate care of
the children. Such failure can lead to child abuse as well as neglect. Some are
'born to fail'. Not all succumb in spite of early massive disadvantage. We need
studies of those who do succeed, success being complete if, when the children's
time comes for parenthood, they can cope with family life in their turn. What
protects them from the damage done by early disadvantages that for others is
crucial to their failure? The general belief is that the correlation is with
emotional adjustment rather than with the level of intelligence. One lesson is
that it is never too late to change when help arrives in the form of fresh opportunity in housing, by retraining and through the formation of fresh personal
relationships.

How far the needs of the baby are fulfilled depends on a parent's understanding
of what those needs are. The baby learns its power from on demand feeding, gets
its sense of security from stable relationships and develops independence through
responsibility. Early socialization, experience of self and self-esteem are other

ingredients in emotional maturation. Inflexible methods of management, unstable
family relationships and isolation limit maturation and withholding independence
follows when mother and child are not so much bonded and welded. The valuable
personality traits include self-confidence, itself related to controlled aggression
(anger may be constructive), self-determination and participation, ability to take
responsibility.

Babies with handicaps put considerable stress on the family and an important
question is the extent to which modern technological neonatology is adding to
their number. Modern parents are better educated and should share in decision
making, given technical information by Health Visitors.

CHAPTER 5

The Family Research Unit's Study of Women from Broken Homes: What conclusions Should We Draw?

STEPHEN WOLKIND, SUSAN KRUK AND FAE HALL*

INTRODUCTION

Over the past twenty years there has been a considerable growth of epidemiological research designed to examine the relationship between aspects of family life and child development (Graham 1977). This growth has been made possible largely because of advances in research methodology. With the aid of sophisticated and reliable semi-structured interviews, we can now examine such important factors as the behavioural adjustment of a child, the psychological health of a mother and the quality of a marriage on an epidemiological scale. Of recent years, in addition, observational techniques developed by the ethologists have been brought in to supplement interview data with measures of a kind which could not be obtained by interview (Wolkind, Hall and Pawlby 1977). With these new aids, epidemiological research has increasingly turned to an examination of issues which have immediate implications for those concerned in a practical way with the needs of families.

In this paper, we shall illustrate this with one set of findings taken from a longitudinal study of child development being carried out by the Family Research Unit of the London Hospital Medical College. Fuller details of this project have been given elsewhere (Wolkind 1979; Wolkind and Zajicek 1981). One of our most important aims in setting up the study was to see whether it was possible, using simply-elicited criteria, to detect during pregnancy women who might be at risk for a variety of difficulties, including difficulties with child-rearing, following the birth of the first child. A number of 'risk' categories were used, but here we will examine only one, namely women who had at some time in their lives been in the care of a local authority. We used 'in care' status not because of any feeling that going into care would necessarily cause problems in itself, but because we felt this might well prove a simple and efficient way of detecting women who had experienced a particularly disadvantaged childhood (Wolkind and Rutter 1973; Schaffer and Schaffer 1968). There is a considerable volume of theoretical work which suggests that a woman who has had a disadvantaged childhood will be more likely than most to have difficulties as a mother and wife (Deutsch 1945).

METHODS

The subjects on whom data will be presented were participants in a longitudinal

---

*Fae Hall took part in the symposium and reported on the results of this study which was conducted at the Family Research Unit, London Hospital Medical College.

interview and observational study of British-born, mainly working-class women
living in a deprived inner-city area of London and expecting their first baby
during the year 1974-5. During that year, all British-born women attending the
ante-natal booking clinics of the two hospitals serving the area were given a brief
screening interview. This provided basic information about the backgrounds and
current status of 534 women, representing about 95 per cent of all British-born
women expecting a first child in Tower Hamlets at that time.

From these 534 women screened in early pregnancy, a total of 233 were selected
for further study. Details of our selection procedures are given by Wolkind and
Zajicek (1981).

Amongst the women selected for inclusion in the study were 33 who were known to
have been in local authority care while under the age of 16 years. Of these,
several were lost to the study, either through infant death, adoption or geographical mobility. The final number available for interview by 42 months was 26, and
12 of these were included in a smaller observational study carried out in parallel
with the main study by interview.

To highlight the special characteristics of this 'in care' group, we propose to
compare them with a group of women selected from a random sample, whose childhood
backgrounds had been stable and without any major separations from the parents
before the age of 16 years. 75 such women were successfully interviewed longitudi-
nally, and at different points in the study, from 20 to 28 of these were participant
in the observational study. For present purposes two further groups are set aside,
namely women who as children experienced family upsets through death, desertion or
divorce but continued to live at home; and women from otherwise stable homes who
as children had spent periods away from home in hospital (Douglas 1975; Quinton
and Rutter 1976). Although there is reason to suspect that these groups also may
be at risk for later difficulties attention is confined to those who were 'in care'
as children, the group appearing from the literature to be the most seriously at
risk. Their experiences are related to those of the group likely to provide the
maximum contrast, whom we call the 'stable childhood' group.

The main source of information for the interview study was a series of very
detailed semi-structured interviews conducted in the home in the seventh month of
pregnancy and when the child was 4 months, 14 months, 27 months and 42 months old.
These interviews ranged widely at each stage over current material circumstances,
the health and behaviour of the child, details of maternal management and attitudes,
the mother's current physical and psychiatric health and the quality of the
marriage. Where observations were made in addition to an inverview, mother and
baby were observed together in the home two weeks following the 4, 14 and 27 month
interview, and in a laboratory playroom situation with another mother and her child
at 27 and 42 months. With children in the observational sample we also carried
out a Reynell language test at 27 months and a Stanford-Binet IQ test at 42 months.

FINDINGS

A few key items, each of which, directly or indirectly, has relevance for the
future outlook for the children of the families concerned, are selected from the
wealth of information available to us.

PREVALENCE OF A CHILDHOOD HISTORY OF BEING IN LOCAL AUTHORITY CARE

Of the 534 women seen in the antenatal booking clinics, comprising 95 per cent
of all British-born women expecting a first baby in Tower Hamlets in 1974-5, 7 per
cent (36 women) were in local authority care for one month or more while under the

age of 16 years (Wolkind, Kruk and Chaves 1976; Wolkind 1977). The type of care, age at admission, the duration of the 'in care' period and reasons for admission into care all varied greatly. Whereas some women had been in care only briefly, others had spent their whole lives in childrens' homes. Among the many reasons for admission into care that were mentioned were parental illness, either physical or psychiatric, family break-up, desertion by a single parent, parental death, homelessness and leaving home due to strained relationships. They type of care included one childrens' home throughout, 'so many homes I can't remember', boarding schools, special boarding schools, girls' hostels and remand and approved schools. Multiple placements were common and among women of this age group only a minority had been cared for in a foster home. Many of the women in the 'in care' group were not Londoners and had drifted into Tower Hamlets on leaving care. Our numbers are too small to allow us to differentiate between the different types of 'in care' experience.

At the time of registering at the antenatal booking clinic, 70 per cent of our final 'in care' sample of mothers were under 20 years of age. The comparable figure for our 'stable childhood' group of mothers was 21 per cent*. Among the 'in care' group more than half were only 16 or 17 years old at the start of this first pregnancy, and there may well have been some even younger, for our study did not extend to girls who conceived while still at school. Not surprisingly, in view of their age. the majority of the 'in care' women were legally single at the beginning of pregnancy, though in the majority of cases they were cohabiting, usually with the father of the child. The majority of the women in the 'stable childhood' group, by contrast, were legally married when the pregnancy began.

OUTCOME OF THE PREGNANCY

Since ours was a longitudinal study, women who stated at the antenatal booking clinic that they were arranging for a termination of pregnancy or had already decided to give the baby for adoption were not interviewed. We thus have no information about the relative rates of elective abortions and planned adoptions in our 'in care' and 'stable childhood' groups. However, of babies who were safely delivered, one baby in our 'in care' group of 33 suffered a 'cot death' at 5 months of age, two were given for adoption before 6 months, and in a further 3 cases the mother relinquished the care of the child permanently to relatives. These 6 children constitute 18 per cent of the 'in care' group. In the 'stable childhood' group, there were 3 neonatal deaths but no children were given for adoption or otherwise relinquished. Thus the corresponding total of children permanently lost to the mother among this group of 79 women is only 5 per cent.

BIRTHWEIGHT

For the live births, there was a much poorer outcome for the 'in care' group than for the 'stable childhood' group as regards birthweight. There was a far greater proportion of low birthweights (Fig. 1) among the 'in care' mothers, and their babies at birth weighed only 2950 g. (6lb. 8 oz.) on average compared with 3281 g. (7lb. 3oz.) for babies of the 'stable childhood' group. The average birthweight over the whole country is 3300 g. (Chamberlain *et al* 1975). We have no information about gestational age at birth but prematurity was only rarely mentioned in the hospital notes and it is more likely that the majority of the poor birthweight babies were small-for-dates.

---

*Here and throughout our paper, an asterisk will be used to denote findings which are statistically significant at or above the .05 level.

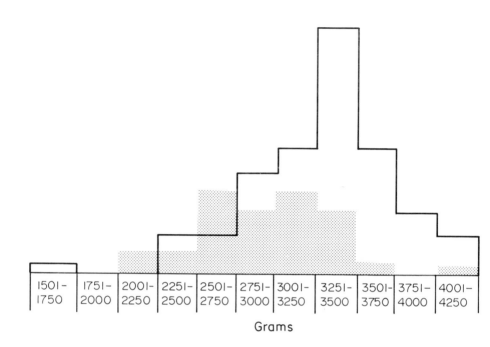

Grams

Fig. 1: Birthweights for babies of the 'in care' group
(stippled) compared with those of babies of the 'stable
childhood' group. (Interview sample).

LATER OUTCOMES FOR THE CHILD

Our main information regarding outcomes for the child comes from ratings of the
child's behavioural adjustment based on behavioural descriptions provided by the
mother when the child was 14, 27 and 42 months old; on direct observation of the
behaviour of mother and child at 4, 14, 27 and 42 months, and on the results of the
Reynell language test given at 27 months and the Stanford-Binet IQ test given at
42 months. We report only on our findings at 42 months.

BEHAVIOUR RATINGS BASED ON MOTHER'S REPORT

Using the Behaviour Screening Questionnaire developed by Richman and Graham
(1971), the mother's description of twelve different apsects of the child's
behaviour was converted into a score on a rating scale with a theoretical range
of from 0-24. A score of 10 or more on this behaviour scale is common among young
children referred to psychiatric clinics and infrequent among children not attending clinics of this kind (Richman, Stevenson and Graham 1975). Such a score may
thus be reasonably assumed to be indicative of the presence of some level of
behaviour disturbance.

The proportion of children with a BSQ score of 10 or more in the 'in care' group
is 31 per cent. This compares with 16 per cent in the 'stable childhood' group.*
The average score for the 'in care' group is 7.00 ± 3.4, compared with 5.8 ± 3.0
for the 'stable childhood' group. From these figures we may infer that at age $3\frac{1}{2}$
years, significantly more women in the 'in care' group than in the 'stable childhood' group were reporting difficulties in their child's behaviour.

OBSERVATIONAL EVIDENCE AT AGE 42 MONTHS

The observational data at 42 months is derived from a detailed running record of
25 minutes of the child's behaviour in a playroom with another mother and her child
or children. This part of the observational data is mainly in the form of total
frequency counts of a wide range of simple behavioural items shown by the child and
by the mother towards her child. The catalogue of behaviour items recorded was
ethologically-based and as far as possible descriptive rather than evaluative. It
included, for example, the number of times mother and child smiled or spoke to one
another and to others. The observational method is described by Hall, Pawlby and
Wolkind (1979).

The majority of a large number of behavioural items examined at 42 months showed
no significant difference between mothers and children of the 'in care' group and
of the 'stable childhood' group. For example, at 42 months there was no difference
in the amount that mother and child spoke to one another or smiled at one another,
nor in various measures of the child's activity and play. There were, however,
significant differences in five measures which together suggest a higher level of
'dependency' and possible insecurity in the unfamiliar situation of our playroom
among the children of the 'in care' mothers. On average, these children spent
more time close to mother*, more time leaning against her*, and more time passively
watching the proceedings of the playroom*. They also cried and fretted more
frequently than the children of the 'stable childhood' group*and were more likely
to be upset by an experimentally-arranged 5-minute separation from the mother*.
Indications of a similar greater 'dependency' and/or insecurity among the children
of the 'in care' group are also present in the 27 month and 14 month observations.
At 14 months and 27 months, however, as at 42 months, on all measures mother and
children of the 'in care' group and of the 'stable childhood' group were statistically indistinguishable. This is in marked contrast with our findings from the
observations made at 4 months (Wolkind, Hall and Pawlby 1977).

The formal observations occupied only a small part of the 42-month playroom
sessions, which lasted a whole afternoon, the observers having ample opportunity
to make informal observations on the child's behaviour in several different situations. These were summarised as a global rating of the extent to which in the
observers' view the behaviour they had seen departed from that of their notion of
the optimally-competent $3\frac{1}{2}$-year old (Hall and Pawlby 1981). Though sometimes a
little on the clingy side, 4 of the 12 children of 'in care' mothers seen at 42
months were, in the observers' judgement, doing well or very well. A further 3
were thought to be showing only mild or dubious difficulties. The remaining 5
were judged to be showing behaviour of a kind which might arouse the concern of a
psychiatrist. This latter proportion of 5/12 children in the 'in care' group
showing behaviour indicative of some definite problem of some kind compares with a
proportion of 4/28 in the 'stable childhood' group.

RESULTS OF THE STANDFORD-BINET IQ TEST AT 42 MONTHS

In a Stanford-Binet IQ test given separately to each child at the end of the 42-
month playroom session, the average IQ for the total number of 94 children partici-
pating in the observational study at this age was 106 (Hall and Pawlby 1981). For

the 12 children of the 'in care' group, the average IQ score was 92.6 ± 8.4, while
the mean score for the 'stable childhood' group of children was 110.5 ± 19.4*.
This represents a group difference of 14 points. Among the 'in care' group,
scores ranged from 65-105. Among childre of the 'stable childhood' group the range
was 65-149. In this group, 16/28 (57 per cent) of scores were above the general
average value of 106 and 36 per cent had scores of 120 or higher.

As described above, children of the 'in care' group had significantly lower
birthweights than those of the 'stable childhood' group of mothers, and there is
a well-established association between IQ scores and birthweight. In our study as
a whole there is a correlation of .32 (Hall and Pawlby 1981); as can be seen from
Figure 2. Even among the relatively small number of children represented by the

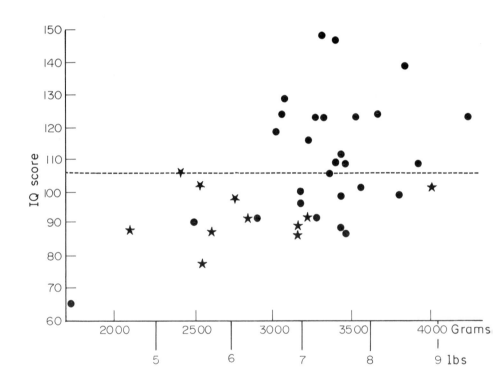

Fig. 2: Relationship between birthweight and Stanford-Binet
IQ score at age 42 months among children of the 'in care'
group (★) and of the 'stable childhood' group (●). (Observational sample) Mean score for all 94 children tested at
42 months shown by broken line.

'in care' and 'stable childhood' groups combined, this relationship is apparent. However, in the small 'in care' group, there is clearly no relationship of this kind and IQ scores remain at the same low level irrespective of birthweight.

We must conclude that some factor or factors independent of birthweight must be operating to depress intellectual performance in the 'in care' group at age $3\frac{1}{2}$ years. Unfortunately, we do not have IQ scores for the parents. However, we do know that in our observations in the home only when the child was 4 months old, mothers of the 'in care' group spent significantly more time out of sight of the baby*, and touched and spoke to the baby significantly less often than the mothers of the 'stable childhood' group*. They also responded less often to the baby's cries by picking him up*. It may also be relevant that when asked the question 'It takes some time to see a baby as a person; do you see your baby as a person yet?', only 33 per cent of the 'in care' mothers answered positively, compared with 78 per cent of the 'stable childhood' mothers*. Since we have also evidence that the 'in care' group of children were retarded in their language development at 27 months (Pawlby and Hall 1979), it is tempting to draw a connection between our 4-month findings and the relatively poorer IQ scores of the 'in care' group of children at 42 months, for there is increasing evidence (Bullowa 1979) that speech development begins far earlier than had hitherto been imagined.

OUTCOMES FOR THE MOTHER

EMOTIONAL DIFFICULTIES

As part of each interview from the seventh month of pregnancy until the child reached 42 months, an enquiry was made regarding a variety of symptoms whose presence would indicate some level of emotional difficulties in the mother of the child. Using a structured and standardised psychiatric interview a rating of definite difficulties was made if the woman described symptoms, generally of depression and/or anxiety, sufficient to impair her life. The general findings from our study using this method of assessment have been described by Zajicek and Wolkind (1978).

Making the most conservative assumption for those occasions when an interview was missed (namely that at that stage there was no disorder present) we estimate that a minimum of two-thirds of the 'in care' interview group had experienced marked depression or anxiety at least once between late pregnancy and the child's fourth year. A similarly conservative estimate of the incidence of definite emotional difficulties among the 'stable childhood' group is about one-third. This high proportion for what we regard as our least vulnerable group of mothers is consistent with findings from our own and other studies regarding the high incidence of depression among young mothers in inner city areas (Zajicek and Wolkind 1978; Richman 1976; Brown *et al* 1975). Amongst our 'in care' mothers, the proportion was still higher, with at least two-thirds having experienced marked anxiety or depression at at least one point during the child's first four years.

QUALITY OF THE MARRIAGE

Another topic extensively explored in our interviews at 14, 27 and 42 months was the current quality of the woman's relationship with her husband or cohabitee. On the basis of the very detailed information obtained using an interview technique (Quinton, Rutter and Rowlands 1976) the overall quality of the relationship was rated as good, moderate, poor or broken. Again the problem of missing data makes it difficult to be exact. At our most conservative estimate, however, at least two-thirds of the relationships of the 'in care' group were non-optimal (i.e. 'moderate', 'poor' or 'broken') at one or more points from late pregnancy onwards,

compared with one-third in the 'stable childhood' group. The proportion of relationships rated as poor or broken, with the partners living apart, was 39 per
cent in the 'in care' group compared with 18 per cent in the 'stable childhood'
group.

CONCLUSIONS

In common with many other researchers, we have presented evidence which points
to the comparative ease with which it is possible to identify groups of people
more than usually likely to develop later problems. There is no doubt that women
in our study who had spent a period in local authority care as children experience
much greater difficulties in many areas of their lives than women with a childhood
history of a stable home.

We must immediately point out that we have no information about the progress
of 'in care' women who have not embarked on motherhood. Working in a deprived
inner-city area, it could be that we may have been studying only the 'casualties'
among this particular group of women although this seems unlikely.

Our contrast group of women from intact homes illustrates how even in our very
deprived area, the majority of working class mothers and their children do well.
The highest IQ in the whole study, for example, was 157. These 'low risk' mothers
not only probably grew up in relatively harmonious homes, but they have continued
to be supported by their family of origin, probably both emotionally and materially
throughout early adulthood and into pregnancy and child-rearing. They often have
both husband and mother to rely on as well as a large extended family. We must
not forget, however, that in spite of their apparently more favourable circumstances, some women in this group too experienced difficulties either on their own
account or with their children.

Our 'high risk' group of 'in care' women by definition lacked support and
stability as children and generally continued to lack them through adolescence and
premature pregnancy. As we have shown, the children of our 'in care' group were
almost uniformly disadvantaged by poor birthweight, and the observational data,
admittedly based on a small sample, show these children to be functioning at a
depressingly low level intellectually as judged by their Stanford-Binet scores.

On observational and interview assessments of the children's behavioural adjustment, however, the picture is less clear. 42 per cent of the 'in care' group of
children were perceived by our observers as having some kind of behaviour problem,
and in our interviews, 31 per cent were described by their mothers as exhibiting
behaviour indicative of some level of behavioural disturbance. If we consider the
emotional environment of these children, nearly two-thirds had at some time been
exposed to a depressed and/or anxious mother, and over one-third to a very poor or
broken marriage, both situations likely to cause unhappiness in the child and
possible disturbance. The 18 per cent loss of our 'in care' sample by infant death
and the relinquishing of care, and anecdotal evidence of family violence and
psychiatric referral are further causes for concern.

However, although this portion of our data is depressing, over half of the
children of our 'in care' mothers were behaviourally at worst, less difficult than
might have been expected and at best doing very well. On our interview findings,
50 per cent had BSQ scores below the mean of 6.2 found in our random sample. And
although maternal psychiatric difficulties and marital disharmony do seem much
higher in the 'in care' group, the severity or occurrence of these problems was by
no means constant at all interviews.

We have shown that though many of our 'in care' risk group have experienced

serious problems, some have done well; and that, conversely, though most of our
contrast group of women with a stable childhood have done well, some among them
have experienced difficulties. As researchers our future long-term aim must be to
try to identify what kind of factors 'protect' some seemingly vulnerable women and
their children from later difficulty, while other families suffer in an ever-
increasing spiral of interwoven problems. Our short-term role, alongside others,
is to consider practical ways in which these families could be helped.

This paper has been in no way an attempt to evaluate local authority child-care
practices of the past. Nevertheless, our findings raise many questions concerning,
for example, the relative merits of the various types of local authority care used
now. We must consider the possibilities for care after the age of 16 years, in
such ways as the provision of a home, financial security and emotional support,
counselling at appropriate times with regard to contraception, abortion, pregnancy,
adoption, marriage, single parenthood, housing when pregnant and the provision of
services to promote the welfare of the child. Perhaps the best way to help some
young children would be to provide support for their mothers before conception as
well as during pregnancy and in the early years. The actual contraction of
services due to the present economic situation is of major concern. To give two
examples, funds have recently been withdrawn from an organisation offering long
term support to grossly disorganised families, and an after-care hostel for girls
without families has been closed. If the former were to result in a proportion of
children being taken into care, or the latter to cause more stress for girls already
at risk for teenage pregnancy, such action must be seen as short-sighted for both
humane and financial reasons.

Nevertheless, the use of 'risk groups' in the caring professions has its draw-
backs. The power of prediction in a statistical sense is less than totally
reliable in real life. It becomes debatable whether resources should be diverted
to the few most in need or the services reorganised, perhaps in fairly simple ways,
to provide a more personal and flexible service for all. An example, perhaps, is
routine ante-natal care, and the present wide-spread arguments about how it should
be administered. In the general field of the caring services, some of the most
innovative and seemingly successful work is often on a small scale — a single
borough or a G.P.'s domiciliary work, a clinic's work with the whole family, the
successful use of volunteers. And there seems to be a need for a more systematic
inter-disciplinary exchange of views on successful and, just as importantly, un-
successful experiments. No less important than theoretical work is evaluation of
services provided, including the consumer's view as to the acceptability and use-
fulness of these services (Page and Clark 1977).

SUMMARY

Our example, namely the early emotional environment and the development of
children whose mothers had been in care, illustrates both the advantages and the
difficulties of attempting to relate research findings to policy. The analysis of
research data usually poses as many questions as are answered, resulting in
cautious conclusions and a feeling for the need for further research.

At present, we are interviewing the sample now that the children are nearly 7
years, hoping to assess how well the children have settled into the entirely
different environment of school. It is too early yet to draw any conclusions, but
the impression is that some of the 'in care' women, whilst still having difficulties, have changed considerably and are better able to cope. Other families, un-
happily, have become overtly disturbed. Perhaps there is a polarisation into
problem and no-problem families, and disturbed and coping children. If so, this
would suggest once again that the early years of child rearing are crucial.

On a more pragmatic level we can conclude that women who have had a severely disturbed childhood deserve particularly sympathetic care during their pregnancy.

One of our initial objectives was to explore the possibility of offering extra support during pregnancy to vulnerable women. Theoretically pregnancy is a good time to intervene, as women are routinely in contact with helping agencies and the possibility exists of preventing the development of child problems later. Whereas this remains our aim, the variablility and longstanding nature of the difficulties experienced by our in-care sample underlines the complexity of their needs. Although they share many disadvantages, each woman's history is unique.

ACKNOWLEDGEMENTS

The research reported was supported by generous grants from the Medical Research Council and the DHSS. We wish to thank our colleagues for their help, and the families in our study who have been so accepting and tolerant of our many demands on their time and patience.

DISCUSSION

Quite simple indications exist for recognising the women who are likely to find difficulty in coping with family life. The identification of such a vulnerable group makes preventive help possible and poses the questions when to intervene and what actual help to give. In one sense these indications provide a screening test with the expected finding that many women in the vulnerable group can in fact succeed. The outcome rests mainly on the three variables — personal qualities, the quantity of stress to be endured and the nature and extent of the support available to the family.

When the home breaks down, everything depends on the kind of substitute care provided. For the care of the children, some institutions can be excellent, but the case against them in general is strong and the question was asked, 'should they exist at all?'. Even institutions themselves try to get children transferred to foster or adopting parents.

The offspring of very young parents are among the most deprived. The form of care given is seldom optional in real life. Often it lasts for too long and when it does the big problem for the 18 year old is how to secure the necessary further protective care.

Is it possible for Health Visitors to be helped to recognise the beginnings of breakdown and to enlist the aid of other services? The future is primarily of mental illness rather than of criminality, but both are concerned. The outlook depends on the availability of psychotherapy or at least of the provision of emotional support.

It was noted that the vulnerability of children up to the age of 8 years in care at any one time does not depend on social class.

CHAPTER 6

Family Policy in a Multi-culture Society

ESTHER GOODY

A CASE AND THE JUDGEMENT

Ann (not her real name) aged nine years, a Ghanaian girl fostered nearly all her life by a white professional English couple in suburban Surrey, can stay in their care, Sir George Baker, President of the High Court Family Division, decided yesterday. He said that he could not bring himself to send her back to Africa, where her real parents wanted to take her ... 'My answer in the best interests, present and future, of this girl — despite the blood tie, the race, despite colour, is that I cannot bring myself to send this child to Ghana, and I, as well as the girl, would feel a rankling sense of injustice were I to do so,' he said (The Times, 5 December 1972).

Mr Justice Baker had begun his summing up by saying:

'The reason why I am giving this judgement in open court is that I think the public, and particularly potential foster parents, ought to know of the practice, indeed custom, of West Africans and other coloured people who come to this country, which is that the husband is a student, often a perennial student, the wife works and the children, particularly those born here, are fostered out privately, often for many years, and often as a result of newspaper advertisements or cards in shop windows or by the introduction of friends. The children are brought up in and learn our British ways of life. When a strong bond of attachment and love has been forged between the children and the foster parents, the natural parents take them away, even tear them away, to go with them to West Africa or elsewhere. There is overwhelming evidence before me of this practice, and there have been two other cases before Judges of the Family Division in the last few weeks' (The Times, 5 December 1972).

MODELS OF PARENTHOOD

Mr Justice Baker said he had decided 'in the best interests of the child' — but how is one to determine this? The foster parents argued that the Ghanaian parents could not have loved their daughter since they allowed her to grow up in another family, (Premiss — 'good parents love their children and rear them at home'.) The Ghanaian parents could not understand how any outsider could challenge their right to decide where their own daughter should live, or their right to take her home to Ghana with them when they returned. (Premiss — 'the true parents of a child have

43

an inalienable right to decide where and with whom the child shall live'.) Both
families acted in terms of a culturally provided paradigm, or model, of the nature
of parenthood. The judge, being English, shared the English model of parenthood
used by the foster parents, and he decided that the 'best interests' of the child
would be served by her remaining with the English foster parents. It is hard to
avoid the conclusion that if he had shared the West African paradigm of parenthood
which stresses not only the parents' permanent rights over their children, but also
their obligation to find the best possible training and sponsorship for them, the
judge would have decided that it would be in the girl's best interests to return
to her Ghanaian parents.

The Birmingham Study

It is surprising how persistent such culturally derived models are, even when
one is aware of their power. In a recent study of private fostering in Birmingham,
Holman (1973) found over 60 per cent of the fostered children to be West African,
and that as a group they differed markedly from the English foster children who
were mainly from incomplete families. In seeking to account for this striking
predominance of West African foster children, Holman recounts the traditions of
fostering in West Africa and then, incredibly, goes on to conclude that the explanation does not lie in West African ideas about the nature of parenthood, but that
the West African parents, like the English ones, had fostered their children
because of a family crisis. This was despite the fact that in his sample apparently all the West African private foster children came from families where the
parents were married and in England. The categories 'West African students',
'unmarried mothers', 'deserted mothers', 'deserted fathers' and 'other' appear to
be mutually exclusive (Holman 1973; Goody and Groothues 1977).

Different Cultural Patterns

Cultural paradigms determine goals and standards of what is right or wrong.
Such models (goals, standards) are shaped and validated both by objective conditions of existence, for example Brahmins and beggars have different diets and
receive different amounts of deference, and also by existing systems of ideas
(e.g. the Hindu doctrine of karma). It is therefore not surprising that societies
in different parts of the world have constructed very different cultural paradigms
of family life. What we have to contend with in Britain today is many transposed
cultural paradigms which shape the goals and standards of immigrant peoples. How
is this any different from saying that people from other cultures have different
customs? On one level, of course, it is the same thing. But by using the idea of
a cultural model I want to stress the largely implicit nature of the shaping
process. Goals and standards may be more easily recognised than the underlying
model which produced them. But unless one understands the underlying paradigm
these goals and standards appear arbitrary and even bizarre. When the model is
clear, the particular patterns of behaviour 'make sense'.

Whether we look at actual patterns of behaviour, such as residence, marriage
arrangements, the rearing of children, or at the underlying cultural models, it is
clear that there is no such thing as 'the family' in Britain today, but rather
many different forms. There are at least four major sources of difference in
family forms: one important source I have already mentioned is the various immigrant cultures with substantial numbers living here. Some like East African Asians
and Cypriots have sought refuge from political turmoil, others, like the West
Indians and the Irish, were invited to come and fill jobs that English workers
avoided. Many, South Asians, West Indians, Italians and Portuguese among them,
came seeking work and a livelihood because their homeland offered none; and some,
for instance the West Africans, have come to learn technical and business skills
with which to return to their own lands. Among these many groups the cultural
differences in family forms are distinctive and profound. They have their own
definitions of 'what is a family', of how and whom one marries, of the basis of

legitimacy of children, and of the roles of husband and wife, parents, siblings and children. Watson (1977) and Khan (1979) give accounts of family structure and models of ethnic minorities in Britain.

Sub-cultures in England

A second basic course of differentiation lies within British society itself. For centuries there have been many sorts of family included under the broad umbrella of English culture. Different occupations lead to different occupational sub-cultures. Studies of mining, farming, fishing, factory workers, soldiers, clergymen and bankers, shows that each of them has distinctive features. Regional differences also exist, though these are only partly documented. We know there are major differences between urban, suburban and rural family cultures. Social class is another source of variation; a recent study (Owens 1981) shows sharp differences between family cultures on a working class housing estate and a middle class housing estate in the same town. Of course some of these sub-cultures overlap, and there are many continuities between one and another. But the general pattern is of a proliferation of sub-cultures within British society.

For the many different immigrant groups, and for the English, there are thus 'normal' family forms. These are the basis of the stereotypes that leap to mind when one thinks of 'The English Family' or 'The West Indian Family'. Yet there is substantial variation around these 'normal' forms, certainly among English families. Single parent families, whether as a result of divorce, death or because the parents never married, are increasingly frequent. Outlooks have changed so much that where single women used to hide the fact that they weren't married, now married women may prefer to be thought single. In cities and towns a surprising proportion of men and women live alone and not as a part of any wider domestic group. A recent estimate in the Guardian (Oct. 1981) placed the number of single adults at around 14 million. In the national sample of households for 1978, 22 per cent contained only one person (General Household Survey 1978). Modern medicine is extending the human life span with the result that there are increasing numbers of elderly couples, and single elderly people living alone as remnant families. Finally, where these 'partial' families re-combine we are seeing new forms of domestic groupings based on step- and half-relations. How these variant forms are represented in the English population is impossible to describe in a meaningful way without taking into account the regional, occupational, class and ethnic variations already referred to. There is even variation in the variation. What we do not understand at all well is the way the general paradigm of 'the English family' (or normal sub-cultural paradigms) affects the goals and standards of people living in variant forms. There is some evidence that members of such families see themselves as individually deviant even when (as with single parent families) there are in fact many others like them (Prendergast and Prout 1980; Rodman 1973).

The fourth major source of differentiation between families is a consequence of their isolation and privatization. For to a surprising extent, families can generate their own worlds; life within a family can create a private paradigm, which acts to re-interpret the dominant cultural paradigm, rather than to displace it completely. And here is a paradox: the one common feature of all these many different forms of domestic family is that they are, for their members, the major arena of daily life. They usually provide both the basic needs of food and shelter, and the only intimate human relationships. This is the world that the developing child first comes to know, and that serves as the measure of his future worlds; this is for most of us the one dependable source of help in sickness, of support in trouble, of resort in bereavement. The intensity and totality of dependence on 'the family' is hard to exaggerate. And yet the ways in which these private worlds are organised, with their own versions of the many sub-cultures of which our society is composed, are extraordinarily varied.

46   E. Goody

PRIVATIZATION

In the pre-industrial societies that anthropologists traditionally studied, the family is embedded in political, religious and economic institutions. Patterns of marriage and child-rearing reflect these close links. No doubt individual family members often experienced the claims of kin and family as restrictive, and we often find resentment expressed as accusations of witchcraft or by migration of a segment of the kin group. But when the migrants settle elsewhere they tend to recreate the same structures from which they had fled, with the domestic family linked to others by political, economic and religious ties. Specific institutions develop to manage the more dominant problems; the Chinese have a custom of adopting an infant daughter-in-law to avoid quarrels later between the mother and her son's wife. Where new problems emerge, new responses may become institutionalized although this does not necessarily happen. And an old adaptation may continue after the problem that it met has disappeared.

Anthropologists studying small-scale societies are often able to see how the constraints of political or economic institutions are reflected in religion or in kinship patterns, and how these feed back into the organisation of political and economic forms. But in modern Western society two things have happened which make this interdependence less immediate and much less visible. First, the scale of some institutions has expanded greatly. This is painfully obvious today when recession is an international phenomenon, unemployment extending throughout the country so that moving from one area to another does not greatly improve the chances of finding a job, and strikes are often national in scope, with even international repercussions. Political institutions are heavily weighted towards the national frame, as the choice of candidates for Parliamentary elections makes clear. On the other hand, for many people religion has virtually disappeared as a viable force. The significant members of 'the family' have shrunk to parents and their children, who as adults may or may not be closely involved with their siblings' domestic affairs. Instead of the family heads also holding positions of authority in economic enterprises and community government as in the small-scale systems we study, they are anonymous 'workers' and 'constituents'. Instead of the systems of political power and relations of production slotting into family roles, each domain has its own dynamic, and they are linked only through individuals who have economic, political and family tasks and constraints to balance.

This individualization of society has resulted in a 'privatization' of the family. Instead of the members of several domestic groups being linked by kinship ties, political, economic and ritual roles into the intricate mesh of over-lapping mutual responsibilities which Gluckman (1966) termed 'multiplex roles', there is no one outside the domestic group who have either the responsibility or the right to intervene in its internal affairs. This is demonstrated in the attitude of the police when called to domestic fights. Even when a woman has clearly been injured, they see their role as 'smoothing things over': recruits are taught in police college never to take sides in a domestic dispute (Faragher 1981). Even where there is an injunction against the husband, including powers of arrest, he is seldom detained (Parker 1981). Such non-intervention sharply highlights the sacred nature of what we call 'private family life', as well as supporting the power of a man to do what he likes in his own home. It is significant that the recognition that infants and small children are sometimes seriously injured by parents has created a climate of public opinion in which it has become the legal obligation of social workers to intervene in domestic violence against children. Studies of violence against wives indicate that the only way they can be sure of getting help against their husbands' attacks is by showing that the children are also at risk. The police are in effect legitimating the husband's violence by not intervening and by permitting it to continue.

This privatization of the family has had another unintended consequence in the tendency to develop private norms, 'private family paradigms', about the nature of family life and family relationships. Because of the very privacy of family life, there is little opportunity to compare the rules in one's own home with those of others. And also little opportunity even to realize that one's own rules are unusual.

In a small-scale social system with overlapping (multiplex) roles, where family members have close links outside the family the norms of the society are readily applied to family life. Families cannot function in isolation if they are to share in community concerns such as religious rituals, economic co-operation (clearing of land, irrigation, herding), or the settlement of quarrels. They cannot find husbands for their daughters or wives for their sons unless the family is known to others and has a good reputation. There is an obligatory interdependence which denies the validity of rigid boundaries around the domestic family. The openness of family boundaries in turn ensures that family norms are continually checked against those of the wider society. For instance, in Gonja, in the north of Ghana, if a quarrel is heard between spouses, those nearby intervene, particularly if the husband is physically assaulting his wife. People agree that beating wives is wrong and are ready to enforce this. People also agree that a woman must never lift her hand against her husband. If she does so, the husband has a right to beat her without interference. In both the cases, where a man's violence is considered illegitimate and where it is approved, behaviour within what we would see as the private family domain is viewed as of public concern. Two norms are upheld simultaneously: that women must submit to the authority of men; and that men must not physically injure obedient women.

And here lies the difficulty. For we would agree with one norm, but dispute the other. Who is right? Because Gonja men support each other in the view that a woman should never raise a hand against a man and act accordingly, this does not make it 'true' in any objective sense, however 'true' it may be for women living in Gonja society. Consensus may create pragmatic validity (when in Rome ...), but this is no guarantee of objective validity. Nor is there any guarantee that the norms of a given society are objectively 'good' although they have usually evolved as relatively effective ways of managing recurrent problems, and even though they do in fact dictate the conditions under which people in that society have to live. Thus the privatization of the family domain not only carries a potential for freedom from the imposition of rejected rules, but also means isolation from the protection of the wider society for victims of destructive family sub-cultures.

PROBLEMS OF A MULTI-CULTURE SOCIETY

A family policy in a multi-culture society faces a two-fold problem. On the one hand it requires an understanding of what are the realities for a given family, what are the objective conditions of existence, and what are the cultural paradigms (including sub-cultural and private paradigms) which determine goals and meanings?

On the other hand, this understanding cannot mean automatic acceptance. There must be a basis for setting minimum criteria of viability for family life and family relations. This is so for two reasons: first, there are some patterns of behaviour which objectively 'don't work'. One example is the placing of an African child with a succession of English foster parents. And there are some patterns which create serious problems in British society today, however well-adapted they may have been to the society where they originated. The attempt to arrange marriages for second generation Asian children is probably an example of this sort of *de facto* difficulty. Because the children have participated in British adolescent culture which stresses adolescent independence and highly valued courtship, Asian parents have difficulty in enforcing their traditional control. Obviously it will be both highly sensitive and very difficult to develop ways of determining which patterns don't work, and

even harder to find ways of helping families recognize the need to modify traditional
paradigms. But the easy alternative, to declare that family space is private space
is not an answer. It cannot be the answer because it leaves the family to carry a
burden for which it has not the strength, and the isolation of the contemporary
family leaves it without the support it has in small-scale societies.

A NOTE ON VIOLENCE IN MARRIAGE

One easy way in which the family is vulnerable is in the prevalence of physical
aggression within it. The domestic family in Western society has recently been
described as 'the predominant setting for every form of physical violence from slaps
to torture and murder' (Hotaling and Straus 1980). Children are obviously particularly vulnerable to damage in destructive families. However it is not only children
who are at risk. There is now a wealth of documentation showing how, in British
families, women can be caught in a violent marriage from which they cannot escape
without some outside support (Dobash and Dobash 1980; Martin 1978). But violent
men may themselves be the victims of pressures they cannot cope with. While it is
true that in some societies, for example the Gonja and Cyprus, violence towards
women is legitimate under certain conditions, and is therefore expected of men under
these conditions (Loizos 1978), it is clear that much of the habitual violence in
marriage in contemporary Western society is a mode of managing frustrations by
attacking someone weaker. When a man holds a paradigm of family relationships that
says a husband has the right to do as he likes in his own home, and that women
'need' to be beaten at times, then violence towards his wife becomes a 'normal'
part of the husband's role.

Violence in marriage is a serious problem in Western societies today; it is not,
therefore, an exotic issue brought into our midst by recent immigrants, or even by
some extreme deviant group in our own society. I cite this example of how the
privatization of the family can convert deviant behaviour to 'normal' behaviour
because the kinds of new problems that immigrant cultures have introduced are no
more difficult to understand, and could not be more difficult to resolve.

DISCUSSION

Many special problems arise in a multi-culture society. One that is basic is the
extent to which the sub-culture is to be encouraged to persist and how far to be
assimilated. The fact that ethnic groups in the U.S. are now seeking to re-discover
their roots suggests the importance to individuals within groups of maintaining
links with their own past. In the Courts what is deemed to be in the best interests
of the child is currently judged by British middle class standards, and sub-cultures
find decisions difficult to comprehend or to accept when they contradict their basic
assumptions. The West Indian concept of British justice seems strange to the Briton.
Education too is dominated by the middle class ethic, and T.V. transmissions reflect
the views of the British middle classes who tend to dominate management and policy
making groups. What must be remembered is that the indigenous British population
while not multi-racial is itself multi-cultural but, while not always followed, the
middle class standard of ethics and of culture serve as and are accepted as models.
In housing, differing family structures create immense and insoluble problems when
they confront a system planned for indigenous citizens and used inflexibly. The
barriers are not only colour and language, which uses the same words with different
meanings, but different concepts and different expectations. Practical difficulties
in giving help can be identified. Self-help voluntary groups could contribute much
and improve the take-up of offered services, through a sympathetic understanding of
attitudes and cultural needs. For example there is reticence over biological
matters. Such Ethnic involvement in groups if officially supported, would enhance
status. Frustration and lack of co-operation thrive on the feeling of powerlessness
which afflicts equally minority groups, members of sub-cultures and the lowest indigenous social classes.

CHAPTER 7

Deprivation, Disadvantage and the Family in Britain*

MURIEL BROWN

INTRODUCTION

From 1974-1981 a programme of research into transmitted deprivation was carried out under the direction of a Joint Working Party of the Department of Health and Social Security and the Social Science Research Council. This programme originated in the concern of Sir Keith Joseph, then Secretary of State for Social Services, to understand the persistence of poverty and deprivation in Britain despite the development of social services and a general rise in standards of living. Under the Joint Working Party, Joseph's original concern with a possible cycle of deprivation within a small minority of multi-problem families was broadened out to cover a wide ranging enquiry into the extent and causes of many forms of deprivation and disadvantage and into the efficacy of policies to deal with them. Twenty-three empirical studies and more than a dozen reviews were carried out by over seventy researchers drawn from a wide range of academic disciplines. A series of books, Studies in Deprivation and Disadvantage, is now appearing, and overall the programme will have contributed substantially to our understanding of the meaning of deprivation, particularly of patterns of continuity and discontinuity in deprivation, and to our range of ideas on how it should be tackled.

In conceptual terms the programme encompassed a considerable variety of approaches to the notions of deprivation and of transmission. Even in terms of definitions, and certainly in terms of explanations, there was no easy consensus among all the researchers but a few general things can be said at least about the scope of the work. The range of enquiry widened from the original narrow concern with the problem families into an examination of many forms of deprivation in income, occupation, housing, education, health, deviancy and family life, and also of patterns of multiple and overlapping deprivation. Similarly the search for explanations ranged across the personal and familial processes involved and moved on to consider the part played by social and economic influences. Essentially a fragmented view was taken of deprivation for the subject of study was not 'the deprived' but 'deprivation'. This operational definition meant, inevitably, that it was impossible to arrive at any single explanation of the phenomenon, or, indeed, to observe

---

*This paper is based on the Final Report of the DHSS/SSRC Programme of Research into Transmitted Deprivation on which the author jointly with Dr Nicola Madge has been working. The Report is now published as Despite the Welfare State by Heinemann Educational Books, 1982.

any single solutions to the policy problems posed. Very broadly the programme concluded with regard to explanations that individuals suffer deprivation as a result
of a complex interaction between their personal and familial characteristics and
the socio economic constraints and opportunities of the structures in which they
operate. For explanations of the levels of certain deprivation such as unemployment or poor housing, the structural factors are regarded as most relevant, while
in explanations of why particular individuals become deprived, the personal factors
tend to predominate. With regard to interventions, therefore, measures to tackle
both the levels of deprivation and the vulnerability of certain individuals or
groups to particular deprivations are seen as necessary.

Although the programme evolved into a wide ranging concern for patterns of
disadvantage, it retained its primary interest in the family. Much of the research
was concerned with families either as the direct focus of study or in terms of the
impact of certain policies, provisions or problems upon the family. It is therefore possible to abstract from the work of the programme some evidence of the state
of deprivation and disadvantage among families in Britain and some discussion of
explanations for its persistence. The implications for policy and practice that
derive from the research can likewise be presented in similar abbreviated form.
Because of the range of the programme much of what follows is likely to echo the
more detailed findings and views of other contributors to this seminar who have
worked to a more specialised remit. But though inevitably superficial, the picture
presented here has the merit of a broad canvas in providing a sense of perspective
and showing some of the relationships between the various problems that families
face. It cannot hope to do justice to the original work of the DHSS/SSRC programme,
because that is both detailed and extensive, but it might prompt some participants
to pursue the separate studies as they become available in the Heinemann series.

EXTENT OF DEPRIVATION AMONG FAMILIES

Families were found to be affected by all the separate states of deprivation
studied by the DHSS/SSRC programme of research. They suffer from poverty and bad
housing and the damaging consequences of unemployment, ill health, deviant behaviour
and poor educational attainment, while family failure, through breakdown and inadequate parenting, involves considerable distress and deprivation.

There is undoubtedly a substantial amount of deprivation in Britain although,
because it is relative to changing standards and lifestyles, it is difficult to
measure it exactly and even harder to map its persistence over time. In any
assembly of data on deprivation and disadvantage certain social groups emerge
clearly as more vulnerable than others and these groups include families, particularly large families and one parent families. Research on transmitted deprivation
showed that deprivation is not only extensive, it is also real, in the sense that
it involves serious suffering and in the sense that it frequently leads to disadvantage, that is, it has detrimental consequences for those who suffer it (Brown
and Madge 1982).

Poverty is fairly widespread in Britain though estimates of its extent depend on
the definition adopted. On a more conservative estimate, from government figures,
ten million people currently live in poverty, and that number includes four million
in families. One fifth of large families and a third of one parent families are
among the very poor, that is they live at or below the prevailing supplementary
benefit rates. Evidence from a variety of surveys suggests that living in poverty
today still means real suffering and deprivation. Families experience actual
shortages of food, clothing and household goods, and what they have is often of
inferior quality with all the consequent dreariness of poor diets, the frustration
of handling broken and defective goods, the danger of cheap fuel and heating
appliances and the stigma of general shabbiness. Low income families have to manage

slender resources, coping as best they can with the unpredictable demands of children and the inequities of inflation, aggravated by poor credit facilities and a
confusing array of means tested benefits, some of which are hardly worth the time
and effort involved in claiming them. They experience the humiliation of dependence, the frustration of being trapped by selectivity and the hopelessness of
seeing no chance of betterment.

The consequences of poverty include isolation, depression and demoralisation,
the near certainty of debt and the risk of fuel supply disconnections and evictions,
either of which may jeopardise the very survival of the family as a unit. Children
suffer from the strains of parental anxiety and discord, from humiliation among
friends, exclusion from some school activities and an enhanced risk of being taken
into care, as well as from the actual deprivations of living in families that are
chronically short of money, and cannot afford treats or indulgence of carelessness
(Ashley 1983).

Housing deprivation is commonly linked to family poverty. Again, large families
and one parent families are more likely to suffer from overcrowding or lack of
amenities than ordinary families. But the extent of official housing deprivation,
though disturbing, is no real measure of the impact it has on family life. There
are currently 1.8 million households living in unsatisfactory housing conditions
but very many more suffer the deprivations of inferior accommodation and poor
environment. Although flats on many public sector estates are usually possessed
of standard amenities, they are often unpleasantly cramped, inconvenient and inaccessible, and their surroundings are dreary and unpleasant. Some estates have
been vandalised, others are isolated on the peripheries of towns with few amenities,
yet others are high rise and inhuman in scale. Most are depressing places in which
to bring up children, lacking in play facilities and destructive of community networks. Meanwhile the multi occupied slums of the inner city remain while some
families are forced into caravan dwelling or outright homelessness by shortages,
high rents and restricted access to public housing.

For many families the basic deprivations of poverty and bad housing are compounded
by the impact of low occupational status, unemployment, poor health and chronic
disability. Each deprivation has its own chronicle of difficulties and restrictions
but most are harder to cope with in families, especially with young children. Just
as poverty is undoubtedly particularly stressful for families, so poor housing can
handicap the development of children and dent parental relationships. Poor health
and disability are always problematic but they may, in addition, severely reduce
the ability of a family to cope with the pressing demands of child care. Disability
among children themselves puts enormous burdens on the caring family and affects
its needs for resources of all kinds. For some families the interlocking web of
multiple deprivation is further compounded by hostility and prejudice whether
expressed as a 'blaming the victim' attitude towards the unemployed on supplementary
benefit or as vicious hostility towards blacks and other ethnic minorities.

The extent of multiple deprivation is difficult to assess but some overlap is
probably quite common and deprivation in terms of low income and low occupational
status is frequently associated with other deprivations. One estimate (Berthoud
1983) suggests that over a million families can be considered multiply deprived
while about 50,000 are deprived, at the same time, in terms of income, occupation,
housing, education, health and family circumstances. Where single deprivations
overlap the impact is intensified and the level of stress experienced may well become intolerable. Problems interact and exacerbate one another: for example,
family relationships are strained by persistent poverty, disability is compounded
by inadequate housing, budgetting is harder with poor education, the burden of child
rearing is increased for isolated lone parents, and so on. Moreover, there is
evidence of continuity both inter and intra-generationally in many deprivations.
While no simple cycle of deprivation exists, it does appear that some groups are

consistently disadvantaged by low incomes, poor health, inadequate housing and low
occupational status. By contrast advantage is even more likely to be passed on
from generation to generation (Brown and Madge 1982). Adverse emotional experiences in childhood, including the experience of being in care is likely to increase
the chance of poor parenting behaviour in adulthood (Rutter and Quinton in Press &
Triseliotis and Russell 1982).

Some parents fail, perhaps not surprisingly, to provide children with good or
consistent care and children are abandoned, or neglected and abused, or are taken
into care by the local authority. In other families, ill health, particularly of
the mother, homelessness, or the child's own waywardness or delinquency may result
in reception into care. All these events are painful, especially for the children.
There is abundant evidence that children are hurt by being taken into care both in
the sense that they suffer and in the sense that they are often damaged by the
experience. The scale of serious child abuse is hard to establish, but it is
estimated that 1 in 2000 children are involved. Around 7 per cent of children at
any one time are likely to be in local authority care some of whom will remain in
long term care throughout their childhood. A considerable though unknown number
of families have difficulties and make contact with social services departments or
voluntary agencies. Most have practical problems usually financial or housing, but
a minority are chronically disorganised and their dependence on social agencies is
likely to be long term.

THE SOCIAL POLICY IMPLICATIONS

Much of the work of the programme was concerned to find ways of intervening to
prevent or alleviate the deprivation described and to reduce its disadvantaging
impact. No real evaluative studies were undertaken of particular interventions
but a good many implications for policy were derived from studies that looked at
the extent of the various deprivations and examined the reasons for their persistence, as well as from reviews of related research.

One general conclusion was that 'we need more overt, explicit and coordinated
family policies'(Coffield et al, 1981), which should involve more provision
specifically for families and also a 'family dimension' in the delivery of all
major social services. Most policy suggestions concerned the statutory social
services but the important role of the voluntary sector was stressed and implications for the community as a whole were clearly discernible.

The work of the transmitted deprivation programme endorsed the widespread conviction that the present social security provision for families is grossly inadequate. It suggests that a thorough review of family income maintenance is
urgently needed. The present level of income support for the poorest families is
simply not high enough to prevent considerable distress and disadvantage. Moreover
failure to coordinate tax and benefit systems produces a poverty trap for families
with low earnings, while families on Supplementary Benefit are confused by boundary
problems between SB and other services. It is also clear from the studies that an
effective housing allowance is needed to tackle inequities in housing finance and
to help poorer families improve their access to decent housing (Murie 1982).
Several researchers pointed out the evidence of dismal failure in schemes to
provide financial support for school age children (Mortimore and Blackstone 1982).

A review of family income maintenance would need to face all these diverse
problems as well as to consider ways of dealing fairly with all families: those
dependent, for long or short periods, on social security and those on low incomes
and those with both parents working. Problems of equity are tricky and the resource implications are sobering but it does seem abundantly clear that more fair,
flexible and generous financial provision must be made for families as a matter of

priority (Brown and Madge 1982; Fuller and Stevenson 1983).

Family poverty has some other implications for policy. The contribution to the family budget of women's earnings was noted. Without it many more families would slip into poverty but the implications for child minding are not always faced. For the preschool child, the need is clearly for good day care facilities that combine the best of nursery schooling with flexible care arrangements. For the school age child reliable schemes for holiday care and imaginative after school provision should be developed. Many mothers, of course, would not wish to work when their children were very small, or not work such long hours, but are forced to for financial reasons. Consideration should be given to the provision of cash allowances for mothers who stay at home, particularly since an increasing number are being forced out of work because of unemployment and reduction in care provision. But women also need better work opportunities, more part time facilities and more career security and provision for training and support when entering and re-entering the labour market.

There was some evidence that many families suffered not only from the deprivation of poverty but from the damaging consequences of debt and disconnection of services. The need for more education in money management was indicated and it was suggested that more money advice centres were needed where families could obtain information, help with budgetting problems and debt counselling. Budgetting advice could help prevent an escalation of difficulties although it was stressed that remarkably little is known about the size of money problems or the exact part they play in deprivation and disadvantage. More forceful consumer protection may be one general approach that would be useful (Ashley 1983).

Apart from the general conclusion of the need to tackle the inequalities of housing finance, the implication on housing that most concerned families were related to the management of the public sector. There is clear evidence of the need to give greater priority to run down estates as well as to the improvement of depressed inner city areas. Numerous physical improvements are indicated, involving the expansion of amenities, but attention should also be directed to social development. There should be more community facilities, more tenant participation in the running of estates and less discriminatory allocation procedures. Most importantly, the local authority must work to avoid the residualisation of the public sector by ensuring that the quality and the quantity of the housing stock are kept up (Murie 1982; Ineichen 1983).

It should come as no real surprise that the provision of a decent income and a good home are seen as central to any attack on deprivation. The work of the programme merely endorses the generally held view of the importance of these environmental factors in the origins and persistence of deprivation. Action to deal effectively with poverty and poor housing would clearly go far to eradicate a substantial amount of deprivation among families and aid them in their crucial caring and parenting roles.

There are further implications on the need for help with parenting. The classic multi-problem families appears to be only a tiny minority of families with difficulties. They need steady support and there are some grounds for optimism in the findings that changes for the better can come at quite late stages in the life cycle and that offspring need not necessarily repeat the patterns of extreme disorganisation and dependency that characterised their parents (Tonge *et al* 1982). But many more families have some degree of difficulty with parenting as well as practical problems. Very young mothers, lacking good emotional support are at risk of inadequate parenting and need special help, including skilled counselling, as well as advice on child rearing and care (Wolkind *et al* 1979). Vulnerable young people include many girls who have had no success at school or work and seek for an absorbing and status-enhancing role in early motherhood, as well as the smaller

FM - E

number who have been emotionally damaged in childhood. Sex education needs to be
vastly improved and, going far beyond the provision of information, to involve
young people in groups geared towards self development through exploration of the
material, social and emotional, as well as the physical consequences of unwanted
pregnancy. Concern for children in care must also be increased, particularly for
those in residential institutions who are highly vulnerable and especially if they
have to face the end of their substitute care by leaving abruptly for a bleak and
friendless world. Hostel provision for children coming out of care, sustained
social work contact into real adulthood and sensitive youth work are all needed for
this group (Rutter and Quinton in Press).

While efforts must be made to help children from institutional backgrounds, it
is important to avoid such backgrounds as far as possible. Care is often necessary
but it does seem that adoption and fostering are preferred alternatives for childre
who have scant chance of returning home to their natural families. And whatever
the care alternatives the need for better planning for individual children in care
has been powerfully demonstrated, planning which avoids undue delays, confusing
and unexplained moves and unnecessary retention in care. Older children clearly
need to be more directly involved in decisions about their future.

The importance of participation and self determination was stressed at many
points in the programme. Invulnerability to the damage of deprivation appeared to
be associated with confidence and the ability to seize opportunities and to act
independently. Individuals need opportunities for self expression as well as
encouragement in exploration and adventure. But the importance of good relationships was regularly shown to matter: loving parents, stable marriage partners and
good friends are shown to be as critically important to overcoming deprivation as
common sense has always claimed.

Families, who are young and unsupported or large and overwhelmed, require more
help with the actual problems of the parenting role. Preventive work with families
has not been well developed by local social services departments, and actual provision for families, rather than children, is negligible. Social work should be
more flexible with some degree of specialisation on family needs and problems.
The potential of group work has not been fully exploited and family centres should
be developed. The voluntary sector can provide activities like family groups, whic
maximise opportunities for peer group learning and community development, but shoul
work through partnership with statutory services, both local or central, particularly for purposes of funding and often for professional support.

Disadvantage in terms of poor health was found to be strongly linked to general
socio-economic disadvantage among families. Reviewing the literature on the health
of children Blaxter (1981) concluded that,

'It is the parent's environment which normally affects the health of the child
... Adults in a disadvantaging environment are likely to produce health deprived
children.'

Nevertheless, although this underlines the need to take action against poverty
and bad housing some improvements to the delivery of health services were indicated
For families with young children the health visitor was shown to be a vital support
and the attachment of health visitors to general practices or health centres was
generally favoured by mothers. The importance of health education, particularly
on matters concerning childbearing and parenting, was demonstrated repeatedly. But
in all aspects of health care it was clear that the most vulnerable families would
only be helped if more account were taken of sociological insights to patient
preferences, prejudices and anxieties in the planning and delivery of services.

In terms of prevention the message of the research was that help is needed for tomorrow's families rather than today's. Young people continue to be born into and grow up in deprived circumstances and their deprivations handicap and disadvantage them into adulthood and across the generations (Kolvin *et al* 1981; Essen and Wedge 1982). Efforts are needed to ensure that young people do not grow up in poverty or face shrinking employment prospects without educational attainments or decent training opportunities, or suffer the adversities of neglect or family breakdown. Young people need hope and confidence in the future and prospects of work and prosperity and self fulfillment if they are to be good parents. The implications of this approach to breaking the cycles of disadvantage are far-reaching as they concern employment opportunities, income policies and vocational training programmes as well as action within social services. But an effective policy for families should start with concern for young people. The evidence is that they are among the relatively disadvantaged in today's society. They need priority attention.

CONCLUSION

The DHSS/SSRC work on Transmitted Deprivation has demonstrated that families in Britain suffer considerable deprivation and disadvantage. While this conclusion is hardly new, the programme has undoubtedly added to our understanding of the meaning of this deprivation for families and of the processes which generate, sustain and perpetuate it. As a result it has helped to emphasise the need for social intervention to prevent or reduce deprivation and clarified some ideas on possible new directions for such intervention. I must stress again that this brief paper provides only a superficial glance on the overall work of the programme. Much is omitted altogether and what is discussed is condensed to the level of generalisation. The aim is merely to provide some indication of the overall scope of the programme and of its relevance to families.

DISCUSSION

Beginning as a quest for the existence of a cycle of deprivation, the studies referred to by Dr. Brown had extended their scope to a large scale study of deprivation itself, with a consequent dilution of interest and intensity. The results suggested that not one but many cycles of deprivation are operating and that the extent of both deprivation and poverty is greater than expected. The question was raised of the justification for such elaborate studies which would need to last for a number of years, would be costly in money and personnel and were unlikely to reveal anything really new. On the question of transmission of the disadvantage that resulted in deprivation, the fault was judged to be less with personal factors, although these played a part, than with the persistence of bad environmental conditions. Deprivation can make life awful for the disadvantaged family by providing a grim environment in which children are brought up lacking the example and the experience of the satisfactions of happy family life. Multi-problem families can be produced and are reproduced by the environment. Deprivation itself is essentially relative to expectation and its effects vary with personality, representing an interaction between the individual and the environment. Two features, often ignored, are loss of opportunity and restrictions of choice, often to vanishing point. This is especially true of housing. A pre-requisite for improvement is a change of attitude. The existing barriers between benefit, tax, employment and housing must be broken down. The two priority areas are financial support and housing. The inadequacy of the former must be recognised and corrected. The main focus of family income should be on dependent children, and work and a wage should be allowed to supplement it. Society's present approach is fragmented, the variations in approach depending on differences in cause and in method of help. Three groups of disadvantaged families are recognised as in urgent need of help: a small number of the multiply deprived, some who merit concentrated

help because they form the lowest socio-economic section of a much larger group
with some deprivation, and some needing complicated and detailed special consideration. Behind it all lay the inadequacy of income maintenance for the proper rearing of children. Present delivery systems should be analysed and revamped on
functional lines, some to continue unchanged, some to be refined and made more
sensitive to the actual circumstances of need. One unsolved problem is how to get
workers in the various statutory and voluntary agencies to work together. Even in
the execution of government policy due consideration of the effect on the family
is lacking so that particular elements are found to be in opposition and working
against each other.

Despite the large amounts of money being spent on services, social, health and
educational problems have not been solved and people have not been helped to help
themselves and in so doing to set a good example to their children. There is room
for experiment in methods of lifting people out of the cycle. With limited resources, perhaps attention should be concentrated on the multiply deprived, where
the inadequate family is overwhelmed by the socio-economic stress. The evaluation
of cost benefit requires a long historical perspective. Meanwhile knowledge
derived from recent and current research studies must be taken into account in
policy planning and spread widely to workers, public and the families themselves.

CHAPTER 8

Housing and the Family — Policy Issues

JOHN PARK

THE HISTORY OF MUNICIPAL HOUSING

The origins of public housing can be traced to the start of the Housing Association movement in the second half of the nineteenth century. Though housing problems are recorded in an Elizabethan Act of 1593, it was the industrial revolution which caused the growth of slums whose horrors have been documented by Henry Mayhew, Charles Dickens and others. The worst conditions were described by a city missionary, quoted by the Earl of Shaftesbury when putting through Parliament in 1851 the Common Lodging Houses Act. He described a house of eight rooms, all let to individuals who furnished and relet them. In one room, 18ft by 10ft, 27 male and female adults and 31 children slept. In the top room of the house, 12ft by 10ft, were 6 beds, and 32 human beings, said the missionary, slept there 'all breathing the pestiferous air of a hole not fit to keep swine in'.

The early Public Health Acts gave local authorities powers to deal, firstly with individual insanitary houses, later with whole areas of bad housing, by clearing unfit houses and developing the sites and so it is entirely appropriate to acknowledge the debt due to the efforts of health workers in connection with housing.

The first developments were achieved by the philanthropic societies which modelled themselves on the pioneering work of Octavia Hill. She undertook the management of three tenement houses purchased by John Ruskin in 1864. Using her ideas, the model dwelling associations sought to demonstrate that wage earners could be provided with dwellings which had a regular water supply, adequate sewage disposal and proper ventilation, at rents that they could afford, without overcrowding, while giving a modest return on capital. A Marxist historian of housing has called it 'Philanthropy at five per cent'. The institutions which did most building were the Peabody Trust, the Improved Industrial Dwellings Company, the East End Dwellings Company, the Guinness Trust, and the 4 per cent Industrial Dwellings Company, most of which were founded by wealthy industrialists such as Peabody, Waterlow, Guinness and Rothschild. Their efforts were concentrated in London. Local authorities were only permitted to build lodging houses, and it seems that Huddersfield, Dundee and Glasgow were among the first off the mark, though a loan of £13,000 is recorded to enable Liverpool to build St. Martin's Cottages.

The Cross Acts of 1875 and 1879 gave local authorities powers to deal with unhealthy areas by acquiring land and building for improvement. Contrary to the intentions of the initiator, Sir Richard Cross, the 1875 Act is said by housing historians to be the turning point which led directly to municipal housing, Liverpool again being among the first authorities to build. The Act had intended the dwellings to be sold off within 10 years. Sir Richard Cross himself said that it was 'not the duty of the Government to provide any class of citizens with any of the necessaries of life, and among the necessaries of life we must of course include good and habitable dwellings'.

Although much space should not be occupied by the history of municipal housing, it is important to understand its origins. Originally, provision was made for artisans. The philanthropic organisations did not permit overcrowding in the model dwellings they provided, but they left insanitary tenements to be filled again and again by people whose prime problem was poverty. Without the concept of subsidised rents, the real problems remained unsolved. The report of the Royal Commission on Housing, 1884-1885, found overcrowding on the increase, particularly in London, and led the way for the Housing of the Working Classes Act, 1890. This Act, by including family dwellings within a definition which had been confined to lodging houses, enabled authorities to provide new homes for working class families without previously clearing unfit properties. To prevent a number of families from having to share accommodation regarded as only suitable for one family the London County Council began to build estates in Acton, Croydon, Tooting and Tottenham, sending families to these suburbs from within what were then the boundaries of the County of London.

Some initial themes emerge from a brief historical survey. The first is that in the early days the philanthropists sought to provide housing specifically for families, and, secondly, that from the beginning it was the artisan class for whom provision was made. These two should be noted because many of the conflicts and much of the anguished debate about what sort of people Council housing is, or should be, for stems from these two ideas. For a long time, when the providers (or 'housers' as David Donnison once described us) of housing had to find ways to ration accommodation, Council housing was limited to families. Indeed, even today many Councils will not accept single people on to their waiting list until they reach a certain age, be it 40 or 60 years as in some cases it is. There is, therefore, a long history of prejudice in favour of families or of housing families: how they are dealt with is another matter. From the second point comes a prejudice which tends to discriminate against the most disadvantaged. One could almost say, that there is a subconscious prejudice among Council tenants against the non-artisan, against, in other words, the non-employed, the one-parent families, the unsocial families who do not pay rent or who cause nuisance. These prejudices come to the surface in discussions on allocation with Tenant Associations when they begin to talk about the people whom they would like to exclude from their estates.

Stressing these two points is not a diversion but raises issues to which this paper must return.

Another question, still in the forefront of the housing debate, can be seen in the early beginnings. Housing has always been bedevilled by the largely political argument about social ownership. The question can be put this way: is it, or is not, a good thing that housing should be provided by the State as one of the necessaries of life? Opposing views over the last hundred years have been based on political theory, and the controversy is far from over. The debate on the Housing Act 1980 showed an old battle rumbling on between the belief that everyone should be/can be self-sufficient and the belief that many people cannot provide for themselves and therefore society, in the guise of the state or the local authority, should ensure that provision is made. The Housing Association movement, the twentieth century descendant of the nineteenth century philanthropists, is stronger than ever and is a major force in housing. The problems that the nineteenth century tried to solve remain.

THE OWNER OCCUPIER

In this century, some new themes can be identified, which have considerably influenced housing policy. The first concerns changes in the cost of money, and,
therefore in the possibility of landlords getting 'a reasonable profit' out of
housing. The second is a fundamental shift in the concept of ownership.

One hundred years ago, very few people owned their own houses. Apart from the
landed gentry with their estates and town houses and the wealthy industrialists
who had built imposing residences near the source of their wealth, most people
lived in rented property. There was an old tradition, best exemplified by Robert
Owen and Titus Salt, that industrialists should provide homes for their workers.
With less philanthropy than self-interest, astute mineowners built the mining
villages so that their employees could live near the collieries. But the number
of houses provided by the employers or by the philanthropic bodies were so few
that they hardly counted. Most property was built by individuals or by firms for
renting at a profit.

After the First World War, following the 'Homes for Heroes' drive, a series of
legislative changes encouraged the growth of municipal housing. The great
'cottage' estates of local authorities such as the London County Council , Manchester, Newcastle, and Woolwich, which went into building in a big way began to
sprout them. Something else happened in the thirties. Five per cent began to
fail as a basis for a fair return on capital, unless you were a Gulbenkian and
volume brought its own rewards. The growth of suburbia and the growth of home
ownership began at about the same time.

It has been estimated that in 1920 some 85 to 90 per cent of property was owned
by private persons and let to tenants. Between 1928 and 1937 the number of Building Society borrowers increased from 534,000 to 1,392,000. By 1939, one quarter
of all householders were home owners. Since then, the decline of the private
landlord has continued, at an increasing pace. Now, more than 55 per cent of all
households are owner occupiers, 33 per cent are tenants of Councils or Housing
Associations, and only 12 per cent of property is rented by private landlords.

I stressed the importance of the cost of money. Perhaps I should also have
stressed the value of money. Whereas my father had to be persuaded to buy a house
in 1937, and my father-in-law never did, believing it to be a 'mill-stone', now
young colleagues of mine take on mortgages of £20,000 to £25,000 without turning a
hair! The private landlord, on the other hand, has not been able to make a profit
as a landlord for many years. In the post-war years some infamous practices arose,
of which Rachmanism is only the worst example: there were too many temptations for
landlords to 'winkle' out their tenants in order to sell the property with vacant
possession, and thus realise a capital profit. It still goes on. Within the last
year, my nephew and a friend were offered £1,000 each to give up the tenancy of a
flat they had rented for less than a year at £50 per week between them.

Obviously, the main growth in housing, both municipally-owned and owner-occupied,
has occurred since the Second World War. While the Public Works Loans Board rates
of interest were low, in the 1945-1951 period, building for the public sector
dominated the construction figures. Public sector building peaked in 1953 and
began to decline, while the number of private sector completions began to rise,
overtaking the public sector figures finally in 1959. Although the positions
changed, for a brief couple of years in the mid-seventies, there have been savage
cuts in housing expenditure since then, so much so that the Greater London Council's
London Housing Appraisal, 1981 can say 'Completions are now at their lowest level
since 1952'.

HOUSING SUBSIDY

Somewhere in the period under discussion the old fear of providing something that people should provide for themselves was resurrected. The 1961 Conservative White Paper on Housing said:

'The Government's aim is to secure that there will be houses for sale and houses for rent in sufficient numbers to keep pace with the rising demand of a prospering society. As real incomes go up, more and more of this need, both for sale and to rent, should be met by private enterprise. For those who can neither afford to buy their own homes, nor to pay economic rents there will be the $3\frac{1}{2}$ million publicly-owned houses — increasing in number as local authorities continue to build for the needs which only they can meet.'

The underlying philosophy, that subsidised housing was only for people who could not afford to buy, pervaded the ensuing six years, despite a change in Government. Owner occupation flourished and was encouraged, and whether or not Councils should control large stocks became a major political issue as 'municipalisation' was embraced as a strategy by many labour authorities.

It would be an over-simplification to say that the old arguments finally came to a head with the 1980 Housing Act, which gave tenants the right to buy and thus forced Labour Councils ideologically opposed to sales to bow to the law. Professionals like me can claim that even if only 10 per cent of the stock is sold, the effect in the total housing picture is marginal, a 3 per cent change overall. But the loss of the best family houses, and the lack of any new provision could still be catastrophic for many families.

To ensure impartiality in describing the current picture, the facts are taken from the latest Greater London Council appraisal, already quoted. The national picture is grim, and the position faced by London is almost disastrous. Though London's population seems likely to continue to decline, by perhaps 2 per cent in the next decade, the number of households is increasing. At the same time, with only 29,000 new units anticipated in the public sector between 1981 and 1986, and sales of more than 45,000, the Greater London Council expect the public stock to decrease by 20 per cent. Waiting lists are now 'as high as ever have been recorded' since the Greater London Council was established' (240,000 in April, 1981), homelessness has grown (London rehouses a third of the country's homeless, 17,500 in 1980) and yet the number of lettings available has dropped. Only 20,000 were housed from waiting lists in 1980.

For council tenants who want transfers, the situation is bleak. Most Councils have systems which enable tenants to move to a new home after a certain period. At their peak time of building housing, Councils were building flats with the most frightening result that nationally there are hundreds of thousands of families literally 'trapped' (a word originally used in an Inner Urban study of Lambeth published in 1977) in blocks of flats or maisonettes. Tower blocks are not the real worry: many authorities have tried to reduce the child population in multi-storey blocks, letting only to adult families without children. For example, in a survey of forty eight tower blocks in the City of Newcastle seven years ago, a majority of the tenants felt satisfied with their accommodation.

The most intractable problems are in the blocks of maisonettes, particularly those with deck access, the miles of 'streets in the sky', like the notorious Aylesbury Estate in Southwark, or the relatively new but terrifying Stockwell Park Estate in Lambeth. In these blocks, families seem to feel herded together, vandalism is rife, and frustration grows as tenants see fewer and fewer opportunities of getting a transfer to a house on a more acceptable estate. The mistake of the past will haunt us for many years. An obvious example is the Kirby Estate in Liverpool, a City where so much was pioneered and so much has gone wrong.

THE HOUSING MANAGER'S POINT OF VIEW

The final section looks briefly at the way families fare in council housing from a Housing Manager's point of view. Current Government policies seem to be aimed at cutting housing costs further. Not only will there be less money to provide new homes, or to improve old ones, but expenditure plans clearly indicate that subsidies to Council housing will be steadily reduced. This means that rents will increase, regularly and inexorably. This may not cause a problem for many 'average' tenants, because it could be said that Council rents are not excessively high. The last available figures from the Family Expenditure Surveys showed average gross incomes for local authority tenants (in greater London) in 1978/79 as £94 per week: average rent and rates, net of rebates (an important point) were £10. This means that expenditure on housing, at 11 per cent of income, seems not unreasonable, as the percentage had been constant for some years. But many tenants are not average.

It is easy for a Housing Manager to say that the average tenant merely wants the key to his house, is willing to pay his rent and wants to close the door behind him and not to be bothered by talk about tenant participation in housing management. Many tenants do not see, and do not need to be seen by, housing management staff from one year end to the next, but perhaps a third of all Council tenants are on some sort of rebate, either rent and rate rebates or supplementary benefits. Many families are still poor. Most analyses of public sector tenants show that disadvantaged groups (the elderly, the disabled, one-parent families, the unemployed, the lower paid workers) are all disproportionately over-represented, and Council tenants are still the most overcrowded.

Housing Management is not an exact science. Despite attempts by many housing officers to raise professional standards, not every estate officer has a sympathetic awareness of the multiplicity of problems that many Council tenants face. The community aspect (to use another cant phrase) is often forgotten.

In an ideal world an estate officer would know all the tenants on his patch, would be able (in a less patronising and less maternalistic way, perhaps, than Octavia Hill a hundred years ago) to ensure that all the other agencies, whose help might be required, could be drawn in to help. It can happen. The best officers are conscious of many needs, will spend time contacting the DHSS, talking to Social Workers, trying to understand. But the pressure on them now is too great.

Like social workers, estate officers are caught in the other vice of general policy. The pressure, both of Government and apparently of public opinion, to reduce local authority expenditure and cut down on local authority staff. The result is that between chasing repairs, doing inspections of vacant properties to ensure their readiness for reletting quickly, taking prospective tenants to see properties offered to them and, with luck, signing new tenancy agreements if the offers are accepted, estate officers are left with little time to do anything else but chase arrears. The scale of local authority arrears can be exaggerated. When a large organisation is collecting an income of approaching £30,000,000 a bad debt figure of 2 per cent does not seem inordinately high; such a figure might be acceptable to a commercial organisation. The actual arrears figure, approaching £13,000,000 in the case of London Borough of Greenwich, makes for unfavourable headlines because public money is at stake. Inevitably, as rents rise, the arrears figure grows. Under pressure, estate officers have less and less time to distinguish between those who will not and those who can not pay.

To present excuses for failure is a sad role for any professional. Sadly, we fail too often. For instance, we should not be seen as creating difficulties for

a pregnant girl who is homeless. Under the 1977 Homeless Persons Act, she is
vulnerable and should be housed, and in Greenwich she would be. But many authorities, conscious of the pressure of demand on a declining stock, will be reluctant
to act until the last moment. Nor should we be seen as failing to explain to
families whether they would be better off on supplementary benefit or a rent rebate
although many of us will, because in the last twelve months, the Department of
Health and Social Security have unilaterally withdrawn the service which they
provided. The Government advice to Councils suggests, in effect, that local authorities might wish to consider whether or not to tell tenants to check whether
they would be better off on reabtes than on benefit, mealy-mouthed advice indeed.
In practice, few Councils encourage tenants to come to them for fear of having
insufficient staff to deal with the expected rush of enquiries.

Council Housing in the future is in danger of becoming residual welfare housing,
with families who cannot help themselves condemned to live in decaying property that
other tenants would not buy. But it will be welfare housing without welfare
services from Housing management.

THE FUTURE

To prevent this, we need positive policies to ensure replacement of family homes
and the refurbishment of the difficult blocks so that they can be let to groups of
people without children. We need determined efforts to improve the standard of
management so that a simplistic landlord view changes to a more consciously caring
role. We need a massive investment of resources in people as well as in bricks and
mortar. More than anything else we need an effort of will, on Society's part, to
recognise that for many families, decent housing is still one of the necessaries of
life, and caring for families who need it one of the signs of a mature and civilised
nation.

CHAPTER 9

Housing Problems of the Inner City Family:
the Practical Outcome of Government Policy

PAMELA HUTCHENCE

INTRODUCTION

The Harding Housing Association in Wandsworth was founded by Dr Beryl Harding in
1962 to provide accommodation for needy families in certain Inner London Boroughs.
Since then much work has been done by the many agencies that are trying to improve
the housing situation in London, but the difficulties facing the young family in
search of a home are increasing rather than decreasing. John Park has set out in
Chapter 8 some of the disturbing facts about the dwindling supply of public housing
in London; in the next ten years the stock of housing in public ownership is
expected to decline by 20 per cent. With one third of the national housing stock
built before 1913, the sharp decline in repair and maintenance work is accelerating
its deterioration.

   This reduction in the supply of housing stock, the deterioration of old properties, and the lack of a consistent policy on housing from successive governments
must adversely affect the chances of a family searching for a suitable home to live
in. A family's housing prospects are affected by other factors such as the unpredictable quality of human nature, the multiplicity of decisions to be made by individuals in all branches of government, research and planning, the way in which
policy is interpreted, and the choices and expectations of the applicants themselves.
However it is the economic situation that dominates the policy making decisions of
central and local government, and it is the interaction of their policies which
governs the standard of housing provision in each area.

HOUSING AND PARTY POLITICS

   The changes in policy due to regular alternation in a council's political
allegiance make it difficult for the officers to administer the housing department
with any degree of consistency, although the lurch from one direction to another
does curb some excesses. But it can also promote extreme decisions form the party
in power, intended to stymie their opponents in the next session.

WANDSWORTH

   For example, the London Borough of Wandsworth regularly swings from Labour to
Conservative majorities and back. Labour dominated councils took full advantage of

the policy of municipalisation in the 1970s, by purchasing property all over the borough.

The combination of a Conservative council and a Conservative central government in 1981 has produced an intense concentration on the sale of council property to the general public as well as to sitting tenants. By March 1981 1,000 council properties had been sold: of these 400 went to sitting tenants and 600 were sold as empty properties. Should a Labour Council be elected in May 1982 the Council will own no land for development, and the municipalised property, originally designated for conversion and improvement, will have been absorbed by the private sector.

The only new council building being started in Wandsworth is sheltered housing for elderly people. Property still in the pipe line, remaining from the previous council's housing programme, will be sold when completed either to private individuals or firms, in order to keep the rates down. Certain newly built rented properties may only be let to families with incomes of over £10,000 a year because the rents are set at between £35 and £50 a week. This virtually restricts the chances of the poorer families to renting only re-lets, which are naturally the older and less desirable properties.

The Waiting List

Many typical Inner City housing problems are illustrated by the housing situation in Wandsworth. The borough housing stock consists of 40,000 units; there are 7,000 people on the Waiting List and 10,000 people on the transfer list. It is agreed that such a waiting list does not represent the whole of the housing need within an area, it is merely the tip of the iceberg. There are many 'hidden' families, who regard their chances of obtaining a home as nil, and so never apply. Nor does a significant proportion of the people who get as far as consulting the Housing Aid Centre who feel that the way the points scheme is constructed would make their application unrealistic.

A points system is devised by each Council in order to assess priority for re-housing, (see Table 1) and in Wandsworth points are allotted for room deficiency, shared accommodation, lack of facilities, badly situated facilities, separated families, ill health, small rooms and length of time on the waiting list. An applicant needs over 45 points to be on the active list, 180 is about top score, and 90 to 100 is good. If a family has a combination of room deficiency, sex overcrowding, shared accommodation and ill health aggravated by unsuitable housing conditions, and survives these ills, they stand a good chance of scoring high points! But there are 6,999 other families also on the Wandsworth waiting list, and only the top 50 receive offers of accommodation. People who reach these heights have generally had to wait a long while and they are understandably fussy about what they are prepared to accept. This explains in part why only 30 per cent of the offers made to the people on the waiting list are accepted.

The factor that most affects the re-housing of those on the waiting list is the sale of Council property to people who are not currently Local Authority tenants; the reduction in the money currently being allocated to housing by Central Government will take its effect at a later stage. The Wandsworth Council's Housing Investment Programme bid for 1981/82 was for £28m plus £2m for Housing Associations. They have actually been granted £18.6m, which with capital receipts of £6m brings their programme up to £24m this year.

The Borough of Wandsworth covers a large area and a wide variety of residential property, from Putney and Roehampton to Battersea, Tooting and Balham. Battersea contains the poorest and least desirable type of units, and its housing problem is particularly intransigent because it is self-perpetuating under present conditions and policies.

TABLE 1   POINTS SCHEME

		Points
1.	Room Deficiency (assessed according to the scale set out below):	
	(a) For each additional room required, (i.e. bedroom, kitchen or living room)	20
	(b) Sex overcrowding — this term indicates either:	
	(i) two unmarried persons of opposite sex (not living as husband and wife) one aged 10 or over, having to share a bedroom, or	
	(ii) a person aged 10 or over having to share a bedroom with a parent of opposite sex.	
	Points are additional to room deficiency points.	20
	(c) In addition, for each member of the applicant's family qualifying for room deficiency points	5
2.	Shared Accommodation and Facilities	
	Living Room	10
	Kitchen	10
	Water Supply (if not in shared kitchen)	4
	W.C. —	
	shared with relatives	4
	shared with non-relatives	6
	Bath —	
	shared with relatives	3
	shared with non-relatives	4
3.	Lack of Facilities	
	No bath	6
	No cooker	6
4.	Badly Situated Facilities	
	Cooker on landing, etc.	4
	External W.C.	4
5.	Separated Families (parents or children separated through lack of accommodation)	10
6.	Ill-health or Physical Disability	
	When this is caused or its effects are aggravated by housing conditions, points to be awarded on the recommendation of the Medical Officer for Environmental Health to a maximum of	30
7.	Small Rooms	
	Where it is necessary for single rooms to be used as a living room or as a bedroom for persons requiring a double room	5
8.	Length of Time on Waiting List	
	For each completed year of current application (including any break in the period of registration of not more than 2 years). ... 10% of total points awarded under headings 1-7 up to maximum of 10 years.	

(NOTE: Transfer of housing applications from another London Borough; length of time of registration on a waiting list of another London Borough immediately prior to removal to London Borough of Wandsworth shall count as equivalent period of registration for the purpose of this points scheme).

Priorities and Transfers

People in a strong bargaining position with the Council, such as tenants who have
to be moved because of major repairs, will only accept property in the most desirable areas, and the Battersea estates are not generally regarded as desirable.
Therefore most offers of properties in Battersea go to the waiting list or to homeless families. Those at the top of the waiting list have been waiting for some
while, and as they will be given more than one offer they are prepared to wait
until they find something attractive. The result is that the Homeless Families
department get the bulk of the lettings in Battersea.

Homeless families are often young, inexperienced and poor, and after a spell in
bed and breakfast accommodation or the homeless families unit, they receive only
one offer of re-housing. If they refuse this they are deemed 'intentionally homeless' and the Council considers that it has no more responsibility for them under
the 1977 Homeless Persons Act. So if the offer that they are made is for a Battersea estate they have no realistic alternative but to accept.

Research in Wandsworth has shown that coloured families are more concentrated in
old accommodation and tower blocks. The reasons are that coloured families make up
a higher proportion of new tenants, and demographically they tend to be at the home
forming stage of the life cycle. The dynamics of the situation create polarisation
and a concentration of coloured people in Battersea compared with the rest of
Wandsworth.

What are the chances of getting a transfer from Battersea, or of a transfer from
any estate in Wandsworth which is less than desirable? The number of transfers has
dropped drastically because of Council house sales and the lack of new property
being purchased or built for the Council. In March 1981 local transfers averaged
3 per week in the whole Borough, and centrally organised transfers, because of
medical grounds or overcrowding, averaged only 10 per week. The amount of movement
here is minimal considering that there are approximately 40,000 Council tenants in
Wandsworth, of whom 25 per cent are on the transfer list.

Tenants judged severely overcrowded by the criteria for statutory overcrowding
are given priority for transfer. There is a recorded, permitted number of people
who can be accommodated in each unit. For instance a 1 bed flat has a permitted
number of 3 people, (the living room is added in for possible use as a bedroom).
Any family that needs two more bedrooms is in a priority group for transfer. Those
who require only one extra bed get less consideration.

Because of the lack of housing stock suited to their needs some families have to
be housed in high rise property. After one year they are allowed to apply for a
'local' transfer, but they are only made an offer within the same area, and as
such offers can only be of an old maisonette, with no central heating, the offer
is often refused.

In the present economic climate a significant increase in the amount of money
available for investment in local authority housing is unlikely. The best possible
use must be made of the present stock with priority for those in the greatest
housing need.

EALING

In Wandsworth housing provision is influenced by the alternation of two extreme
political views in control of the Council. The complexity of the problem can be
illustrated by contrasting the situation in Ealing with that in Lambeth.

Political control of the Council in the London Borough of Ealing changes frequently, but here because the Labour party is not very left wing and the Conservative party is not very right wing, there tends to be little difference in policy on housing apart from the issue of owner occupation. Currently the Conservative Council is not only selling to sitting tenants, but pursuing a policy of 'move and buy' so that when a vacancy occurs they try to find someone interested in buying the property rather than renting it. The housing department's small building programme is aimed at relieving the situation in Southall which has the highest level of overcrowding in London.

Ealing made a Housing Investment Programme bid of £19½m; they were granted £14m and cut their estates improvement budget by £1½m. The shortfall of £4m is being made up by injecting receipts from local authority house and land sales. Therefore the only immediate effect of the cut in Central Government funding has been to delay estate improvement. In the long term it will certainly delay progress with the waiting list, although this is in step with their current local authority policy of disposing of housing stock.

HACKNEY

In contrast to Ealing, which is reasonably affluent, the London Borough of Hackney has the lowest average household income in London and the South East. It has been Labour controlled for many years. In the past the Council distrusted the private sector. Property was acquired and housing provided at the expense of encouraging industry and business. There was a low rate base, a deterioration of amenities and little employment in the Borough for local residents.

The Council appreciated that these policies would have to change and was encouraged by Hackney's designation as a Partnership Authority, despite the fact that 25 per cent of the money had to be raised by the Local Authority itself. The rates soared as a result. However, in the first year of the Conservative government this activity lapsed; the government black-listed Hackney for spending too much on revenue expenditure and penalised the Borough by cutting £15m from its budget. In effect they were penalised for spending their partnership money and attempting to make good some of their past neglect.

The re-organisation of the housing department to carry out the massive improvement and building programme required in the Borough coincided with cutting of the Housing Investment Programme bid from £58m to £21m, and the shattering of these plans led to an ebbing of morale amongst members and officers. The overall effect of the housing cuts in Hackney has been to reduce all activity by half. Empty houses cannot be dealt with and all estate improvement has been postponed. The Council might even have to consider the sale of land to raise capital for its projects.

In all these three London Boroughs the immediate effect of the cuts in housing has been to delay improvement programmes for the existing housing stock. Virtually all new building programmes are in abeyance, and in Ealing and Wandsworth the sale of large quantities of housing stock has had a significant effect on delaying progress on waiting and transfer lists. The area, amenities and standard of property in Hackney have not attracted many would-be purchasers who are not already sitting tenants.

PROBLEMS OF COMMUNICATION

Discussion with health visitors and social workers reveals that there is no

regular accepted formula for communication between local authority departments.
Each individual has to build up a network of friends and contacts in other departments in order to get the help that they require for their needy families. Those
who are keen succeed in building up these relationships, but the less able can be
overwhelmed, and consequently their clients get less consideration.

The difficulties are aggravated by the differing methods of organisation used in
the various local authority departments; for instance the housing department tends
to be hierarchical, social workers are organised in teams and health visitors work
in small isolated groups dotted about the Borough in Health Centres. Two simple,
practical measures could improve communication. Firstly, during professional train
ing time should be allotted to working in other closely related departments, so
that problems related to the welfare of the family could be viewed from all angles,
and the problems inherent in the work of other disciplines appreciated.

Secondly, regular opportunities should be provided for staff working in the same
area, but in different departments, to meet to discuss problems related to their
work and the community. This would facilitate the exchange of information and the
establishment of a positive, rather than a negative relationship between the groups

THE HOUSING ASSOCIATION MOVEMENT

Inevitably changes in Government policy have a radical effect on Housing
Associations. The Housing Association movement has traditionally provided family
housing, as well as catering for special needs such as sheltered housing for the
elderly and projects for disabled and disadvantaged people. In many cases we have
a higher proportion of staff to tenants than the local authorities can provide,
and with a special interest in welfare we are able to give individual help and
attention to tenants who need our assistance.

However details of proposals for the Housing Corporation spending next year just
published suggest that we may have to alter our traditional emphasis. Two themes
emerge from the proposals: firstly a reduction in the programme of housing for
poorer and more disadvantaged people, of about one third or two thirds if not of
100 per cent depending on how much the Government decides to allocate to the Housing Corporation, and secondly an increase of over 25 per cent in spending on Home
Ownership initiatives.

The Housing Association movement would greatly prefer to see private funding
being used for these Home Ownership Initiatives so that they do not absorb the
public money needed for housing less well off people. In times of financial
stringency such money as there is available for housing should be used for those
who are less able to manage for themselves. There are many families with young
children in London and other Inner Cities who are still living in appalling conditions, and the quality of their present and future lives depends to a considerable extent on our ability and willingness as a nation to provide the housing that
they urgently need.

DISCUSSION

The discussion of these two papers showed the great importance placed by the
group on housing. Many of the practical problems stemmed from the inevitable
tensions between housing viewed as a commercial undertaking, with proper concern
for finance, and housing accepted as an intrinsic part of a welfare service. The
two things that had in the past helped to reduce this tension had disappeared.
Housing and health were now divorced both centrally and locally and the Housing
Services Advisory Group had been destroyed.

A forum was undoubtedly needed to provide access to the Minister and his Civil Servants for those concerned with the social content of housing. It was unfortunate that at present housing policy is used as a political football with really deep differences between the Parties in alternating control.

From the point of view of priority for the family with dependent children the inbuilt problems of housing policy can be especially harsh. The housing authority has at its disposal much property 'unlettable' through obsolescence or because of its situation on a run down estate and it has the big problem of rent arrears, some certainly planned by the tenant but much due to family incapacity. The disadvantaged family, including both single parent families and those with a large number of children, easily join the ranks of undesirable tenants and of those in arrears. The temptation to house the undesirable in the unlettable is obviously strong. Whose job is it to study the family so as to distinguish the totally helpless from the intentionally homeless family? The local authority housing departments lacked the funds to employ caring personnel and their Housing Officers lacked both the time and the training for making social studies on families. On the other hand, the Housing Associations which are designed to help disadvantaged families can make such studies. The former manage about 700 tenants per officer compared with the latter's 350. A solution might be for Housing Associations to take over some of the more difficult families.

Although there are exceptions, the Housing Departments do not co-operate closely with their parallel Social Services Departments and the suggestion was made for swapping personnel, say for six months periods, between departments. One area was quoted where the area nurse gets the Health Visitor to look at families in 'bed and breakfast' accommodation who are mainly women with young children. Collaboration has developed between the Housing Officer and the Health Visitor with access to the General Practitioner especially in the antenatal period. The Community Physician has a part to play.

In general it pays to be in maximum need. To be pregnant before marriage is a great help although it may be necessary to suffer an eviction. Should the well-behaved be rewarded? and if so, how?

In the discussion on finance, suggestions were made about tailoring housing costs to life cycle so that heavy outlay could be avoided early and late in life with major costs met during working life. Available money should be put into new rather than old housing. Poor housing could be sold cheaply with assistance provided to bring it up to standard. The effect of a unified housing benefit on different stages of family life should be studied much more closely. Such benefits, which are not really housing problems, ought certainly to rest with central government.

Among other subjects discussed, which have less impact on disadvantaged families, were shared tenancies for larger accommodation, more suitable, though with many practical difficulties, for students and transients, and the problems of transfers. For Housing Associations, grants should be allocated by bed-space rather than units and preferably for a 3 year period at a time.

The unresolved problem remains of how far the State should be concerned with housing. During the century of Municipal Housing the population's housing needs have changed. General standards have vastly improved and an estimate was given that 70 per cent of men aged 30 are buying their own homes. Would it be an advance or the reverse if State housing contracted down to become welfare housing?

CHAPTER 10

Housing Atypical Households: Understanding the Practices of Local Government Housing Departments

VALERIE KARN AND JEFF HENDERSON

INTRODUCTION

The theme of this chapter is the impact that the allocation policies of local government housing departments have upon households that do not conform to preva- lent ideas of what constitutes a conventional family. Despite changes that have occurred in the form of British households, housing authorities persist in regard- ing two parent nuclear families with one to three children as a norm and other types of household, (except possibly the elderly and young married couples without children) as somehow deviant. The effect of these attitudes is that one parent families, large families, joint families, unmarried cohabiting couples and single people receive unfavourable treatment either in being less likely to be accepted for council housing at all, or in receiving a disproportionate amount of the worst property on the worst estates.

As one might expect, these attitudes are seldom made explicit in policy state- ments. However, we have obtained a confidential document prepared for a Housing Committee, which we quote in detail because it gives the flavour of housing manage- ment attitudes to the types of household mentioned above. It indicates managers' tendency to apply negative stereotypes to such families and label them automatically as 'problem families'.

REPORT TO HOUSING COMMITTEE OF AUTHORITY X

Purpose of Report: To consider the problems of:

a) Housing applicants who, if housed are likely to create problems as anti-social tenants, and

b) Existing tenants who cause problems to the Council and their neighbours by anti-social behaviour.

The housing of socially undesirable families amongst tenants who do not accept this behaviour is more of a problem now than it has been in the past. The reason for this can be argued fourfold

a) More low standard families are being housed because in the past Housing Authorities would not always house those known to be potential trouble makers, e.g. children of existing problem families, ex-tenants of known repute, persons on probation and those discharged from prison, and the homeless.

b) The deterrents of Notice to Quit, threat of eviction, have reduced considerably in recent years. It appears likely however, that the Tenants' Charter
   which gives both Local Authorities and tenants greater responsibilities, may
   result in the tenants pressing the Council to remove anti-social families.
   Tenants expect to live peacefully and expect the Landlord to protect their
   interests.

c) The present waiting list is made up of a high proportion of persons who from
   the start we know are more likely to have or cause problems; single persons,
   single parent families, persons affected by matrimonial disputes, owner-
   occupiers in financial difficulties, dubious ex-tenants, discharged
   prisoners, people with psychiatric problems.

d) The reduction of parental control, the refusal to accept discipline from
   organisations as wide apart as the Church or the Armed Forces; the problems
   of unemployment; ... the number of marital break-ups; reduced Social Service
   in a higher population; are all factors which illustrate the social problems
   of the last five years, both nationally and more specifically in this area a
   which produce more groups of persons who will be unacceptable as neighbours
   to good tenants.

The view of certain sectors of society, that people of all types and social
behaviour should be mixed to everyone's advantage, does not appear to be acceptab
at the present time. Past experience also shows that whilst it may be good in
theory it rarely achieves its objective, and good tenants are rarely able to 'lif
a tenant with unsociable characteristics.

All research would suggest that anti-social behaviour is normally only acceptab
by persons of the same character. Some congregation of such families would appea
inevitable.

PROBLEM TENANTS

It may be helpful to define what is an anti-social family; difficult family; or
problem family. There appear to be three groupings:

(i) Those whose behaviour is bizarre, sometimes related to mental illness, or
    old age.

(ii) Those who are scruffy, noisy, use foul language, refuse to obey any rules,
     have untidy or filthy habits, behave in a threatening way.

(iii) Those with an unusual life style, including radically (*sic*) sexual life
      styles, habitual drunkenness, drug addiction or similar excesses.

In addition, certain categories of applicants or tenants are liable to suffer
more problems than average, and generally make heavy demands upon tenant welfare
services:

(i) the very elderly; (ii) the young; (iii) single-parent families.

Not all these households have problems, but generally they do contain a higher
percentage of anti-social families with problems than other categories. Very few
tenants like to live next door to a criminal, particularly if being discharged fr
prison with a record of violence or sexual offences; single parent families must
often be housed in dwellings with large gardens that they cannot cultivate; the

very young single person is normally unaware of the responsibilities of being a
tenant, and usually moves on within six months (over 50 per cent of all single
persons who register on this waiting list do not pursue their application to the
point of allocation).

The elderly of course also have problems. These may cause difficulties to their
neighbours and certainly make demands upon the Local Authority services.

Difficult tenants, therefore, pose a housing problem for this Council which is
caught in a web of conflicting responsibility with the public. There is a duty to
look after the housing stock and to prevent tenants from abusing the fabric. There
is a duty to ensure that rent is paid regularly. There is also a duty to ensure
that tenants do not cause annoyance to their neighbours. At the same time we are
expected to look after tenants who cannot cope. The question of whether the
solution should be provided by Social Services action or those of the Housing
Department, must also be posed.

The problem is complex and the solution difficult. What needs to be done is to
isolate certain issues and try by prevention, good management and remedies, to
restrict it to an acceptable level. It is often difficult to differentiate
between anti-social families and those families who need additional help and
assistance, and sometimes they are one and the same — sometimes they are not.'

HOUSING MANAGEMENT ATTITUDES

The quotation shows up housing managers' tendency to inflate half truths into
whole truths, and then even to exaggerate these. Thus the report within a few
lines in one paragraph moves from listing those who 'are liable to suffer more
problems than average', on to speaking of 'anti-social families', on to 'criminals'
and 'sexual offences' and then back to single parent families and the single. In
the next paragraph it groups damage to property with rent arrears and annoyance to
neighbours.

The report also rationalises a policy of housing 'problem families' in groups.
In practice the question of unpopular minorities in council housing relates very
clearly to the question of the unpopular stock, in that unpopular stock can, to a
limited extent be, allocated as a 'punishment' to difficult tenants. But invariably there is much more unpopular stock than there are difficult tenants. On
the other hand there is fierce competition for the best properties on the most
popular estates. The degree to which there is competition for council housing is
influenced by the state of the local private housing market, that is the availability of cheap, good quality alternatives to council housing, and within the
public housing sector it is crucially affected by the variability in quality of
council housing; the degree of match between the types and number of properties
and the types and numbers of households needing accommodation; and the degree of
match between the location of council housing and the areas of the town where
people tend to want to live. In every housing authority some estates and some
types of property are the subject of competition while others are difficult to let.
The allocation system has to find some way of judging between applicants, on a
basis considered legitimate and justifiable. For the officers, the allocation
process, is by its very nature, one of discrimination between one applicant and
another or one class of applicants and another in the distribution of a scarce
resource. The points system, based mainly on housing need, can provide only the
most general guidance and is, in any case, only one of the factors which determine
the nature of allocations.

Other variables tend to be introduced into the allocation process to help to
differentiate between applicants or even to disqualify some competitors completely.

Some of these rules are the subject of official council policy. These are
typically the exclusion or differential treatment of groups who are regarded as
less in need of housing (commonly, for example, single people and ex-owner-
occupiers) or of those who are regarded as being less deserving of priority (again
commonly new arrivals to the district and those judged to have poor housekeeping
standards but, also in places, groups such as unmarried cohabitees). At the
officer level, judgements of the applicant's 'worth' and 'respectability' are also
brought in, both as factors in their own right and in combination with judgments
about the applicant's acceptability to other tenants. Officers tend to ask about
a good property 'What sort of applicant deserves the property?' and about a bad
property, 'What sort of applicant would accept it?. As Niner (1980) says:

> 'It is normal practice, if a 'very good' standard applicant and a 'less good'
> one are competing for a very good vacancy, to allocate the property to the
> higher standard applicant. Such a policy is seen to enhance estate management.'
> (Niner, 1980).

But tenant 'suitability' is only one of the factors which ultimately enter the
allocation process. As we saw in the extract from the report to a housing
committee, housing officers have to weigh up a series of conflicting aims of the
housing department. In so doing they have to exercise discretion as to which of
these aims they should pursue in each individual case. The sorts of aims of
allocation processes they have to weigh up are as follows:

1. To let properties fast, in order to avoid rent losses and vandalism and to
   rehouse people rapidly;

2. To meet people's preferences for properties and areas as much as possible;

3. To avoid subsequent management problems as a result of tenant complaints,
   rows between neighbours, etc.;

4. To observe the allocation rules (points system) concerning the priority
   to be given to various types of applicant and to discourage 'queue jumping';
   to house those in housing need;

5. To avoid wasteful expenditure of management time and staff resources;

6. To keep the stock in good repair.

Let us take an example of how such conflicting aims can affect allocations and
produce areas of discretionary behaviour often unrecognised by senior management.
Say, for instance, a two bedroomed flat on an unpopular estate is to be let. If
the allocation officer follows Aim 4 (observing the points system) he will allocate
this property to the person with the most points at the top of the two bedroom
queue. However, if the area is particularly unpopular, a family with high points
and hence high priority for housing is likely to refuse it. To offer it to this
person, therefore breaches Aim 5 (waste of time and staff resources), Aim 1,
(letting the property as fast as possible) and Aim 2 (the meeting of preferences).
In practice, because of the overriding importance of rapid lettings, what is likely
to happen is that an allocation officer offers this property to someone he thinks
is likely to accept. This is likely to be someone who is desperate for somewhere
to live, a homeless person for instance, one who has not accumulated sufficient
points for an early allocation of good property. Alternatively, the property may
be offered to someone who is expected not to mind living in that area or to
deserve no better. This is where ideas and stereotypes about different groups
come into operation. One more example brings this out from a different angle.
This time let us suppose the property is a three bedroomed house on a popular
estate, and that the person at the top of the 3 bedroom queue requesting the

estate is a woman on her own with four children, one of whom has been in trouble
with the police. The chances are that, despite the fact that this allocation
meets Aims 1, 2, and 4, Aim 3 (avoiding trouble with neighbours) will become the
crucial element in conjunction with Aim 5, (waste of staff time) and that a
different allocation will be made which breaches rule 4 (the priority system
allocations) and rule 2 (meeting people's preferences).

Where there are conflicting aims of this type, officers tend not to notice that
the degree to which they emphasise particular criteria or institutional priorities
varies from case to case. In effect, allocations become a very discretionary
exercise indeed, even when the system is described to the public as 'computerised'.
All that the computer does is to store the data upon which discretionary decisions
are made. In addition, even in departments with computerised allocations,
considerable information is kept about applicants in personal files and this, too,
is available to those involved in the allocation process. An initial decision to
allocate a property may be reversed at a later stage when the applicant's personal
file is inspected. These discretionary allocation processes are random neither in
the criteria they use nor in their outcome, which is to let the worst estates to
desperate applicants, 'potentially difficult' tenants or those whom other
'respectable' tenants would not welcome, and to offer the best property or estates
to those who are expected to refuse the worst. The end result of the whole series
of decisions is that council housing allocations take on a pattern which is far
less egalitarian than either the professed aim of council housing or the publicly
stated allocation rules would lead us to expect.

This approach has a material effect upon certain types of households. The
evidence presented comes mainly from a study of council housing allocations in one
city. The main theme of that research was the impact of race on allocations but
it was central to our analysis that race was only one of the measures of
'respectability' upon which housing departments base their allocations. While
much of the empirical evidence used here comes from this one study, corroborative
evidence is quoted from studies of other housing authorities which shows that the
approaches are very generally adopted (Parker and Dugmore 1976).

ATYPICAL HOUSEHOLDS

For the purposes of this chapter, five types of 'atypical' households are considered: single persons, cohabiting couples, female-headed one parent families,
large families, and Asian joint families. We first describe the ways in which the
rules and practices of a housing department handicap such families in obtaining
good council housing and then give an explanation of how this happens, and why,
despite policy changes which have improved the situation, there are underlying
factors which make it very difficult to improve the less favourable treatment of
'atypical' households.

SINGLE PEOPLE

Most housing authorities in Britain have not, until recently, seen themselves as
having a housing responsibility towards the single. In our study area, up to 1973
no single men under 55 or single women under 50 were allowed on the housing
register. These limits were lowered to 40 in that year, to 30 in 1976, to 25 in
1977 and finally to 18, the same as for married couples, in 1980. These restrictions have had a harsh effect upon single people because of the shortage of
accommodation in the private rented sector, its high cost and poor quality. When
the waiting list was opened up to those under 25 in 1980, there was a massive increase in registrations.

Apart from its direct impact, the restriction on access for single people has
had an effect in combination with other rules. It has combined harmfully with the
rules about unmarried co-habitees, as we shall explain below. It has also
combined with a restriction on owner-occupiers in the following way. During the
late 1950s and 1960s there was, as in many other cities, large scale migration
into the study area, particularly from the West Indies and the Indian sub-
continent. Many of the new arrivals, particularly the Asians,*were men on their
own, who intended to establish themselves in jobs, obtain housing, and then send
for their families to join them. For the purposes of council housing they were
treated as 'single men' and were therefore ineligible for the waiting list. However, as a condition of obtaining permission from the immigration authorities to
bring their families in they had to show they had housing for them. To do this,
many of these men bought old cheap properties of poor condition in the inner city.
Subsequently, however, when their families had arrived, if they wanted to obtain
newer, better standard housing by moving into a council house they were yet again
ineligible to register because they were owner-occupiers. In this way the legacy
of the age restriction on single people remains, even though the age limit has now
been dropped to 18.

COHABITING COUPLES

A series of regulations about unmarried co-habitees has adversely affected the
housing circumstances of cohabiting couples. The impact has been particularly
marked on West Indians, amongst whom common-law marriage is particularly common.
Until 1979 the condition of registration on the waiting list in the study area for
unmarried couples was that the relationship has to have lasted five years for co-
habitees without children and two years for those with children. In 1979 the
regulation was changed so that co-habitees with children were accepted on the
same basis as married couples, that is without a time qualification placed on their
relationship. A qualification of five years was, however, retained for co-habitees
without children. Those who had lived together for less than five years either
had to wait until they qualified or register as a single woman with a male lodger.
This made the woman subject to the age limit for single people, which meant that,
until autumn 1980, women under twenty-five did not qualify. The bulk of West
Indian co-habitees without children would have been excluded in this way. Although
the situation has been improved by the reduction of the single person's age limit
to eighteen, the problem did not disappear, since at first a quota of only 250
allocations a year was earmarked for single people from eighteen to twenty-five.
Only since the summer of 1981 have single people from eighteen upwards, and hence
cohabiting couples without children, been accepted on the waiting list on an equal
basis with those who were married. In contrast, married couples without children
have now become one of the largest groups receiving housing from the waiting list.
They made up over 40 per cent of the non-elderly housed between 1971 and 1978.
The impact on West Indians shows up in that 33.6 per cent of white families
registered on the waiting list in 1978 had no children, compared with only 18.4
per cent of West Indians. In addition only a small proportion of childless West In
dians registered were under thirty. They were mostly older households with grown u
children. Amongst whites the majority were under thirty. The explanation appears
to be that young West Indian couples without children are not usually married and
therefore have not had the same access to the waiting list. The co-habitation
rules may well have been partly responsible for the large numbers of single West
Indian women with babies amongst those families rehoused because of homelessness.

---

*Throughout the article we designate as 'Asian' all those applicants or tenants
  who were of Indian, Pakistani (East or West Pakistan prior to 1971), Bangladeshi
  or Sri Lankan origin.

Their inability to register has an added significance in this context because homeless families with points on the waiting list are more likely to be housed
directly into permanent accommodation, albeit often of poor quality, whereas the
homeless without points have a greater likelihood of initially being put into a
hostel or bed and breakfast accommodation.

LARGE FAMILIES

Large households are regarded as very abnormal by housing departments. They are
often, almost automatically, assumed to be 'problem families'. Nationally there
is a strong correlation between numbers of children in a family and parental
social class. Of those couples marrying between 1956 and 1965, for instance, only
5 per cent of women from the Registrar General's social classes I and II had four
or more children, only 10 per cent in social class III but 16 per cent in social
classes IV and V (Dunnell 1979b). Judgments based on family size then can be
roughly equated with discrimination based on class.

It emerged from our detailed study that large families are particularly likely
to be given older housing: thus 23.6 per cent of white households containing six
or more people were allocated a pre-1919 property in our study area compared with
13.4 per cent of those families containing five people and about 6 per cent of
those containing less than five (Table 1). In cities like the one studied, however, large family size is now much more clearly related to race than to class.
The Asians in particular have large families; so do the West Indians, although to
a less and a declining extent. As a result, these two groups are particularly
affected by the official attitudes to large families. They also receive older
property irrespective of family size, and this is particularly true of Asians. In
Table 1, 58.1 per cent of the Asians with six or more in their household received
pre-1919 property, as compared with 31.0 per cent of West Indians and 23.6 per cent
of whites. Moreover, over 40 per cent of Asians with less than five in their
household received pre-1919 property, compared with about 6 per cent of whites and
10 per cent of West Indians.

This indicates that the explanation of the allocation of pre-1919 property is
not just related to its being of a suitable size for large families. The shortage
of purpose-built council houses with four or more bedrooms, which has existed for
many years, has not been remedied by new construction or by the conversion of
existing properties. The justification has always been the cost, but behind this
may well lie a resistance to providing expensive new properties for families that
are regarded as irresponsible in having had so many children.

Table 1: Age of Housing Stock by Race and Size of Household:
Tenants allocated 1971, 1974, 1976 and 1978.

	\multicolumn{6}{Number in Household}
	1	2	3	4	5	6 or more
	Proportion given 'Acquired' (Predominantly pre-1919) stock					
White	8.7	5.2	6.7	5.2	13.4	23.6
West Indian	17.7	8.8	8.4	12.1	14.4	31.0
Asian	28.3		51.5	41.6	36.7	58.1

ASIAN JOINT FAMILIES

Asians suffer from a particular problem in the way their family structures are
approached by the local authority. Many Asian households are constituted by joint

families, based on the relationship of members of the family with the grandfather.
Cousins and brothers are regarded as being in the same relationship to each other
and within the same family, whose head is the grandfather, whether or not the
latter is actually present. The Housing Department studied regards such families
as being a grouping of several nuclear families and requires them to register for
housing as separate units. Invariably brothers or cousins will be required to
register their families separately. The authority has more sympathy with the
desire to register the grand-parents along with one of their children's families,
but this is often impossible because the parents are frequently owner-occupiers
and therefore ineligible for council housing. The justification for the practice
of splitting joint families is that there are not houses large enough to house
them, although this is not always the case. Sometimes the authority finds itself
owning extremely large houses which are impossible to let to nuclear families.
Moreover the needs of joint families can be met in other ways than finding one
house. Two or more adjacent houses, or flats or maisonettes in the same block for
instance, can be and occasionally are let together. At present there is no way in
which the various applicants within one joint family can ensure that their
applications are considered as a whole, rather than as isolated parts. More
sensitive consideration of the needs of Asian joint families could well pay
dividends, not only for the Asian tenants, but also, by ensuring that elderly
Asians have family support, for the local authority, which may be relieved of
some of its social welfare responsibilities. Furthermore, if whole families could
move together, many might be willing to widen the range of areas they are willing
to consider, rather than feeling the necessity to stay close to elderly parents
in the main inner city areas in which Asians tend to be concentrated in the
private sector.

An example taken from our field work with housing visitors will help to convey
a sense of the impact of such rules. We visited a Pakistani applicant, Mr. Patel,
(the name is fictitious). He lived with his wife, his daughter and his mother and
father in the house of his brother. The brother's family consisted of his wife
and three children. Mr. Patel's wife was expecting her second child. The entire
extended family lived in a three-bedroomed terraced house. The reason for Mr.
Patel's housing application was that his brother's family needed extra space. On
the application form Mr. Patel had indicated that he wanted his mother and father
to be rehoused with him. The Visitor told the applicant that it was not Housing
Department Policy to rehouse two families together, and consequently his parents
would have to submit a separate application. Mr. Patel pointed out that his
parents were quite old, and as neither of them spoke English it would be difficult
for them if they had to live on their own. The Visitor asked if Mr. Patel's
parents could continue to live with their other son and his family. After a con-
versation with his parents and his wife, Mr. Patel reiterated that his brother and
his family needed the extra space, and in any case his brother did not get on well
with his parents. In response the Visitor repeated that it was not possible for
'two families' to be rehoused together in the same property. The Patels eventually
agreed to submit separate applications but the old parents were disappointed and
upset.

SINGLE PARENT FAMILIES

Female-headed single parent families even more than large families are frequently described as 'problem families', about whose presence tenants complain to
the housing authority. The parents are regarded as being sexually promiscuous,
neglecting the younger and having no control over the older children. Like large
families, they receive an undue proportion of the least popular properties in the
least popular areas, a finding common to all studies of poor quality estates. In
our study we found that one parent families received houses, as opposed to flats
and maisonettes, far less often than did two parent families with the same numbers

of children. Amongst whites, only 21.9 per cent of one parent families received houses as compared with 43.5 per cent of two parent families. For West Indians, the figures were 16.7 per cent and 37.7 per cent and for Asians 35.6 per cent and 78.7 per cent (Table 2). Controlling for numbers of children still leaves a large difference between one and two parent families; for instance only 14.7 per cent of West Indian one parent families with two children obtained a house compared with 36.5 per cent of two parent families with two children.

Table 2: Type of Property Allocated to One Parent Families
1971-78.

	White			West Indian			Asian		
	One parent	Two parent	All with* children under 16	One parent	Two parent	All with* children under 16	One parent	Two parent	All with* children under 16
House	21.9	43.5	40.8	16.7	37.7	31.3	(35.6)	78.7	78.7
Maison-ette	24.0	19.9	10.6	19.2	29.4	23.9	(16.8)	11.2	9.1
Flat	54.0	36.1	38.1	62.3	32.5	43.8	(44.7)	10.0	11.9
Other	-	0.5	0.4	1.9	0.4	1.0	(2.9)	-	0.4
Weighted N =	160	452	656	292	329	668	44	203	351

*Including households with children and with more than two adults present.

EXPLAINING THE ALLOCATION PROCESS

POLICIES AND PRACTICES

Although formal policies and explicit practices account for some of the processes through which 'atypical' families receive inferior treatment, an approach to organisational explanations which concentrated solely on these would clearly be inadequate. Though there were rules about single people, co-habitees and joint families, the authority studied had no explicit rules about the treatment of large families or one parent families. In fact in the case of one parent families, it was officially assumed that the Housing Department accepted and operated the recommendations of the Finer report (Finer 1974) that there should be no distinction between the treatment of one parent and two parent families.

In explaining the types of allocations received by 'atypical' households, and by single parent families and large families in particular, we therefore need to look beyond the level of formal policies and practices and to turn our attention to the informal, or at most semi-formal, decision-making processes within the organisation. This concern led us to examine the sub-cultural practices of the organisation's personnel, especially their interaction, how they generate their 'understanding' of particular applicants, properties and areas of the city, and the use to which they put their discretionary powers. Earlier work in organisational sociology (Dalton 1959, Cicourel 1968, Zimmerman 1971) has stressed the significance of organisational subcultures and 'subterranean' practices for the achievement, or indeed the partial deflection of 'organisational goals', whilst the 'managerialist' tradition within urban sociology has directed attention to those 'gatekeepers' responsible for the allocation of private as well as publicly produced urban resources (Pahl 1975). These bodies of literature helped to alert us to the need to examine allocation decision-making in practice, that is, the ways in which such decisions are produced on a day-to-day basis. To penetrate empirically the Department's decisions in this way, the adoption of ethnographic or qualitative research techniques was necessary (Schatzman and Strauss 1973, Agar 1980).

Combining work on official policies and formal rules with the study of informal
managerial processes could still not offer us a totally satisfactory explanation.
How did it come about that all the housing departments studied by us and others
have produced broadly similar profiles of housing allocations, despite different
internal structures and relationships? Why do housing departments in general
produce broadly the same type of allocation of scarce urban resources as other
public as well as private agencies in Britain? How is it, in other words, that
discretionary practices by different individuals in different resource-distributing
organisations tend to produce broadly similar results?

Organisational Perceptions

Here help comes, especially from Batley (1982), from a new body of literature,
which stresses the need to understand organisational 'behaviour' as well as the
perceptions and practices of personnel, not just in themselves, but in terms of
their structural relationship with the wider society of which they are a part
(Benson 1977, Heyderbrand 1977, Salaman 1978, and Ranson *et al* 1980). In our
case it was important to understand a Housing Department's policies as well as the
behaviour of its officials in relation to the structured inequality existing in
British society and widespread legitimated beliefs about the sorts of households
which deserved to be in recept of scarce resources.

Studies of the allocation of resources in the National Health and education
services have tended to concentrate on distinctions between the treatment of the
middle and working classes but this is irrelevant in council housing, which is
concerned with the allocation of housing to people who are predominantly from
manual working class backgrounds. However, social classes are not homogeneous
even within ethnic groups. They are internally stratified, according to material
position, life chances, social prestige and status of the people concerned. In
relation to the allocation of council housing, a very broad distinction within the
working class between the 'respectable' and 'disreputable' working class or the
'deserving' and 'undeserving' is the most crucial (Matza 1967, Valentine 1968,
Douglas 1970). Perceptions of respectability, disreputability and acceptability
influence the housing that different sorts of applicants receive. People's life-
styles offer bureaucracies certain cues or codes through which they can be classified. The most important is probably family structure, the negative cues being
offered by being, for instance, a single parent family, an unmarried couple or a ve
large family. Then there are unemployment and other more specific factors such as
housekeeping standard, quality of furniture, and rent paying record. Some authorities even go through the local newspapers cutting out any items which refer to
their tenants' involvement with the police, even down to speeding offences. A numb
of studies have given examples of the sorts of comments made by visitors about
potential tenants. For instance, Owen Gill (1977) gives, amongst others, these
descriptions of tenants allocated to Luke Street, a severely deteriorated estate:

> 'Applicants are a likely problem family for housing department.'
> 'This large family will go anywhere'.
> 'Rough type of family'.
> 'Have no idea how to care for a house'.
> 'Not suitable for good property'.

He concludes:

> 'The criteria by which the individual families in Luke Street were judged were
> at best crude and at worst entirely subjective. The data presented above hardly
> suggest a sensitive attempt to distinguish the particular characteristics of in-
> dividual families ... the key point is that their difficulties should have led to

positive rather than negative discrimination. In effect the housing department
had (i) selected individual families who were facing major difficulties, (ii) revised the perspective, saying that they were a problem to everybody else rather
than that they faced problems, ...' (Gill 1977).

In using these cues or codes an officer is in effect classifying an applicant
or tenant along a disreputable/respectable dimension. So the importance of the
cues lies in the meaning ascribed to them; not the meaning of each individual one
but rather the composite picture which housing departments and officers construct
about particular applicants as a result of the combination of a number of the
codes.

THE ATYPICAL HOUSEHOLD

Without a description of the whole allocation process, certain ways can be outlined briefly in which classifications of households as in some way deviant are
effective within the process, either through formal or informal mechanisms.
Discrimination against 'atypical' households is seen, not as an anomalous outcome
of individually prejudiced officers, but as a normal part of the allocation
procedure. Two of the previous examples are used, large families and single parent
families, because these were the ones about whom the Housing Department had no
explicit rules.

There are four ways in which 'atypical' households are differentially treated in
the allocation process. The first is that 'normal' families receive abnormally
good treatment. This may take a variety of forms. For instance we observed cases
in which 'respectable' homeless families were allocated brand new flats whilst the
poorer properties reserved for the homeless were ignored. 'Respectable' families'
cases were also advocated by (desk) interviews, visitors and other personnel, and
'bids' for properties made on their behalf to central Allocation Control.
'Bidding' for properties in this way is in this authority an officially recognised
process, using duplicated forms on which each 'bid' is recorded. Other than a
very general and fluctuating 'points level' indicated at any time for particular
properties in particular areas, there are no defined criteria on which 'bids' are
based. Remarkably, however, they constitute perhaps a third of all allocations
made in this authority.

We observed the process of differentiation of non-conforming household types
amongst interviewers who dealt with people coming in to see how their application
was progressing. We found that, in a group of twenty West Indian non-homeless
families interviewed, only 25 per cent of the single parent families were advocated
to Allocation Control compared with 38 per cent of the two parent family cases.
It seems then that interviews treated 'respectable' two parent families differentially well. In fact interviewers and clerks were often heard commenting that
it was unjust for properties to be allocated to single parent families when they
could have gone to two parent families.

These views are shared by the public who frequently write in to complain about
one parent families being given property. Their complaints are of two types, first
that they do not 'deserve' the property and second that they lower the 'tone' of
the neighbourhood. Tenants, who came in to complain that they had not received a
transfer when a neighbour had received one, often said that they thought it was
the 'decent' families who should receive preferential treatment.

SUITABILITY GRADING

The second type of differential treatment is abnormally bad treatment for

'deviant' families, of which we give two instances of the approach to allocation.
The first is the use of formal grading of housekeeping standards. Up to 1975 the
authority studied operated a policy of grading applicants' housekeeping standards
according to their 'suitability' for different types of property. The grading
referred specifically to the type of property for which families were considered
suitable. In descending order the grades were (1) Post War (2) Early Post War
(3) Inter-War relet and (4) Central Area or Substandard Property (i.e. nineteenth
century). As Table 3 shows, there was an extremely strong relationship for all
groups, but amongst whites in particular, between low grading and size of family.
The relationship for West Indians and Asians was less marked because, they both,
and Asians in particular, tended to be given poor grades whatever their family
size.

Table 3: Suitability Grading by Size of Household and Race,
         1971-76 % Graded 'Inter-War' or 'Central Area/Sub-
         standard Property'.

Size of Household	White	West Indian	Asian	Weighted N White	Weighted N West Indian	Weighted N Asian
1/2	6.7	15.6	33.4	179	115	18
3	7.3	4.3	50.0	149	117	32
4	9.8	11.1	58.1	102	81	31
5	25.0	21.0	63.0	52	38	30
6	30.0	41.4	64.2	26	29	28
7 or more	74.2	42.5	65.5	31	40	58

Our observations also suggested a bias in the attitudes of Housing Visitors about
women's housekeeping standards. Where the family was less than perfect in its
housekeeping, the Housing Visitors seemed much less sympathetic when there was a
woman present. Some of their comments indicated that they did not expect the same
standard of cleanliness and tidiness from a man as they did from a woman, whether
on her own or with a man present. 'He's kept the place fairly clean under the
circumstances' was a frequent comment on a single male, whereas after a visit to a
woman with children in a flat of similar tidiness, the Visitors would remark 'She
could keep the place better than that'.

The grading system was dropped in 1975. However given the sorts of easily
identifiable factors, such as family size and quota, which contributed heavily to
suitability gradings, it was likely to continue informally through the allocation
process, even if it had been formally dropped. Allocations in 1978, after the
grading system had been dropped, showed that large families still received a
disproportionate share of pre-1919 property. This is a clear example where the
presence or absence of an explicit policy or practice may be irrelevant to the
outcome, given no fundamental change in the philosophy behind allocations.

THE INFLUENCE OF RESPECTABILITY

Besides the suitability grading system, we found another mechanism through which
'disreputable' applicants are filtered to 'suitable' vacancies. After a potential
allocation has been identified from the computerised data by Allocation Control,
it is possible for this allocation to be 'blocked' by an Area Officer before the
offer reaches the prospective tenant. These officers have access to the applicants'
or tenants' file which contains much more detailed information than is stored on
the computer. This information includes comments by Visitors on the original
application form, the 'history sheet' which constitutes a record of the applicant's

contact with the Department, more detailed information on the nature of and the reasons for refusal or withdrawal of previous offers, plus letters from external agents, such as social workers, councillors or other tenants. The file therefore gives a much more complete picture of the family, from which their relative 'respectability' can be deduced.

In addition to this data the Area Office inspects the homes of transfer applicants and their rent books to see if they have good decorations and a clear rent record. If they do not, it is policy as in most authorities to refuse a transfer. In addition many offers are withdrawn for more nebulous reasons. In one case that we observed, a woman on her own with four children lived primarily on social security payments. The 'history' sheet in the case papers contained a reference to the need for social work support and there were a few letters from neighbours complaining about the woman's 'unruly' children. The officer who was vetting a transfer offer which had been made to her commented as follows:

'They've caused a lot of trouble, so they're not really suitable for the offer ... in this road there are some owner occupiers and there has already been trouble, ... so we don't really want another problem family in there causing more trouble. So I'm not going to sign this one (the offer). I shall send it back to the other area and say we can't have this family.'

The third way in which respectability influences allocations is through the stereotyping of people's preferences and expectations. In the city studied there is a shortage of houses which families with children overwhelmingly prefer. At interview with us over 90 per cent of applicants with two or more children in 1978 said they preferred a house, although a very different picture was presented on the application forms. The applicants themselves did not complete the item on 'type preference'. It was completed by the Visitors. It emerged that different preferences were recorded for one and two parent families. Only 31 per cent of white and 34 per cent of West Indian one parent families were recorded as wanting houses as compared with 64 per cent and 52 per cent of two parent white and West Indian families. In interviews with us over 80 per cent of West Indian one and two parent families said they wanted houses. There was a very close relationship between recorded preference and the type of property actually allocated, so the fact that recorded preferences are not produced in a fashion which is independent of household type and racial origins is crucial to the outcome of the allocation process.

These are some examples of the ways in which management imperatives to let, as quickly as possible, a stock of properties of varied quality and location and, in so doing, avoid trouble with the majority of tenants and applicants, interact with generally shared (and legitimated) beliefs about race, class and gender, the result of which is a very unequal distribution of council housing. Housing departments are not alone in producing a non-egalitarian distribution of resources. Despite the fact that welfare state institutions such as the National Health Service and state schools are supposed to redress some of the inequality created by a purely market provision, it appears that the distribution of 'their' resources is by no means egalitarian. Indeed the evidence is now overwhelming that the unequal distribution of resources, publicly as well as privately provided, broadly parallels the class and racial structure of our society, and that gender is also a strong factor (Reid 1978, Townsend 1979, Goldthorpe 1980, Halsey and Heath 1980, Smith 1977 and 1981, Wilson 1978).

In the housing service, categorisation of households according to their relative respectability has the function of making possible the rationing of a scarce resource of unequal quality. Without it, an officer might just as well draw lots between applicants for similar properties in the same area and points band. This would create much work by increasing the rejection rate of properties by the 'respectable'. It would also admit that the publicly purveyed impression of objectivity in the selection of tenants is fallacious. But officers need to retain this impression to keep public dissatisfaction under control. The adoption of judgments of the worth of households enables the individual officer to justify to himself or others what otherwise must appear arbitrary and often harsh decisions. Without such rationalisations the job would probably become intolerable. So officers categorise and stereotype in the cause of what Satyamurti calls 'occupational survival' (Satyamurti, 1981). If one can assure oneself that single parent families prefer flats, then it usefully disguises the fact that a family with children has had to be housed in high rise property. Or if a homeless family is given an otherwise unlettable flat, it is helpful to be able to argue (to oneself as well as to others) that a really homeless family should be willing to accept anything. All these beliefs of course contain partial truths, and it is by unconsciously inflating these to the level of whole truths, that actions based upon them can be legitimated.

Measures of respectability have the advantage as criteria for rationing scarce resources in that they are legitimated via the social structure and hence publicly supported. There is, therefore, a widespread belief that the 'disreputable' should change their ways before they are helped. This accords well with the needs of a service which is always in dread of being inundated with demands which it cannot meet. Typically housing managers fear that if they help some homeless people, everyone will make themselves homeless; if they accept owner-occupiers on the waiting list, all owner-occupiers will register; if they are lenient with one family in arrears with rent, all the tenants who hear of it will stop paying. They even say that if they rehouse women who have left their husbands, they will merely encourage marital breakup. With this 'siege' mentality, the housing service naturally adopts a practice of separating the interests of the 'respectable' from those of the 'disreputable', rewarding the former and punishing the latter. This happens at all levels, through both rules and discretionary decisions. Class discrimination in this sense is an integral part of what is regarded as good housing management practice.

SUMMARY AND CONCLUSION

The examination of the actual operation of a housing department has shown how central are judgments of 'respectability' to the allocation processes of housing departments, even when, officially, allocations are based on a points system of 'housing need'. We have traced how class attitudes in the wider society become invested with official status as they are absorbed into the housing authority's rationing processes, both of a formal and more informal nature. In fact, as we have seen most clearly in the case of large families and 'suitability' grading, there is at some levels really no distinction between formal and informal practices.

For a number of reasons this analysis is not encouraging for the prospects of improving the treatment of 'atypical' households in council housing allocations. First, though present allocation processes run counter to the interests of those who are regarded as less than 'respectable', the principles upon which they are based receive widespread public support. Second, even if the 'respectable' were to be offered estates and properties on a random basis, they would reject the worst and wait for a better offer, or possibly opt out of the public sector altogether. Here is a major dilemma. In egalitarian terms, council housing must be run in the interests of those for whom the private sector provides least well. Yet moves in this direction would make council housing less attractive to the better off working class, would lead to their leaving and would make council housing even more a 'welfare' tenure, with all the problems of a stigmatised service with intensified segregation of the poorest.

Despite these problems, reform is imperative. Council housing is far too important to the life chances of those most adversely affected for it to continue to be
run in the present way. The dropping of restrictions on the single and of formal
housekeeping gradings, and the adoption of equal opportunity policies by some
authorities, show that progress is possible at the policy level. These changes
need to be accompanied, however, by a willingness of housing authorities to behave
in advance of public opinion in the treatment of stigmatised groups, both at the
formal policy level and, more importantly, at the level of informal organisational
practices. Such unpopular decisions are made much harder when the public sector
is being starved of resources so that competition for the best properties is
greatly increased and the quality of the worst is further eroded. In current
conditions, we must apply to the public sector as much as to the private, Townsend's
comment that:

'The housing market must be perceived as an institution which is doing far more
than mediating housing supply and demand. It reproduces and indeed creates inequality within society' (Townsend 1979).

ACKNOWLEDGEMENT

We are grateful to Bill Brown who carried out much of the data collection and
analysis. The responsibility for the views expressed here, however, is solely
that of the authors.

DISCUSSION

Dr. Karn's paper dealt essentially with the difficulty in allocating a scarce
resource and the contrast between formal arrangements intended as guides to
practice and the informal methods used. Just as there is an inevitable tension
between the housing department's commercial and its welfare functions, so the
formal guide and the informal application are in conflict. This has been shown by
studies of allocation in other areas than in the one studied. Pragmatism is likely
to prevail over justice as long as some housing stock is sub-standard and some
families rated as undesirable as tenants and indeed as neighbours. Poor quality
housing and unattractive estates are recognisable; who constitute undesirable
tenants requires study. There is a real difference between those families which
become problems because they cannot cope with family stress and families who
create difficulties by reason of an unacceptable lifestyle or inconsiderate and
anti-social behaviour. The lifestyle may be in itself normal, for example a need
for loud out of doors music or for a gypsy life, but it does not mix with the
middle class model which is accepted as normal by many tenants and by the majority
of administrators. Stereotypes of what groups are undesirable develop early during
training and once formed in the worker's mind are hard to change. The results are
prejudice and unfair discrimination. Would some training of housing officers
alongside social workers help? Linking timetables presents serious problems,
motivation needs to be strong and funding at present is impossible.

More study is needed too of how caring agencies as well as statutory services
can diminish the influence on their decisions of sub-consciously accepted status
lists of family respectability and acceptability. Present habits of mind tend to
increase the deprivation of families already disadvantaged. At the same time their
presence stigmatises an estate as undesirable, one result of transferring the
problem families to estates where social service is more readily available.
Estates can be upgraded and enhancement of the environment and the amenities as
opposed to the condition of the buildings themselves plays an important part. The
publication of allocation 'rules' and the provision of an appeals procedure might
lessen the influence of prejudice. Perhaps most important would be mitigating the

cost of housing in favour of families with dependent children difficult as devising
such a scheme would be. So too more flexible allocation and easier transfers would
introduce an element of choice at present weighted against the homeless. The local
authority housing department is not an estate agency: it could and should seek ways
of giving greater importance to its welfare function. Changes in the training of
housing officers and greater co-operation with social service departments could
help to lessen the stress of housing problems on families finding difficulty in
rearing children.

CHAPTER 11

Tax and Benefit Policy for the Family

JONATHAN BRADSHAW

INTRODUCTION

What is really remarkable about the financial treatment of families with children
in Britain is that despite there now being general acceptance that child poverty
and deprivation are widespread and that social security and fiscal policies
actively discriminate against families, so little has been done about it. In the
early 1960s we used to talk about the 'rediscovery of poverty'. It is not unreasonable that it would take time for the facts to emerge, to permeate and be
absorbed by the key policy making institutions. The means to respond to family
poverty not unreasonably took time to design and legislate. Yet here we are nearly
two decades later with probably more families in poverty than when it was rediscovered. The latter part of this paper will address itself to a discussion of why
it is that so little has been achieved in the last two decades to improve the way
the tax and benefit system operates to relieve poverty among families with children.
First however I will rehearse the most recent evidence on the number and nature of
poverty among families with children and present a critical review of current tax
and benefit policy.

CHILD POVERTY

   The most authoritative data on the number of families with children living at and
around poverty level in Britain is provided (now biannually) by an analysis of the
Family Expenditure Survey carried out by DHSS statisticians. The latest analysis
is of the 1977 Survey. Table 1 shows that in December 1977 6.3 million parents and
children were living on incomes which were less than 140 per cent of the supplementary benefit (SB) level. 3.5 million children — about one child in every four in
Britain — lived in these families.

Table 1: Estimated number of persons with incomes at various levels
relative to supplementary benefit level at December 1977 (thousands)

Family type	Income below SB level	Receiving SB Persons	10%	Income with 20% of SB level	40%
Couples with children	670	700	500	1520	3690
Single person with children	110	900	70	180	290
TOTAL	780	1600	570	1700	3980

Source: Social Security Statistics 1980 HMSO Table 47.07.

There are, of course, a number of reservations to be made about these findings.

First they relate to December 1977: nearly four years ago. For a number of reasons we can expect the number of families with children living at the margins of poverty to have increased since 1977 — most obviously because of the increase in unemployment but also because the level of family support has not improved and the tax threshold has declined.

Second, all estimates of the numbers in poverty are very sensitive to the definition of poverty being used. The conventional supplementary benefit definition which is being used in this case has been criticised as an inadequate index of the needs of families with children. Piachaud (1980 and 1981), in two striking papers, has shown that the scale rates for children need to be increased by as much as half again to meet his estimation of 'modern minimum requirements', described in *New Society* as 'frugal to the point of inhumanity'. If the SB level is adjusted to make adequate allowance for children (by increasing the scale rates for children by 50 per cent), then the number of children living in poverty increases by more than half.

Third there is the question — what does living on or near to SB level of income actually mean? The supplementary benefit scale rates, it might be argued, have more than doubled in real terms since 1948 and therefore can they really be regarded as an index of poverty any longer? The reply is that poverty is a relative notion and the SB scales bear roughly the same relationship to average earnings as they did in 1948. If anyone doubts that the income provided on SB provides no more than a boring basic diet for a good manager, let them try and live on it for even a short while. If anyone wants a sense of the restricted nature of the experiences of children living at these levels of income, then they could obtain a vivid picture from Piachaud's studies of what the SB rates can purchase.

INEQUITY

Even if there is still room for argument about whether or not a substantial minority of families in Britain are poor or hard pressed, there can be no doubt that their relative living standards — that is relative to the single and childless — have deteriorated over the years and the differential is now remarkably narrow. The evidence on this has been explored in depth in a recent paper for the Study Commission on the Family (Bradshaw 1980). Here we can only review and update the most important of those figures.

Table 2: Net disposable resources of families (Post November 1981 upratings)

| Gross earnings | Childless couples | Families with | |
		One child	Three children
70	43.19	53.03	75.78
140	81.23	86.48	90.98
210	125.58	130.83	141.33

Assumptions: Net disposable resources = Gross earnings (single wage earner) less income tax, NI contributions, rent £10.50 per week, rates £4.25 per week, fares to work (£3.55 per week) plus any child benefit, FIS, rent and rate rebate and the value of free school meals.

Observe that on an average wage (£140 per week) the couple with one child has net disposable resources only £5.25 more than a childless couple. This is the total value of child support in Britain today. A good deal more is given to families with lower earnings. At half average earnings (£70 per week) a family with children receives (if it claims them) a rent and rate rebate, free school meals, family income supplement as well as child benefits. But these benefits are withdrawn as income rises so that the three child family on £140 has only net disposable resources of £21.20 more than another family on £70. So for a difference in gross earnings of £70, net disposable resources differ by only £21.20. This is the phenomenon known as the 'poverty trap' where tax and benefit rules conspire together almost to wipe out differentials in net incomes at earnings below national average. At the present time it matters not whether you earn £60 or £110, your net disposable resources will be the same with a three child family.

These absurdities are created by two interlocking factors in tax benefit policies for families. The first is that our universal provision for children is inadequate and second because of this, families have to receive subsidies of one kind or another which are means-tested. Only Denmark in the European Community is as reliant on means-tested benefits or withdraws benefits as sharply as income rises.

What horizontal distribution could be considered equitable is of course, a moot point, but two pieces of evidence indicate that horizontal redistribution is inadequate in Britain. The first is the decline in the value of child tax allowance/family allowance/child benefit over time.

Table 3: Changes in the relative value of child support.

	Value of child tax allowance/ family allowance/child benefit for a married man on average earnings as percentage of gross earnings of manual worker. (2 children 11-16)	Proportion of average earnings paid in tax by a couple —	
		without children	with 2 children
August 1946	10.1	16.3	6.0
April 1979/80	8.1	25.2	23.3

The result of this trend against the family with children is that such families have begun to pay income tax at a progressively lower point on the income distribution. This has increased the severity of the poverty trap and undermined the effectiveness of income support measures.

The second piece of evidence in support of the contention that horizontal redistribution is inadequate is comparison with other countries. Of course, these kinds of comparison are notoriously difficult to make and always out of date but in a recent comprehensive study the UK was found to come third from bottom in the league table of countries in the value of child support at average earnings, just ahead of Ireland and Italy. The UK is relatively more generous at lower and higher income levels but the equivalent purchasing power of these benefits in the UK are about half that of countries such as France, Belgium and Luxembourg (Bradshaw and Piachaud 1980).

Why is it that our tax and benefit system operates so inadequately and inequitably for families with children? There are a number of ways of answering that question and the first is by pointing to some of the main failings of the tax and social benefit system. However, why these are as they are, raises more fundamental questions about the position of the family in national values and institutional arrangements and these also will be briefly discussed.

The easiest way to deal with tax/benefit arrangements is by client groups, that is the main groups of families.

SINGLE PARENTS

Single parents are a rapidly expanding population with a high risk of living in poverty or being hard-pressed. About half of all single parents are dependent on supplementary benefits. The Beveridge scheme covered widows with an insurance benefit but the divorced, separated and unmarried have to depend on maintenance payments and earnings or on supplementary benefits. The Finer Committee (1974) proposed that there should be a comprehensive single parent benefit but the Labour Government rejected their proposals because the benefit was means-tested and because of the cost. Single parents in work benefit from family income supplement where the hours rule has been reduced from 30 to 24 for them and there is a supplement to child benefit of £2.50 now called One Parent Benefit. Single parents on SB now receive the long term rate after one year and from November 1980 a tapered earnings disregard was introduced to encourage them to work part time.

Single parents who earn more than the tax threshold benefit by £4.45 per week from the additional personal allowance (APA) which is the equivalent of the married man's tax allowance. The Green Paper on the Taxation of Husband and Wife has discussed the possibility that this tax allowance should be abolished and the revenue used for an increase in one parent benefit (Inland Revenue 1981). The main constraints are that there would be some net cost from extending the additional benefit to those earning below the tax threshold and increased take up of one parent benefit. However welcome such a reform is, it would not help those single parents unable to get into the labour market and dependent for all or part of their incomes on supplementary benefit.

FAMILIES DEPENDENT ON INCOME FROM WORK

The living standards of families with children where the head is in full time work is dependent on earnings, any earnings of the spouse, child benefits and the family income supplement. Although earnings are the main source of these families incomes it is not to improvements in earnings that one should look for improvement in family living standards. Indeed this lesson is just beginning to permeate discussion of these issues in trades unions. Historically, wage bargaining has been conducted using notions of the 'family wage' — enough for a man and a dependant wife and one or two children. Unions are beginning to recognise that partly because the majority of wives are now not dependent and partly because wages are an expensive and relatively ineffective means of compensating for children that unions should press for family benefits rather than the narrow 'family wage' (Coussin and Coote 1981). Low pay is endemic in Britain and many families live in poverty because their breadwinner earns too little. Although there may be a strong case for increasing the earnings of the low paid, there are more cost effective ways of improving the position of families with children.

Now that child tax allowances no longer exist, the most important mechanism is child benefits. As already noted, UK child benefits have fallen in value and are lower than in most other European countries. An increase in child benefits would have a number of beneficial consequences apart from helping families. It would lift families off means tested benefits such as Family Income Supplement, rent rebates and free school meals and improve work incentives. However the problem with child benefits is the revenue cost of increasing them. Every 1p increase in child benefits costs an extra £5.5 M. per year. Unlike other social security benefits, they are not formally linked to an index though there is a recent commitment to increase them in line with prices 'subject to economic circumstances'. In

fact, every year a major campaign still has to be mounted in parliament and elsewhere to protect child benefits. All this has led to a consideration of whether
child benefits could be made more selective. Having considered the advantages and
disadvantages of a number of different selective schemes, one study group concluded
that universal, flat rate benefits were the preferred option (Bradshaw 1980).

However more recently the subject has been reconsidered in the context of the
Green Paper on the Taxation of Husband and Wife (Inland Revenue 1981). About
£3,000 M is now foregone by the Revenue each year in the married man's tax allowance
(MMA). Yet almost everyone, including the authors of the Green Paper believe the
MMA is now anomalous, in that it results in the tax system treating the incomes of
married men differently to married women and gives an allowance in respect of a
wife regardless of whether the wife is working. The Green Paper devotes most
attention to whether or not the MMA should be made transferable. This is not the
place to go into the arguments. What is important and missed by the Green Paper is
that the resources tied up in the MMA could be paid as a benefit in recognition of
dependency, both for dependent children by improving child benefits and for dependent adults by extending invalid care allowance to married women. To abolish MMA
and leave no family worse off would require a child benefit increase of £4.45 per
child. However a way to concentrate the benefit on families with children dependent
on one earner without creating a disincentive for the spouse to work, would be to
pay an enhanced rate of child benefit to a family with a child under five years.
There are very strong arguments in favour of doing this. The proportion of families
with two earners increases very rapidly after children are aged over five and it is
in families with one earner that resources are most hard pressed. If an enhanced
child benefit were paid to families with a child under five, then in order to leave
a one child family with a child over five no worse off than at present and avoid
increases in public expenditure, it would be necessary to make an enhanced payment
to the first child of a family (Lister 1981).

FAMILIES OUT OF WORK

Families out of work are the final group affected by the tax/benefit system.
Their incomes are constrained by the scale rates of benefits. By far the largest
and most hard-pressed group of families with children living on benefits are the
families of the unemployed. The unemployment benefit system has completely broken
down. It was designed for small scale, mainly short term unemployment and with
mass and increasingly long term unemployment it no longer copes. Unemployment
benefit lasts only one year; earnings related benefit lasts six months, is payable
to less than one person in six and is being stopped from next year; unemployment
benefits have been abated and are no longer keeping pace with inflation. In particular the child scale rates of unemployment benefit have fallen in value. The
result is that over half of the unemployed are now dependent on supplementary
benefit and unlike all other claimants, however long they have been on benefit they
can only ever receive the short term scale rates.

In my view there is no justification for discriminating against the unemployed in
the way current legislation does. In particular the long term rates of supplementary benefit should be extended to the unemployed now. The first constraint is the
cost of doing this, which is £130 M per year. This money could be raised by lifting
the ceiling on employees' National Insurance contributions. The second constraint
is the unemployment trap. If the incomes of the unemployed were improved relative
to the incomes of those in work, it is argued that fewer would work. In fact
despite the commonly held views of politicians and members of the public, it is very
difficult to receive more in benefit than in work. There are families with a number
of children or high housing costs and with an entitlement to earnings related supplement or tax rebates that may be better off out of work than in work. There are
many families with lower net earnings in work than they could get out of it. But

whether this affects behaviour is a different matter. Research by economists on
the impact of the replacement ratio on labour supply tends to suggest that it is
very small and has no impact on unemployment durations up to 20 weeks. Also as
the last report of the Supplementary Benefit Commission (1980) pointed out:

'incentives to work can only be effective if there are opportunities to work.
To increase incentives, while unemployment accelerates upwards, is like trying
to encourage somebody to jump into a swimming pool while the water is being
drained out'.

Even if the unemployment trap is unlikely to exist in its full form there is for
many families very little difference between net disposable resources and benefits
A three child family earning £85 per week would get 90 per cent of their net disposable resources when unemployed. The narrowness of differentials and popular
ideas about incentives are likely to remain a powerful block to any improvement in
benefits unless and until incomes in work are raised. The reason why child
benefits are so crucial, is not just to help families with heads in work, but also
to enable the incomes of the unemployed to be lifted.

The discussion so far has explored the failings of the tax/benefit system but it
has not really answered the question why has the family with children done so
badly in Britain in the last twenty years? The three different propositions now
discussed, none of which is entirely convincing, nevertheless may present the basi
for argument.

                    ATTITUDES

The first proposition is that the fault lies in British national attitudes to
children. The argument is that in our collective provision for children we
illustrate a relative disdain for them. Not just in our cash benefits but in our
child health services, children's homes, nursery school provision and other aspect
of provision which will, no doubt, be discussed at this symposium. Apart from an
oft quoted report by the European Commission (1977), there is little empirical
justification for this view. That study found that the British were more likely
to blame poverty on such factors as laziness and lack of will-power than other
countries. Those of us, who over the years have tried to argue in public the case
for more generous support for families with children, have been struck by the
public antipathy to family allowances. There appears to be a national stereotype
that family allowances in particular encourage 'feckless breeding' and are mis-
spent, commonly at bingo!

ABSENCE OF A POLITICAL COMMITMENT

These national attitudes have been reflected, perhaps, in the absence of a
central concern with the family and children in successive government programmes.
Whatever the commitments in manifestos or the rhetoric of politicians, the fact is
that the family has not been at the centre of the political stage. Of course, all
recent governments have been obsessed with economic problems and the need to
control public expenditure. However, we have learned from the political diaries
of Crossman and Castle, from the outstanding case study of Banting (1979) and
particularly from the leak of cabinet papers during the battle for child benefit
in 1977 that in the ranking of priorities the needs of children receive no particu
lar priority in the minds of politicians.

LACK OF SOCIAL PLANNING

Cabinet battles are partly a reflection of interdepartmental rivalry for resourc

Despite the existence of cabinet committees and the Central Policy Review Staff, policy making in Whitehall and particularly policy making for families is not coherent. Over cash benefits, this has most obviously been revealed in the disjunction between fiscal and benefit policy. There is still no single government department responsible for scrutinising the distributional consequences of policies. The changes in tax announced annually in the budget by the Chancellor are still not scrutinised in advance for their impact on benefits. Tax allowances, despite their recent recognition as tax expenditures in the public expenditure white papers, are still not treated as benefits although they have identical consequences for the public sector borrowing requirement. The most recent example of this lack of integration in planning in Whitehall is the Treasury's Green Paper on the Taxation of Husband and Wife which goes out of its way to draw on distinction between 'fiscal arguments' and 'social considerations'. Some writers have blamed a great deal on the dead hand of the Treasury in domestic social planning (Townsend 1980). But it is not just divisions between DHSS and the Treasury. There are also important conflicts in income maintenance policies for the family between the Departments of Health and Social Services and of the Environment over housing benefits and the Departments of Health and Social Services and of Education over educational welfare benefits.

These problems have *inter alia* resulted in calls for a Minister for the Family, family impact statements, the establishment of the Study Commission on the Family, the Family Forum, the short lived Children's Committee and is part of the background to this symposium.

CONCLUSION

The propects are very bleak indeed. With a depressed economy, mass unemployment, and with public expenditure cuts a major aim of this Government's economic strategy, there is little prospect of any new resources being found for improvements in cash support for families. Indeed the rumour is that social security benefits, including child benefits, are likely to be increased next year by less than the rate of inflation. The best short term hope is that the Government can be persuaded to redistribute all or some of the revenue tied up in the married man's tax allowance to families with children. For that to happen the childless must be prepared to carry the costs.

DISCUSSION

If families with young children are to be given priority in our society, some review and reorganization of fiscal policy is essential. While Jonathan Bradshaw's view that the reason for the low priority in political commitment given to the family is that the British hate children did not receive general support, all agreed that the disjunction between different sectors of the policy-making machinery and the absence of any consideration of the impact of fiscal policy on households did disadvantage the family. First, public attitudes must change. Too many children are being brought up in families at the Supplementary Benefit level of poverty, and consideration of the issues in family support were hampered by worries over incentive. Supplementary Benefit assessment, which does not reflect the cost of child maintenance, discriminates against families with children, who fare badly in comparison with their past situation in this country and with what is now done in other countries. It was felt by some but not all that the re-instatement of the child tax allowance would be a good way to differentiate families with children from those without. The importance of child benefit as a source of income for the mother is not disputed. Another method would be to use the married man's tax allowance, allocating any proposed increase instead to children under 5 years. Could tax and benefit be related to the family life cycle? The cost of maintaining

a child varied with the child's age, being highest for teenagers. On the other
hand the mother of young children was less likely to be working out of the home.
There followed a brisk discussion on competition for benefit between children and
the elderly, disagreeable as this polarization is. Elderly dependants become more
expensive and their proportion in the population is increasing. The re-allocation
of resources means that one group's advantage is at the expense of another group.

There has been some Trade Union pressure for the adoption of a tax allowance
system instead of wage-bargaining for a 'family wage'. Public opinion would need
to be mobilised, but first the prejudice against the large family, stereotyped as
feckless and particular to Asian and Roman Catholic families, needed clearing away.
Lobbies favouring the single parent family and the elderly had accomplished much
for these groups. What is needed is moral indignation on the part of the public
about the deleterious effect on young children of being reared in poverty.

CHAPTER 12

Work and the Family

PETER MOSS

BACKGROUND TO THE PRESENT SITUATION

Two post-war trends are of particular relevance to any discussion about 'Work and the Family'. First, there has been a substantial increase in employment rates among women with children (see Table 1)*. In the 1950s, these rates grew fastest among women with older children, of secondary school age. But in the 1960s the trend became firmly established among women with younger children, the fastest increase occuring to women with primary school children. Rates of increase in the 1970s have been greatest among women with pre-school children (see Table 1), and

Table 1: Proportion of mothers economically active and working full-time by age of youngest child, 1961-80.

Age of youngest child	1961(1)		1971(1)		1975(2)		1981(2)	
	a	b	a	b	c	b	c	b
0-4	11	5	20	6	28	6	30	7
5-10(3)	24	10	51	14	63	16	62	14
11+(3)	34	16	59	22	70	29	71	29
All with dependent children	25	11	39	13	51	16	54	17

NOTES: a = Economically active
       b = Employed full-time
       c = Employed full-time + part-time

(1) = From Census; covers married women under 60
(2) = From GHS; covers all women 16-59
(3) = 5-9 and 10+ for 1975, 1978

---

*Unless otherwise stated, the statistical material presented in this paper is drawn from Moss (1980), which provides a fuller description of the circumstances of parental employment.

perhaps fastest of all among those with babies. In a recent study of maternity
rights in the United Kingdom (Daniel 1980), 24 per cent of women having babies in
early 1979 were economically active within eight months of the birth: by contrast
in the 1971 Census only 9 per cent of all recent mothers were economically active
as long as twelve months after the birth. More than half of all mothers are now
employed at any one time, a position first reached in the mid 1970s. As Table 1
shows, two-thirds work part-time, with the average working week (in 1975) being 23
hours: indeed, the growth in maternal employment has been almost entirely due to an
increase in part-time working.

Women with children, and especially those with pre-school children, move into and
out of the labour force frequently, undertaking a lot of temporary or other casual
work. This means that the numbers employed over a period are considerably greater
than the numbers employed at any one time. In the Child Health and Education in
the Seventies (CHES) study, a national survey of 13,000 five year olds, 37 per cent
of these children had a mother currently employed, while a further 17 per cent had
non-employed mothers who had worked at some stage since the child's birth. Less
than half (45 per cent) of the mothers therefore had never worked during their
child's pre-school years (Butler *et al* 1982), compared to 74 per cent in a similar
cohort study undertaken twenty years earlier (Douglas and Blomfield 1958).

The propensity of women with younger children to work intermittently is reflected
in the different and lower employment rates derived from the General Household
Survey and the Census compared to those based on Family Expenditure Survey data.
The FES uses a wider definition of economic activity, including more paid work
undertaken on a casual basis. The 1977 FES for instance showed 33 per cent of
women with children aged 0-1 year economically active and 45 per cent of those
with children aged 2-4 years (1.2 per cent and 0.7 per cent of these totals
respectively were accounted for by unemployed women and a high proportion, 12 per
cent and 14 per cent, by women described as self-employed): the GHS for the same
year showed only 27 per cent of women with a youngest child under 5 to be employed.
The difference between the FES and GHS is much less for women with older children,
whose FES rates also show a much lower proportion self-employed. It seems likely
that many of this 'self-employed' group are in very marginal and intermittent
employment, often home-based, squeezed around the heavy demands of child-care for
young children, and that as children get older, increasing numbers of mothers
take more regular, if still mainly part-time, work outside the home. This is
consistent with GHS data which shows that 14 per cent of employed women with pre-
school children work at home, compared with 6 per cent of those with a youngest
child over 5 years.

Since 1975, the rate of increase in maternal employment has almost come to a
halt, reacting to the second significant post-war trend, the growth in unemployment
that began in that year. Up to and including 1980, the increase in unemployment
has not actually reduced employment rates among mothers, though the surge in
unemployment occuring in 1980-81 may yet bring about some reduction. Apart from
increasing the numbers of women with children unable to find jobs, rising unemployment will have increased the number of fathers out of work, though unfortunately
there are no current or time-series statistics that discriminate between men with
and without children. A 'one-off' analysis, in the GHS for 1977, showed that 8.4
per cent of married men with dependent children had been unemployed for part of
the twelve months preceding interview, though the level for men with three or more
children was more than double that for other fathers (14.7 per cent against 6 per
cent), whose rate in fact was similar to that for all childless married men.
Given a near doubling in male unemployment since 1977, it may be the case that
about one in six families experience a period of paternal unemployment at some
stage in 1981.

SOME PROBLEMS IN THE PRESENT SITUATION

About three-quarters of all parents are now employed, while parents make up rather more than two-fifths of the workforce. The relationship between work and the family has become increasingly close and complex, but in its present form has a number of damaging consequences. Among the most serious of these consequences are:

1. Many women who wish to work are unable to do so, not just because of the high level of unemployment, but because of child-care and other domestic constraints. Studies have shown that between a quarter and two-fifths of mothers are dissatisfied with their employment status, either because they currently work, but would rather not, or because they don't work and would prefer to. These studies also show that the latter group is two to three times larger than the former.

2. Employed mothers are a very disadvantaged group of workers on almost any criteria, including job status, pay, conditions of employment and future prospects. In 1975, for instance, the hourly earnings of employed mothers were only 61 per cent of those of employed fathers, while in 1974, 52 per cent of employed women with pre-school children had semi-skilled or unskilled manual jobs, compared to 21 per cent of employed married women aged 16-45 but with no children.

3. As well as these short-term effects, having children has a massive detrimental effect on women's long-term employment and earnings prospects. As well as the disruptive effect on employment of having children at home, the expectation of having children to care for affects women's educational and vocational aspirations and behaviour before they have children (Polachek 1975).

4. Many women and probably some men with children face undue tension, strain and other difficulties in attempting to combine work and family life, which detracts from their enjoyment of and contribution to both of these important areas of life.

5. Men work the longest hours of their working lives when they have young children and are often also making a major investment of energy and effort in career advancement. These factors contribute to many having insufficient time, energy and inclination to take an adequate share of family responsibilities and activities.

6. Most children of working parents are either cared for by their own parents or relatives while mothers or fathers work, or else are at school. 'Formal day care' (i.e. nurseries, minders, other paid help) is used for only a minority of children, mainly those with mothers working full-time. While there has been little study, at least in this country, of either informal methods of care or of formal care in nurseries or by nannies, there is evidence that some children at minders receive unsatisfactory standards of care (Mayall and Petrie 1977, and in press: Hughes *et al* 1980). There is also evidence that many parents who use child-minders would opt for alternative forms of care if they were available (Bone 1977).

7. These problems penalise not only parents and children but employers and society as a whole, by wasting much of the employment potential of women and the domestic potential of men, and by reducing standards of performance in both work and family life.

One could add, more speculatively, that present circumstances, where most fathers work full-time and feel little effect of parenthood on their work lives, while most

mothers either do not work or work in marginal employment, have more pervasive undesirable consequences. They contribute to the economic dependency and lack of
political influence of women, and therefore of those most directly involved in the
care and upbringing of children; they maintain a low status for the task of child-
care and are dysfunctional in a society where women are increasingly likely to find
themselves unable to rely on men to provide a secure source of family income,
because of the growing incidence of both unemployment and lone parenthood.

CONSEQUENCES FOR CHILDREN

The growth of maternal employment has generated much hostile comment, with frequent assertions that working mothers are harmful to the family in general and
children in particular. Paternal employment, by contrast, attracts little or no
popular attention as an issue, and little serious research into its consequences
for children and families. In fact a considerable body of research, reviewed by
Wallston (1973), Jobling (1973), and Hoffman (1974, 1979), has failed to support
these assertions by showing any clear or consistent relationship between mother's
employment and harmful outcomes for their children. This is despite the lack in
most countries of adequate services and other policies to enable working mothers
to combine work and parenthood with less strain and difficulty. Perhaps surprisingly, least research has been done on the effects of maternal employment on
infants and other very young children. Hoffman (1979) however concludes that

'studies of older children, as well as common sense tell us that other aspects
of the situation will be more important than the sheer fact that mother is working. What is happening to the child when the mother is at work? Is the child
in a stimulating, affectionate and stable environment? In what way is that
environment different from the way it would be if the mother were at home? What
is the quality of the mother-child interaction when the mother is with the child?
(p. 861).

Hoffman also points to potentially positive aspects of maternal employment,
especially for school-age girls:

'There is much in the situation of the working mother that fits quite well the
needs of school-age children and is better suited to the new adult roles they
will occupy. This is especially true of daughters. There is a great deal in the
family of a working mother to increase the daughter's academic and occupational
competence and to contribute to positive adjustment generally ... it is not
surprising (therefore) that there is a fairly consistent picture (from research
studies) that school-aged daughters of working mothers are higher achievers and
show more positive adjustment on several indices ... (adolescent) daughters of
working mothers are more outgoing, independent, active, highly motivated, score
higher on a variety of indices of academic achievement and appear better adjusted
on social and personal measures'. (p. 862).

Other interesting consequences of increased maternal employment have been identified by Hoffman (1979) and Rutter (1981). First, when mothers work outside the
home, fathers tend to take a more active role in family life, and mothers are more
likely to encourage independence in their children, who in turn accept more household responsibilities. Secondly, most studies find that employed women have a
greater sense of self-esteem and personal satisfaction in their role, compared to
non-employed housewives. Thirdly, maternal attitudes have an important mediating
effect on the consequences of maternal employment. Women who are dissatisfied with
their role, either as working or non-working mothers are likely to perform less
satisfactorily as parents. Finally, data obtained from school-aged children suggest
that one of the reasons why maternal employment has not had negative effects may be
that working mothers, particularly in the middle class, often compensate for their

absence by increasing the amount of direct interaction with their children when at home. In other words, to quote Rutter (1981), 'it is not self-evident that day care will necessarily reduce the amount of exclusive, intensive parent-child interaction'. (p. 174).

Research to date has emphasised that the relationship between maternal work and the family is an interactive one, rather than a one-way process, and a complex interaction at that, mediated by many factors and capable of producing a wide range of outcomes. It has also illustrated how child-rearing practices and organisation, and the values underlying them, exist within a social, economic and demographic context, and that these practices and values are probably beginning to alter in response to changes occurring in this external context.

POLICY OPTIONS

Successive post-war governments in Britain have largely ignored the changes occurring in parental employment, and indeed the whole field of the relationship between work and the family. There has been virtually no official discussion of the issues involved or of possible policy options with the exception of a short report by the Central Policy Review Staff (1978). The increase in married women's employment was put forward, again by CPRS (1975), as a candidate for the proposed Joint Approach on Social Policy, but again nothing further has been heard of this proposed initiative. Action has been limited to the running down of council day nursery places after the War, removing the State from involvement in any provision made explicitly for children of working parents, and the introduction of a statutory maternity leave provision, modest in the extreme by European standards where six months is now the standard for paid leave. Furthermore, this new provision was introduced in isolation, without any accompanying measures to support women wishing to take advantage of the option such as provision of child care or entitlement for leave to care for sick children.

This approach exemplifies the first of five alternative policy options defined by Sheila Kamerman (1980), which countries can theoretically apply in response to recent developments in women's employment. The idea of making any specific policy response is rejected and individuals are left to work out their own solutions in the market place. The other four options proposed by Kamerman are that:

1. A country can decide that all adults should work and therefore subsidises child-care services so that children may be well cared for at a reasonable cost to parents. In East Germany, for instance, in 1976, group care was provided for 80 per cent of 1 and 2 year olds and 85 per cent of 3-6 year olds, with further expansion planned.

2. A country can decide that traditional gender roles represent the best way to minimise the strain between work and family life and subsidise one or a lone parent to remain at home. In Hungary, for example, a child-care grant is paid to women (men are not eligible) who stay at home until their child is 3 years old. The grant is equal to about 40 per cent of the average female wage, per child.

3. A country can decide to permit parents in a two parent family to choose whether one or both parents will work and leave a similar choice regarding work to a lone parent. However parents would be assured of good quality child-care if they made one choice, and protection against economic penalty if they made the other. This represents the official French position.

4. A country can decide to make it possible for both parents or a lone parent to manage work and family responsibilities simultaneously, without undue stress

for any family member. One country, Sweden, has actively begun to pursue this as a principle for policy development. The measures taken in Sweden include: a programme to expand child-care provision for pre-school and school-age children with the aim of providing places for all children of working parents who need such care; a six month post-natal leave entitlement: a further six months leave entitlement, which can be taken at any time up to the end of the child's first year in school at 8 years, either as six months full-time leave, twelve months half-time leave or twenty-four months quarter-time leave; up to sixty days leave per year per child under 12 years to care for a sick child, to visit a welfare or school health clinic or day care centre, or to undertake other specified parental duties which include taking time off 'if the person who customarily looks after the child is ill,' including a parent, childminder or relative, and to enable fathers to care for children if the mother is in hospital giving birth; and the right for a parent to work part-time, say for 6 hours a day until his or her child is aged 8 years. All periods of leave, but not the 'part-time' option, are linked to insurance benefits which provide approximately 90 per cent of lost earnings, and all are open to both parents. In the case of the six months leave period after post-natal leave, which to be taken until the child is 8 years, the period should be shared equally between the parents: other leave entitlements can be shared between the parents in any way they choose, or can be taken entirely by one parent.

CHOICE OF OPTIONS

The choice between these options must depend on the relative weight attached to various values and principles. Basically, should Government take an active role in the management of the relationship between work and family, or adopt a *laissez-faire* approach? If the former, on what basis should this involvement take place? The central issue is how 'the problem' is defined. Some countries insist on viewing it as a 'women's problem' or 'a woman and child-care problem', designing solutions that take account of the needs of women and children only. Such a response Sheila Kamerman (1980) concludes 'alleviates a portion of the immediate problem but will not address the more fundamental tension between work and family life ... nor can the needs of women, children and society be satisfied if men are not part of the solution'. The next stage involves defining the problem as one of parental employment and the changing roles of men and women. There is however growing awareness that the 'fundamental issue is not just these changes in gender roles, but the nature of the relationship between work and family life in a society in which all adults are likely to work yet children are wanted and the society needs them, and indeed needs them to be well cared for if the society is to survive' (p. 108).

Two values will primarily determine which of Kamerman's definitions of the problem is chosen and therefore which set of policy options is followed. First, the importance attached to the attainment of equality of opportunity between the sexes. Any option such as her second, aimed only at women and concerned with encouraging them to drop out of the labour force, is incompatible with this goal. Secondly, what importance is attached to child-rearing relative to paid employment? If greater importance is attached, implicitly or explicitly, to paid employment, options like her first will be chosen that make no demands on the organisation of employment, requiring adaptations to be made only by the family or society at large through, for example, the provision of child-care services or by both.

My position would be that equality of opportunity should be a prime goal of society and that child-rearing should be accorded equal importance with paid employ-ment. This leaves her third and fourth options to be considered, 'free choice' and 'combining work and family'. The former, while attractive and a 'popular option on the level of discussion in countries yet to develop a distinctive policy has several disadvantages. In practice, it would require day-care for all who wanted it, plus a cash benefit equal to lost earnings to all parents who chose to stay at home. Pursued to these lengths, the option would be extraordinarily expensive: in practise however, the option is liable to abuse through half-hearted application, providing inadequate cash benefits and child-care.

More realistic is to offer real choice at certain crucial periods in parenthood, and at other times provide extra support to help parents manage both work and parental roles. Option 4 provides such opportunities, through a package based on the Swedish model, i.e. a range of child-care provisions for children under and over 5, post-natal leave, leave to care for sick children and undertake other parental duties, and a further period of leave kept in reserve, to be used when needed during the early years of parenthood, on either a full-time or part-time basis. All leaves would need to be linked to benefit payments providing adequate compensation for lost earnings. Each parent would have his or her own leave entitlement, which might be exchangeable in part with the other parent's in certain circumstances: for instance, each parent might be entitled to six months paid leave after the birth of his or her child, to be taken at any time in the child's first twelve months, plus a further period from three to six months to be taken at some time in the child's first 5 to 7 years. Lone parents would have a 'two parent' entitlement.

The one omission in this blueprint is the Swedish entitlement for parents to work part-time. Part-time work as an option raises difficult problems. To make it a real choice for both sexes, it should involve compensation for lost income, which could prove extremely costly unless confined to a very limited period, as for instance the period of leave proposed above to be taken at some time in early parenthood. Moreover, as currently constituted, part-time workers are both mainly women and heavily concentrated at the lowest level of occupational status and earnings, with little or no prospects and few occupational benefits. Any extension of part-time working may only exacerbate this current situation, providing a second-rate option used predominantly be women. Finally, it can be further argued that it would be better to reduce everyone's working day, rather than provide more part-time work for certain groups.

On the other hand, part-time work has been the one area of employment growth in recent years and is likely to be the only sector of employment to hold up over the next five years; in other words, it is unlikely to go away. The number of part-time workers increased from 1.96 million in 1961 to 4.57 million in 1980 and is projected by Warwick University MRC to increase to 4.61 million by 1985. By contrast full-time employment fell from 19.66 millions to 17.79 millions and is proposed to fall further to 16.67 millions (Lindley *et al*, 1981). Part-time work appears to fit the needs of many parents, at least at certain stages of parenthood, while a reduction of general work hours to a level comparable to average part-time working, say 20 to 29 hours a week, though desirable could take many years.

Given these conflicting arguments, some sort of compromise may be necessary, involving a 'reserve' period of paid leave to be taken as, say, six months full-time leave, twelve months half-time leave or twenty-four months quarter-time leave, plus a right to part-time employment for all parents. No compensation would be paid for lost income, either in their former job or its equivalent, until their youngest child reached a certain age. Parents would therefore not need to forfeit their job if they wanted to work part-time, and jobs at all levels could be filled by part-time workers. It would be difficult to ensure that the job prospects of parents were not damaged by opting for part-time work, while the option would be more viable for higher income families who could more readily afford to work shorter hours.

FURTHER ISSUES

Cost — the proposals outlined above will involve additional public expenditure (as indeed would any of the other options described, except for continuation of the existing *laissez-faire* approach). How can these costs best be met? Benefits could be incorporated into the existing national insurance system, as has been done in Sweden, though this would obviously involve an increase in contributions. Adopting the principle would place parenthood, or at least early parenthood, as a comparable event to old age, unemployment and sickness, that is a frequently experienced life event with severe implications for earnings, which should and can be collectively provided for without any attempt to relate contributions to risk. Parental benefits therefore would come through redistribution, both from those without young children to those with, and between different periods in the family life-cycle.

The other major sources of funding might be the married man's tax allowance, now widely regarded as an anachronism, costing the Exchequer £2.5 billions in foregone revenue in 1979–80. While there is a strong case for a large part of this allowance being used to support higher child benefit-payments, a proportion could be redirected to support both capital and revenue costs of expanded child-care provision, including an allocation to research and development work to improve quality of care and, possibly, an Exchequer contribution to the cost of parental benefits.

Adapting paternal behaviour. Most of the adaptations required by the increase in maternal employment have been made by women. Apart from providing more part-time jobs, employers have done little, government has virtually ignored the issue and men's advance on the domestic front has been modest (Moss in press), chiefly by providing the main source of care for children whose mothers work part-time. This is hardly surprising since paternal employment patterns remain based on continuous full-time working through parenthood. The argument so far is that a better relationship between work and the family requires adaptations not only by employers and government, but by men as well as women. Measures outlined above provide a framework within which such paternal adaptations can proceed.

How can 'take-up' of these measures by men be encouraged? Several approaches need to be considered: education at school, during pregnancy and through a publicity campaign as in Sweden to encourage fathers to use the available benefits: through the behaviour, attitudes and expectations of maternity and child welfare services and staff: and through the example of men prominent in public and professional life. But perhaps most important is likely to be the financial and employment situation of women. In Sweden, post-natal leave is two or three times more likely to be taken by husbands with wives in professional and managerial occupations than by those with wives in less skilled manual jobs.

Men's behaviour and attitudes seem to be influenced by the job status and earning capacity of their wives, both because wives with 'good' jobs are likely to demand more of their husbands who accept the value and validity of their wives' employment aspirations. In this chicken and egg situation, progress to equality of opportunity and the attitudes and home conditions to support it are interrelated. Progress breeds further progress, so that improvements in women's employment position, having reached a certain point, might largely become self-perpetuating. That point is still a long way off. In the meantime, active policies to provide better employment opportunities for women must play an important part in reshaping the relationship between work and family life.

STARTING THE PROCESS

The prospects of significant policy innovations in the field of work and the family are not promising. No political party has a strong body of opinion ready

to press for action, the small support for action being outweighed by general
disinterest if not active opposition. Considerable weight of public opinion is
disturbed by the economic, social and moral implications of change in family life,
including work-family relationships. Without serious public debate, opinion is
generally badly informed and unaware of the issues involved. Until we get past
discussions about whether mothers should or should not go to work, to accept that
they do and have a perfect right to, and that the problem is not just one of women
and child-care, little can be achieved in terms of raising public consciousness.

Other pressures that might force the hands of political parties to pursue change
are also largely absent. Trade unions are generally unwilling to attach priority
or clout to the excellent positions they often take on paper, and more traditional
concerns such as pay, unemployment and the impact of technology are likely to
assume even greater importance in times of recession (Coote and Hewitt 1980).
Labour shortages have stimulated change, both in other countries and in wartime
Britain, but are clearly not applicable now, while there is no widespread concern
about the birth rate that might encourage measures to help women combine having
babies with continuing at work as part of a package of pro-natalist policies.

Perhaps the only possible source of change may lie in the prospect of continued
high unemployment, though this might backfire to produce inequitable measures to
persuade women to drop out of the labour force rather than policies to produce a
more equitable work-family relationship. Even more worrying than the current high
levels of unemployment and their persistence envisaged in most projections, is the
lack of credible solutions which could provide some hope of work for those, including many women with children, who have been too discouraged even to try to
join the labour force.

The feasibility of achieving the traditional remedy of sustained economic growth
seems a remote prospect. Even with economic growth, new technology could drastically affect the demand for new labour. New approaches, therefore, at least
deserve serious consideration.

One obvious source of additional jobs is through growth in the number of people
employed to provide care, support and education to dependent members of the
community, including children, and chronically sick, disabled and elderly people.
The recent Report of the Jay Committee (1979) recommended a doubling in staff
needed for the mentally handicapped if residential services were to be provided in
a civilised and integrated fashion in the community rather than in existing
hospitals. A second part of the programme to tackle unemployment might involve a
move to the general reduction in workhours, first to a 35 hour week which is
already accepted in many occupations, especially in the non-manual sector, combined
with the introduction of the sort of parental leave and part-time entitlements outlined above. The end result might be that men spent more time in the home and
women more time outside it. Such a change would imply an acceptance that the care
of children, and indeed of other dependents, is work, and that it constitutes a
major contribution to the resources and well-being of the community. The need
therefore is to redistribute work both in the home and out more equitably between
the sexes and to reduce the total workload, both paid and unpaid, of all those
caring for dependents.

        DISCUSSION

Increased employment of women has intensified the tensions that exist between
work and family. If current trends continue, the problems will increase and
enough policy options must exist to allow for real choice. Child-bearing and the
care of children make part-time work preferable to whole time and cause discontinuity in employment. Nevertheless part-time work should be better organized and

integrated into career structure. Many women who would like to work cannot do so
and vice versa. A number of supports should be available for critical periods.
Women have to rely on their man's earnings unless good and sufficient child care
opportunities are provided. At the same time, fathers are interesting themselves
more and more in the care of their children and this should be reflected in their
terms of employment. Equality of opportunity in employment and the interests of
family policy conflict. The question of recognition of child-rearing as a form
of 'work' and whether it should be paid or unpaid work were discussed. If sex
equality is important, it would be wrong to pay mothers to stay at home. In any
case, the level would be unlikely to attract any but the poorest. Benefit should
be for the child.

Research is needed on the effect of parental work, especially paternal, on the
family and information may be available in the General Household Survey. An
annual 'Child Care Audit' could be helpful by showing how children are cared for,
by whom and in what sequence.

Unfortunately both women and the care of children enjoy low political status.
Government policies pay insufficient regard to the needs of parents at the shop-
floor level, and to the provision of alternative methods of child care should
mother wish to work or be forced to work through financial stringency. Whether
or not government wishes women to work, priority should be given to removing
obstacles that prevent her from working if she so wishes or otherwise jeopardise
the future of her children. Britain lags behind other countries in its arrangements for maternity and paternity leave. Nursery and pre-school care and child
minding are far from adequate. These should be extended and 60 days' paid leave
allowed each year for sickness and other childhood emergencies. Responsibility
rests with Trades Unions no less than employers to adapt work arrangements to meet
the needs of workers with families, especially the young ones.

CHAPTER 13

A Family Service?

JOAN D. COOPER

In 1970 the Local Authority Social Services Bill was introduced to Parliament as providing the machinery for a family service. The Secretary of State's welcome was clear enough: 'the primary purpose of the Personal Social Services is to strengthen the capacity of the family to care for its members and to supply the family's place where necessary'. The legislation was essentially related to organisational matters, and this chapter is mainly concerned with the organisational issues.

During this century, we have experimented with unified and with separated social services. The 1905-09 Royal Commission on the Poor Law, in its concern for the family, was itself divided on the organisational issue. The Minority Report, signed by Beatrice Webb, favoured separate education, health and welfare services, and this view eventually found full expression during and after the World War II reconstruction period (1944-48). In less than twenty years, the separate services which reflected age, condition or symptom had come to be regarded as divisive; they required people to shop around bureaucracies for the services they needed, and they failed the family as a unit, which was just what the Majority party on the Poor Law Commission had feared. By the middle of this century, systems revision, with the object of supporting the family, was again contemplated in Britain, and the reorganisation first occurred in Scotland.

SERVICE ORGANISATION IN SCOTLAND

A major reconstruction of services in Scotland developed from concern during the fifties over rising rates of juvenile delinquency, always seen as a touch-stone of family functioning. The Kilbrandon Committee (1964) set up by a Conservative government, recommended the combination of children's, special education services and child guidance in a social education department within the Local Education Authority. This was a proposal for an organisation based on a limited age range, with special attention to particular conditions such as delinquency, educational subnormality or maladjustment. The proposal gradually came to be regarded as a narrow concept, resting on too restrictive a knowledge base about human needs and behaviour and overemphasising cognitive development.

Under the political leadership of Judith Hart, the Joint Parliamentary Under Secretary of State for Scotland (1964-66) who was appointed when the new Labour Government came to power, a working consensus of academic, education, health, legal

and social work interests was achieved. This transformed the Kilbrandon proposal
into a wider initiative. The argument used by Judith Hart (1965) was that services
for children affected a quarter of the population; the inclusion of their families
was essential and would extend to half the population, and from such a base it
would be 'absurd' not to create a service for the whole community. The Social
Work (Scotland) Act 1968 resulted, with unified services for all age groups, including the Probation service, so that one social work system served all families.

ENGLAND AND WALES — CONFLICT OVER A FAMILY SERVICE

The Scottish development exercised no powerful influence on the decision to
examine the case for a family service in England and Wales. Here, a conflict
between rival interest groups concerned for children and families, and for single
adults and the elderly population emerged.

The Ingleby Committee (1960), set up under a Conservative Government, had
examined the case for increased powers to prevent or forestall the suffering of
children through neglect in their own homes, and had devoted the first two chapters
of its report to a discussion of children and families. Its basic premise for
helping families was effective professional and service co-ordination. There was
a tentative suggestion for a family service in the long term, but organisational
proposals were baulked. The Children and Young Persons Act 1963 legitimated the
work that many Children's Departments of local authorities were undertaking to
avoid family breakdown.

The Longford Committee (1964), a group of opposition Labour supporters, published
'Crime, a Challenge to us all' in which they saw problem behaviour as essentially
related to family dynamics, and a family service as an essential social mechanism.
Nine of the fifteen members of the Longford group received Ministerial Office in
the 1964 Labour Government, and the Queen's Speech declared an intention to legislate.

The prospect of legislation activated Home Office and children's interests, but
these were counterbalanced by an equally powerful lobby which impressed upon the
political leaders in the Ministeries of Health and of Housing and Local Government
the case for equivalent treatment for the social needs of elderly and adult handicapped people. The Government, faced with acute rivalries at central and local
levels and among professional interests, reacted by setting up the Seebohm Committee to study the issues and deflate the conflict which covertly related to social
justice and overtly to professional and service rivalries. The social policy
issues were not new but changes in demography and family structure gave them
prominence.

SOCIAL POLICY

Twentieth century concern for the family, and its child centred ethic, has to
take account both of the expansion of opportunities and the relief of distress.
The relevant social measures are based on classified benefits which have collective and personal elements in varying degree, and an inherent tension between
family and individual needs. Social policy, in the interests of equity and of the
management of social relationships free from the extremes of violence, has adopted
the simplest of formulas for the receipt of benefits. These are based on age,
employment position, ascertainable physical or mental condition or legal status.
Entitlement to benefit may be a citizen right, but benefits such as health care,
education or personal social services are also forms of social control
(Donajgrodzki 1977). On the benefit — control axis, individual and family claims
may conflict and may sometimes be seen to do so acutely in the mental health and

child care fields where judicial action may be involved. On the system — family
axis, conflict occurs when pressure on health care facilities exploits family care,
or alternatively, families exploit services by a refusal of care. Furthermore,
systems reject people and behind the systems are professional backers; schools
reject truants into the judicial system, and bargaining occurs between health and
personal social services over geriatric care.

The formulas based on entitlements according to age and condition, as in equity
they probably must be, also define systems, and serve as controls on professional
and bureaucratic power. But formulas make for difficulties in determining
priorities for particular social groups, of which the family is one. The ambiv-
alence over social benefit and social control is an obstacle to the continuance of
the same priority over time; the recent emergence of juvenile unemployment is an
example of a priority switch. Existing systems have to be flexible enough to
respond to new social demands, or fragmentary services have to be created in the
short term. An overall egalitarian framework poses hard questions about priorities
for social investment in the individual, in ancestry and in progeny, and attitudes
constantly shift. It was these kinds of conflicts that the Seebohm Committee had
to face, though they were presented to them by their witnesses in concrete form
and the committee kept closely to a concrete frame of reference.

The problem is, as the Committee discovered when they set out the services to
help the family and examined the emergent pattern, that social provisions and
entitlements to benefit interact with random effects. '... in a theoretical sense,
retirement insurance has acted as a form of children's allowances ...'. A reduction in the extent of filial responsibility for elderly relatives frees parents to
regard children as their first priority (Schorr 1980). Looked at in this way, it
is simplistic to develop policies other than comprehensive ones which recognise
the needs of all age groups in society. A housing policy which provides for
separate accommodation for grandparents may reduce marital stress among parents of
young children, or alternatively remove the emotional and practical support that
could reduce the chances of child abuse. And social disorder or civil disturbance
affects all age groups.

The Seebohm Committee proceeded pragmatically, rather than philosophically, but
it was concerned with social justice, open access and community involvement and
responsibility. The Committee set itself a practical problem solving exercise to
make the personal social services more 'legible'.

        THE SEEBOHM COMMITTEE

The Committee was appointed in December 1965 and reported in July 1968. As
already noted, there was no political issue over a family service; the conflict
was about boundaries and organisational forms. The terms of reference were clear
enough:

    'to review the organisation and responsibilities of the local authority and
    personal social services in England and Wales, and to consider what changes are
    desirable to secure an effective family service'. (para 1)

The Committee found no difficulty in persuading politicians and civil servants
that the terms of reference could cover all age groups. There was no generally
acceptable definition of family. An arbitrary definition is useful in a symposium
but not for policy formulation. The national census definition was inadequate for
the services under examination:

    'Either a married couple and their never married children, if any, or a lone
    parent with his or her never married children'.

This definition excluded unmarried couples with never married children, married couples with married children or without children living with them, and unmarried people not attached to their parents' household. The Committee's view was more comprehensive:

'We decided very early in our discussions that it would be impossible to restrict our work solely to the needs of two or even three generation families. We could only make sense of our task by considering also childless couples and individuals without any close relatives: in other words, everybody'. (para 32)

What the Committee recommended was logical enough. It was a new local authority department to provide a community based service available to all. They proposed the combination of the local authority services for children, for the aged, for the mentally ill, and for physically and mentally handicapped people of all ages; together with the addition of child guidance and school and housing and welfare. The subsequent legislation avoided confrontation by excluding the last three. The Committee's stated purpose was to 'meet needs on the basis of the overall requirements of the individual or family rather than on the basis of a limited set of symptoms'. (para 111)

Their own study of the services and the balance of the evidence had favoured the organisation of personal social services on a comprehensive basis. The Committee stressed accessibility through local offices, and 'bringing the services to the people'. One reason for disliking the term 'family service' was its ambiguity which might prove to be a deterrent to some individuals seeking help but afraid that a family service was not appropriate to their situation. Although the Committee had regarded the evidence presented to them as defensive, it was, nevertheless, illuminating in disclosing:

1. rivalry (or deeply felt loyalty) among professional interest groups and managers of service systems which had to compete for scarce resources of money, skilled manpower, research investment and physical plant;

2. failure of co-ordination as a policy for meeting family needs (the Ingleby solution);

3. powerlessness among small departments representing low status clients in comparison with large systems manned by prestigious professions;

4. shortage of administrators, psychologists, psychiatrists, and social workers;

5. housing difficulties as an important component in an estimated 30 per cent of social problems;

6. neglect of particular groups such as children under five, and especially those under three with mothers in employment; and of chronically sick and disabled people; undervisiting of elderly people who were not receiving the current equivalent of supplementary benefits;

7. Lack of a family perspective in the face of professionals seeking clients.

An analysis of the situation as they found it led the Committee to propose machinery for pooling and sharing out scarce facilities. Unification, as distinct from co-ordination, was their remedy for reducing specialist rivalries, endorsing an overall preventive policy, and developing community resources to supplement family and professional ones. Equity was their aim, and good husbandry their purpose.

It is possible to argue that this strategy represented propaganda for a predetermined case of special pleading for the elderly under-served population, that the treatment of the terms of reference was cavalier, that 'community' was substituted for 'family' and that this was exchanging one indefinable term for another. It can also be argued that a comprehensive service required the Committee to press for a radical revision of an inherited array of confusing and conflicting legal powers and duties which conferred statutory protection on some children and adults, and that a simplified legal code was a pre-requisite for a universal service.

What is important is that the Committee based their recommendations on the recognition of the interdependence of social needs and did not rely upon the powerful economic argument that parallel services for families (parents and dependent children) and for adults lacking family support would be expensive and wasteful.

PRIORITIES

The importance of local study to identify local needs and resources was stressed, but the Committee singled out two general priorities: children under five and very old people (para 5). It was their numbers, particularly of the very old and frail that justified priority for the elderly. In the case of young children, the Committee were impressed by research findings that at least one child in ten would need special education, psychiatric or social work help before the age of eighteen years (Appendix Q). Their own enquiries pinpointed the inadequacy of day care for the under fives and not only for children whose mothers were in employment but for children's social and environmental advantage. It is in this context that the immigrant population, otherwise largely ignored, is referred to:

'Particular mention should be made of the young children of immigrant parents who may suffer from many of the problems of low income, bad housing and pressure on mothers to go out to work, and whose difficulties may be greatly accentuated by barriers of language or colour' (para 200).

Secondly, the Committee were impressed by expert opinion which emphasised the significance of childhood experience on future development. In determining priorities, systems theory and the interactive nature of social provision and professional intervention — the underlying thesis — was well illustrated:

'There are also young children from homes where the parents are mentally or physically unable to provide a suitable environment or where the harmony of the family is threatened by a child's difficult or abnormal behaviour. In such circumstances, day care becomes part of the process of support, assistance and treatment ...' (para 199).

Priority heightens the issue of who is the client, patient or consumer, and the convergence or conflict of interests among the contenders. The much criticised and misunderstood proposal for basic generic training for social workers, prior to any later specialisation, was in part a response to conflicts of interest aroused by narrow specialisms or, in reverse, a contribution towards seeing problems in their full social rather than individual context.

A FAMILY DIMENSION

Starting from different stances, the development of comprehensive personal social services was the product of thinking through the appropriate response to social need in the different settings of Scotland, England and Wales, and later in Northern Ireland. Comprehensiveness was the common feature, though to differing extents and within different structural patterns. In England and Wales, the basis of allocation between health and personal social services was determined by a formula, announced in the First Green Paper on the National Health Service, as a primary skill test. This formula was not simply an administrative convenience; it was intended to assist the maintenance of knowledge, competence and ethical standards through professional groupings. The reorganisation of the services was concerned with structures based on the principle of universalism: this, in itself, lays a responsibility on professions to adopt an individual, a family or a communit dimension, and to influence structural procedures accordingly.

Within organisational frameworks, specific programmes can be developed, and both national and local priorities can be accommodated, but in elective systems of government, priorities are subject to political determination which, in turn, is influenced by public sentiment which is not constant. Furthermore, family patterns and family behaviour seem strikingly unregulated by public policy; witness the rapid increase in the employment of women despite difficulties in securing alternative child care, the abuse of children despite the mass of nineteenth century child protection legislation the extent of which is a cause of surprise to some Commonwealth immigrants, changing marriage and child rearing patterns, or the self determination of elderly people in guarding their way of life even when it involves calculable risks. State and family relations are in constant flux (Moroney 1976). This is well recognised. Where the professions stand in relation to this tension is a question more rarely debated. The family dimension can be recognised or ignored in terms of income maintenance, health, housing, employment, education and personal social services, just as it can be recognised or ignored in the commercial and entertainment sectors and in employment unions. In these influential power systems, professionals rarely enter into debate.

Privileges, or norms, intended to promote positive family functioning can be varied and are very variable as indicated by cross-cultural studies of family or social policy (or women's policy?) in industrialised countries. These policies may include minimum to generous maternity leave, job protection with proportionate wages for either parent during a child's first year of life (Norway, Hungary), subsidised vacation schemes for families (Austria, Finland), equal pay for men and women (Sweden), preferential home loans for large and young families (Hungary), or cash housing allowances (France). It is noteworthy that variants relate to social as much as to family policies, and sometimes to population policies, although, as in the commercial world, they may be 'packaged' as family policies (Kamerman and Kahn 1978). Income support seems a favoured means of assisting families, but traditionally it remains tied to the assumption of a male breadwinner rather than to the parent who cares for the children. Traditionally, the professions maintain a neutral stance, and perhaps a degree of conservatism in practice, leaving demographers to pursue a lonely course in analysing trends. It is sometimes pertinent to ask whether traditional policies and traditional professional attitudes are in collusive alliance in lagging behind changing social patterns.

There is another problem of collusion. There is an enduring problem about the attraction of high professional skill to high cost programmes for family replacement rather than family support systems. Institutional and acute services in health, education and personal social services drain preventive, day and domiciliary resources. It is the absence of family, family collapse or family violence that mobilises resources and devalues the notion of 'shared care between public and family provision'(Moroney 1976). The less dramatic, and perhaps less professionally rewarding practice of organising family support to modify the roles, to organise the tasks and ease the relationships in family management that is relativel underdeveloped and has less professional status.

Yet it may be the professions that have to play a key role by modelling in their practice recognition of the family dimension, in whatever shape it is found to exist in the particular set of relationships confronting the practitioner or discovered by him (which was the Seebohm approach). It may be the professions who

are important in re-evaluating parental and family roles which have been lacking
in prestige and power so long as the work ethic has prevailed over the nurturing
task and so long as the importance of the maternal role has been so emphasised.
When individuals or families are in need of help, it may be that a family dimension
calls for early analysis of the roles and potentialities of all the actors, not
excluding the contributors from the community, and that this assessment may be the
significant one to make at a high level of skill. In this connection, so far as
the personal social services are concerned, it may be appropriate to take note of
the profile of consumer demand as it presented itself in Goldberg's research study
(1978).

Demographic analysis generally confirmed that high demand is associated with
social disadvantage (the complex of low socio-economic status, unemployment,
large families and poor housing), but that these factors are less pronounced in
the case of elderly people who represent a wider cultural and economic spread and
show a willingness to use services, especially practical ones. About one third of
all referrals are elderly, physically frail and disabled. Nearly a third are
young families with material problems which are normally within the province of
other social systems and advocacy over income, housing or other sources if required.
About a sixth of referrals may be disturbed families exhibiting material difficulties, serious stress and violent reactions and these are the families which consume
social work attention over long periods. The time commitment to these disturbed
families whose difficulties are chronic and whose crises are frequent has been
noted by other studies (Stevenson and Parsloe 1978). In a sense the social policy
provisions either pass them by or confuse them, but in order that they may be
helped more effectively than they have been in the past, it may be important to
redirect material and professional resources to planned nurturing and social learning schemes and to other strategies, which can be compared and evaluated, by
shifting some resources from family replacement to the family support programmes.
It will be objected that our knowledge is inadequate; this is so. If the family
dimension is to have any permanence, investment in increasing knowledge and skill
is overdue.

DISCUSSION

The idea of a social service for families is not new. So far a number of
difficulties have stood in the way of its achievement, some of which are administrative and some due to the operation of human nature, to which both client and
social worker are heirs. A basic problem, as Sir Edmund Leach showed in his opening paper, is that the family is difficult to define in any terms and particularly
in terms of policy. Most people are involved in family for most of their lives
and are interdependent so that, for example, helping the old frees parents for
their children. The present system, following Seebohm, is a universal social
service for all age groups although their requirement for cash or service, both
being needed, varies in its proportions. The old mop up money for gadgets while
children and their families consume personnel. The universal system was designed
to defuse the conflicts that arise from professional loyalties and jealousies with
their resulting competition for limited resources, and because replicating services
for various age groups is uneconomic. In theory nothing prevents social workers
from taking a family perspective, yet in practice the policy of training generic
workers fails to take into account any predilection for special types of work.
There is, too, the probability of 'burn out' with its heavy toll among workers for
the handicapped and in mental institutions. The objectives of social control are
threefold: humanitarian, economic and the prevention of social disorder. Unfortunately some clients refuse offered help. Old people refuse the health system while
with the young it is the educational system. Within the family there may be a
conflict of interest between the different members. Many obstacles separate the
workers in different departments. In the conduct of social work, important

questions of training, of career structure and of administration remain unsolved.
Because a profession needs prestige if it is to work alongside other professions,
a university course aiming at a higher standard than may be necessary for the actual
work done is rated more highly than practical experience, although it is the latter
which breeds confidence. Power and influence are necessary for resource allocation
Is the training relevant to practise? Could more be done to mobilise voluntary help
This tends to be more flexible and innovative. Conformity was established too earl
before we had sufficient knowledge, and there is room for experimentation through
projects that do not have to turn into permanent provision or to be absorbed into
institutional or career structure. This does not help career prospects. Non-
dramatic interventions carry little *kudos*. A local community system, which might
be advantageous, is a dead end and the use of skilled professionals in managerial
positions downgrades the value of social work practice. Voluntary services provide
a network of support at low cost. Enthusiastic projects mushroom but there are
financial implications. Fortunately, although time brings rigidity and bureaucracy
ability to innovate and to identify gaps in provision survive. The relationship
between voluntary and statutory services is haphazard and perhaps voluntary
societies now need a Seebohm analysis. Client groups multiply and with encouragement are able to work together, local co-operation proving immensely valuable.

Many problems of administration were discussed. How to attract workers to unattractive places? Health visitors are badly needed in inner city areas. Local
government political organization makes it difficult to bring together the work of
the different departments. Housing, education and health are not viewed nor
managed as interdependent, an attitude which obstructs the growth of mutual confidence and co-operation between the workers themselves. With the abandonment of
regional autonomy for central control, there is little encouragement to explore
what works well in a particular area so that its modification and general application can be studied. It would be advantageous if thinking time could be built
into the career, so that a body of people could be thinking about what needs doing.

CHAPTER 14

A Question of Inter-agency Collaboration for Family Health

SUE DOWLING

INTRODUCTION

I start by apologising for the jargon which surrounds the subject of collaboration. No attempt is made to define the terms collaboration, co-ordination, co-operation, consultation and communication, the c's of an exhortatory rhetoric which urges the various family care agencies*to work together. All these words refer to the complex processes involved when individuals and agencies are coming together or moving apart, about which too little is known for the accurate drawing of demarcating lines of language. This chapter focuses on some practical aspects of the ways in which different agencies can work together for family health. First comes the case for collaboration from the public health perspective. Then some of the evidence is outlined which points to formidable organisational and professional barriers that impede progress. Finally some examples are described of local initiatives which are trying to find ways around these barriers.

THE CASE FOR INTER-AGENCY COLLABORATION FOR HEALTH

Although the basic case for collaboration may seem self evident, it needs to be stated. This justification is necessary because of the costs involved in bringing together those who normally work apart (DHSS 1978), because, having brought them together, there is a need to establish commitment to such ways of working (Bruce 1980), and because of the importance of defining clear objectives whose success can be measured.

---

*Among 'family care agencies' are included government departments concerned either directly or indirectly with family policy and services, in particular the DHSS and DES, Health Authorities and their various services, such as Family Practitioner Committees and General Practitioners, Local Authority departments concerned with policy issues or services which impinge on families, in particular, Social Services and Education: and voluntary organisations (national and local) and their intermediary bodies and the more informal sector of family care such as family members, friends and neighbours.

THE DEFINITION OF HEALTH

For health, the case for inter-agency collaboration stands or falls on the definition of that concept. If health is interpreted as a state of non-illness, one
which can be maintained largely by hospital and curative services, the case for
inter-agency collaboration is probably marginal. If, however, health is truly
'Everybody's Business' (DHSS 1976a) and the National Health Service is seen as only
one in a spectrum of agencies for health promotion as well as prevention and cure,
the need for collaboration is paramount.

In Britain today it seems that a curative and rather limited concept of health
still persists. Health professionals, especially doctors, exert considerable power
over health information and have major influence over the shape of health policies.
Not surprisingly, with their training in modern scientific medicine their attention
has tended to focus narrowly on the NHS, and mainly on services based in hospitals
rather than in the community. Unfortunately, the 1974 NHS reorganisation abolished
the post of Medical Officers of Health who led a global Public Health movement,
fighting the social causes of ill health, such as infected water supplies and air
pollution. Since then, the new specialty of Community Medicine has had its attention drawn from public health to the more immediate and parochial problems of
service administration and management (USHP 1979). Today its voice is deafeningly
quiet in public debates about the continuing but fundamental social causes of
family ill-health, such as poverty and inequalities in educational opportunities.

Despite this, a growing international and national voice is calling for an
urgent re-shaping of the concept of health, and a re-consideration of the way in
which health policies are formulated and services delivered (Blaxter 1981). Here
the remit of health is interpreted as extending far beyond the boundaries of health
services, involving a whole range of other and complementary services. The following are some of the characteristics which emerge from this broader view of health:

1. Health is a fundamental human right, which should be given high status in
   policy making at national and local levels. In the case of family health, it
   sets parents and children, rather than the service provider(s), as the *raison
   d'être* of health policies and services.

2. Health is not merely the absence of disease, but the achievement of a maximum
   potential of physical, intellectual, emotional and social development. The
   positive promotion of these attributes is important, as well as the prevention
   and cure of disease.

3. Health is an ideal state which is impinged upon to different extents by
   adverse factors which operate in a variety of ways at different times in human
   growth and development. These are reflected in a number of different
   categories of health needs, medical, educational, environmental and social/
   welfare. Not all of these can be met by the health services nor be influenced
   by the individual by modification of lifestyle. These health needs are
   central to the argument for inter-agency collaboration for health and require
   elaboration.

   The medical health needs of families range from needs created by medical
   emergencies such as severe gastro-enteritis in infancy and road traffic
   accidents through chronic medical conditions such as physical and mental
   disability to emotional and behavioural problems and are usually met by health
   professionals. They include such preventive medical needs as immunisation
   and the early detection of developmental abnormalities.

   The educational health needs of families arise from parents, the children and
   the services themselves. Parents need and desire information with which to

make important decisions about health behaviour and medical care (Cartwright 1979) as well as other factors which affect health such as nutrition and income maintainance. For children with educational disadvantage the Headstart programme in North America has shown how carefully designed and supported pre-school educational programmes can improve their intellectual and educational development (Lazar *et al* 1977). And from the services themselves comes the need to learn about families' own perspectives of their health needs and health services (Garcia 1981).

The environmental health needs include the provision of clean air, food and water, protection from the adverse side effects of social planning, for instance, the hazards of positioning noisy and polluting traffic and industry next to families' homes.

Social and welfare health needs stem from factors such as poverty, unemployment and the erosion of social and family support systems. These factors probably all contribute to 'family stress', a concept which, though tantalisingly difficult to define, may be crucial to family health. Haggerty (1980) has pointed to the association between 'upsetting' life events, such as loss of a job and death of a family member, and an increase in vulnerability to infection. Brown and Harris's study (1978) of the aetiology of depression in mothers with pre-school children has shown its association with severe life events characterised by loss and disappointment, and that factors, such as social support through having an outside job or intimate friendship, may protect protect people from depression who would otherwise be at risk due to their stressful lives. This type of evidence suggests that support for families by neighbours, social services, social security or whoever, may be of critical importance to their health.

SOME OBJECTIVES

This concept of health points to the importance of inter-agency collaboration in policy making both national and local and in the planning and delivery of family services.

From the public health perspective, objectives of such an approach could be:

1. to provide information on the health impact to families of policies and services arising from agencies outside the N.H.S. e.g. with regard to transport, income policy and the nuclear defence programme (Outer Circle Policy Unit 1978). Health Impact Statements have been in operation in the USA for several years with the intention of making agencies more sensitive to the health consequences of their actions.

2. to sharpen the definition of families' health needs. Input from each of the statutory, voluntary and informal agencies contributing to family care would emphasise the learning process of planning and would broaden the vision of the health field currently available.

3. to improve the knowledge of other agencies' skills, roles and resources. This would develop an informed and realistic baseline for collaboration, improve inter-agency referral and might bring a more coherent 'wholeness' to the various family services, helping families find their way around them.

4. to increase the availability of scarce resources by decreasing unnecessary overlap of function between agencies.

THE PROBLEMS OF COLLABORATION

THE ORGANISATIONAL MACHINERY

Each of these broad objectives could be translated into a variety of policy making or service providing programmes from the national level of cabinet ministers and government departments down to the local level of the statutory and voluntary agencies and the individuals working in them. To assist in such collaboration in family services, certain organisational structures have been established (see Table 1). The paucity of information about inter-agency co-ordination at the national level limits this chapter to evidence concerning the local statutory and voluntary sectors of family care.

Organisational Problems

Webb and Hobdell (1980) summed up one of our major organisational problems in these words:

'It is unfortunate that in Britain we have hardly begun to analyse what it is we are urging upon practitioners; why it is we are doing so; how much we think it is worth paying for better co-ordination, or how we might recognise good co-ordination — or teamwork — when we see it'.

In a strangely back-to-front manner the structures designed to help the different agencies plan and co-ordinate their services more closely together have been established before the answers to these basic questions have been found (DHSS 1976b). One need only consider the Joint Consultative Councils and the Joint Care Planning Teams. And now that these structures are established there seems a difficulty and even a reluctance to monitor the way in which they work, their successes and their failures.

A small amount of research has examined the organisational aspects of inter-agency collaboration, but this has almost exclusively focused on the agencies. There is still little evidence on the impact of the collaborative procedures on the health and wellbeing of the families themselves. Undoubtedly we should be asking about the adverse consequences for families as well as the positive effects. Two important questions which urgently need asking and answering are: when and how does the co-ordination of different agencies' work jeopardise the confidentiality of private information? and could the results of certain types of joint action reduce families' choice of access points to services?

At the Local Authority/Health Authority level many organisational factors operate to confound attempts to collaborate in policy making and planning. These include major variations between the different services' management structures, their ways of being financed, their direction of accountability, their planning systems and timing of their planning cycles and their geographical boundaries (Norton and Rogers 1977; Rowbottom and Hey 1978).

Unfortunately the re-structuring of the health service in 1982 will do little to iron out these difficulties. Indeed, there is a danger that the situation may be worsened by increasing the number of small health service units with which local authority departments have to liaise (Wistow and Webb 1980).

In their study of relationships between health and local authorities, Norton and Rogers (1977) found that service planning did not usually have a rational basis. This tended to undermine attempts at joint planning. 'To be successful, rational planning requires a context where values are agreed and explicit, broad objectives can be agreed, information is complete and the tools for its analysis available and an environment which is relatively certain'. There is now sufficient evidence to suggest that such a basis rarely exists either in local authorities or in health authorities (Hunter 1980).

Table 1:   Examples of Structures to Facilitate Inter-Agency
Collaboration.

NATIONAL

Consultative group for under fives (representatives of central government
  departments)
The DHSS's Children's Committee (abolished October 1981)
National 'federations' of voluntary organisations who liaise with central
  government departments, e.g. The Voluntary Organisations' Liaison Council
  for Under Fives (VOLCUF) and The Maternity Alliance.

LOCAL

Joint Local and Health Authority Structures

Joint Consultative Committees
Joint Care Planning Teams

Health Authority Structures

Area Review Committees
Health Care Planning Teams, e.g. for child and maternity services
District Handicap Teams
The School Health Services
Liaison posts, e.g. Specialist in Community Medicine (Social Services)
  and Area Nurse (Child Health)
Community Health Councils

General Practice Structures

The primary health care team
Patient Participation Groups

Local Authority Structures

Liaison posts, e.g. Social Services' Health Liaison Officers, Pre-School
  Officers
Environmental Health Officers
Pre-School Co-ordinating Groups/Committees established and serviced by some
  Local Authorities

Voluntary Sector Structures

Some Pre-School Co-ordinating Groups/Committees
Liaison/co-ordinating posts, e.g. Voluntary Service Co-ordinators in the NHS
Local intermediary voluntary bodies, e.g. Councils of Voluntary Service,
  Rural Community Councils

As well as making joint local/health authority planning difficult, this lack of
rational planning also serves to confuse voluntary organisations trying to work
with the statutory services. Leat and colleagues (1981) were led to recommend that
the policy making process of statutory authorities should be further examined and
clarified for the public; and that volunteers and their organisations should
develop political skills and knowledge of the machinery of local government.

For voluntary organisations there are other types of problems which come under the 'organisational' heading. For instance, their work tends to be family and child centred, embracing a wide range of needs which cut across the statutory services' divisions between health, education, housing and social services. Issues of representative democracy can also impede collaboration between the voluntary and statutory services (Hatch 1980). Local authorities, with their electoral accountability, may feel constrained in working closely with voluntary groups who have no such accountability.

Other organisational issues include the independent contractor status of General Practitioners, which has been referred to as a barrier to joint planning with health and local authorities. The separation of this part of primary care, which is outside the Health Authorities, appears to make integration difficult in collaborative schemes. A different type of problem is created by the negotiating/ bargaining nature of joint agency work. With the present resource constraints there are rarely any financial benefits which can be offered to 'buy' collaboration.

Interpersonal Problems

Organisational arrangements in themselves are not enough for collaboration. The attitudes, skills and knowledge of the individuals within the statutory and voluntary agencies also seem to be important. Studies of interprofessional work have shown widespread ignorance about the training roles and perspectives of other professions (Hallett and Stevenson 1980), and also a lack of congruence between the self-perception of particular professions and the way others perceive them (Olsen and Olsen 1967). Research on interprofessional work in primary health care teams and with child-abuse cases shows how inadequate knowledge about other professions may lead to negative stereotyping. (Bruce 1980; Hallett and Stevenson 1980). This may result in a failure in trust and a reluctance to share information between professions. Though there is little evidence on multi-agency work involving volunteers, here too there are often problems of inappropriate attitudes and inadequate information about skills, knowledge and roles (Leat *et al* (1981).

Training programmes for professionals and volunteers in multi-agency work are often proposed as a way of ameliorating these problems (Hallett and Stevenson 1980) Though these may remould attitudes and provide the necessary information about other groups of workers, little is known about effective ways of carrying out such teaching.

Bruce (1980) in his study of primary care teams in Scotland, identified three critical factors for collaboration: physical proximity, social proximity and positive motivation. Teamwork, as he observed it, was a developmental process which did not result automatically from the presence of any of these factors. Instead, it appeared to grow 'step by step as the frequency of contacts increased, as the relevance of such contacts became clearer, as a better understanding of roles emerged accompanied by the disappearance of stereotypes, as social proximity increased, as mutual trust began to grow and problems of confidentiality to shrink' Other studies suggest that Bruce's three factors maybe important in many other multi-professional situations.

SOME EXAMPLES OF LOCAL COLLABORATION FOR FAMILY HEALTH

THE CPAG/DHSS STUDY

From this discussion it appears that the goals of co-ordinated service planning and operation may be hard to achieve. Indeed, with so many organisational, attitudinal and educational maladaptations one can only wonder that attempts to co-ordinate family services ever materialise. Yet they do.

In a project sponsored by the Child Poverty Action Group and funded by the DHSS,

I have been studying initiatives which were attempting to increase the availability
and access of health care for families (Dowling 1982). Among the material collected
were many examples of ways in which agencies were working together to pool local
resources and skills for families. The value of such a study is its record of
ideas and experience as a learning resource with which family services for health
can be examined further and developed. Among other things this record suggests the
importance of the 'bottom-up' approach to service planning and innovation, with
management and policy-makers responding to the experience of families and field-
workers, rather than vice versa.

It is important, however, to emphasise the limitations of this descriptive,
rather than evaluative study. With little evidence of the successes and failures
of the schemes described it was hypotheses forming rather than hypotheses testing.
In addition, because there was a deliberate attempt to seek out the more innovative
fringe of family care, the unusual and the rare were identified. The schemes
encountered could not be said to be typical of care in the ante-natal or pre-school
periods, the two time-spans studied. One might conclude, therefore, that such
initiatives are so marginal as to be unimportant. I suspect they are not. Being
an optimist I prefer to think they will remain marginal only so long as service
managers and policy makers continue to ignore their struggles and fail to support
them with finance, morale and, most importantly, with organisational changes to
iron out some of the problems already described.

The initiatives selected for description all illustrate aspects of Bruce's hypothesis (1980) that collaboration is facilitated by positive motivation and the
opportunities for members of different agencies to meet and get to know and understand each other. They have been divided into two groups: those that bring people
together by sharing and working from the same premises and those that bring people
together by neighbourhood based organisation.

COMING TOGETHER BY SHARING PREMISES

Gloucestershire's Family Centres are examples of the different Child and Family
Centres which have developed throughout the country. Though these types of centres
vary in the way they are managed, funded and the range of services they offer, they
all try to make the child and family the prime focus of their work. They bring
together in one place partnerships of parents, volunteers and professionals.
Gloucestershire's centres, each situated in an area of high social stress, were
instigated primarily by the County's Education Department. However, other agencies
are closely involved. For instance staff of the Health Authority have helped
organise pre- and postnatal groups, there are professionally supported playgroups
and many voluntary and informal activities such as mother and toddler groups and
coffee mornings. Though a full-time teacher is employed in each centre to co-
ordinate the work there is considerable parental involvement in running the centres
(Jackson 1979).

Surprisingly few health centres and general practices were found to be exploiting
their potential for being community resource centres for health in its broadest
sense. Those encountered suggested the range of ways in which this could be done.
For instance, a G.P. in Birmingham's inner city worked with the local community
group to acquire a derelict site adjoining the surgery for an adventure playground.
Money was raised for a play leader to join the primary health care team. As the
play facilities were available to all children, whether or not they attended the
surgery, it was hoped that the leader would provide a link between the health
professionals and the local families. This practice also worked with the children's
library and set up a small collection of books in the surgery waiting area.

In Stockwell, another inner city area, a community health group composed of local

people has successfully negotiated with the District Management Team to be involved
in the planning of their new health centre. In their proposals (Mawbey Brough 1979
the health group have indicated their wish for community involvement in the management and running of the centre and also in the contribution to its resources. In
a survey they identified over twenty other groups who wanted to work with the new
centre. These included mother and toddler groups, women's health groups, tenant's
associations, parent-teacher associations and playgroups.

Another example of a general practice fulfilling the role of a community resource centre comes from Barnsley. Here a general practitioner has helped to
establish in the rooms above his surgery a resource centre for self-help groups
concerned with health issues. The groups are offered, free of charge, a well
equipped meeting place as well as office facilities and any medical advice which
they request. The centre also acts as a clearing house for local enquiries about
self-help groups.

COMING TOGETHER WITH NEIGHBOURHOOD BASED ORGANISATION

'Patchwork' or the zoning of agencies' work to geographically distinct populations has been the subject of recent debate on the organisation of the personal
social services as well as the primary health care services (DHSS 1981c: Hadley and
McGrath 1980). Valuable professional as well as voluntary and informal resources
may be wasted by the mis-match of their working areas, resulting in unco-ordinated
effort and poor channels of communication. A small but increasing number of
Social Service Departments have changed from centrally based area fieldwork teams
to dispersed 'patch based' teams who work within geographically defined communities
of between five and seven thousand. Accounts from some of these suggest that as
the social workers get to know the local GP's and health visitors, so they are
gradually evolving ways of working more closely together.

This type of re-organisation of social work teams on to a neighbourhood basis
ideally should be matched with a similar organisation of primary health care.
The need for this seems particularly great in urban, particularly inner city areas
(London Health Planning Consortium 1981). In some urban areas general practitioners already voluntarily restrict the neighbourhoods from which they accept
patients. However this does not seem common.

In view of the large geographical overlap of the practice populations of many
urban GP's some Health Authorities have reorganised the work of their health
visitors and district nurses. Whereas their caseloads were previously limited to
the scattered patients on GP's lists, now by covering the populations of geographically defined zones they include patients of all the GP's who work across
the area. Barnsley Area Health Authority has monitored the effect of this re-
organisation of their community nurses. For General Practitioners liaison work
has increased a load not surprisingly at first resented. For the community nurses,
their new way of working has increased their contact and collaboration with mid-
wives and social workers, the numbers of families visited, and their job satisfaction. This streamlining of services has been appreciated by families too.
Whereas before they often had to deal with one health visitor at home, another in
the clinic and yet another at school, most of them now have the same health
visitor in each.

Turning to other ways in which neighbourhood based networks of family care
agencies may be fostered it is important to mention local pre-school co-ordinating
committees and groups. Bradley's survey (1981) of local authority procedures for
co-ordinating the statutory and voluntary services for the under fives has shown
the growth of these groups in recent years and their variety of structure, representation and function. The impression gained from their experience is that an

effective type of organisation may be one which attempts to knit together the four different levels of local services: the families who use the services, the field-workers (statutory and non-statutory), the service managers and those with policy-making and resource allocation power, such as councillors and members of health authorities. In one London Borough a network of Family Forums developed with one Forum in each of the social service districts. Health visitors, social workers, pre-school playgroup organisers, and volunteers belonged to these Forums. They aimed to develop their local resources to meet the needs of families and to identify gaps in existing provision. To link the ideas and work of these Family Forums together and relate them to the management and policy making bodies of the statutory services, an 'umbrella' advisory committee was established with repre-sentatives of each of the Family Forums, officers of the Health Authority and the Local Authority Departments together with elected members of the council.

The pre-school co-ordinating groups throughout the country are engaged in a variety of health related activities. For instance, they are providing resource information points for parents, volunteers and professionals needing to know the availability of certain facilities in the area; multi-disciplinary courses have been set up to discuss health topics; play and educational material has been provided in clinics and surgeries; some of the groups have helped initiate links between health visitors and playgroups, childminders and nursery schools and classes.

The final example is of a neighbourhood based training scheme (Poulton and Campbell 1979). This attempted to increase the collaboration between all those providing pre-school care in six different neighbourhoods in Hampshire. Groups were established to study the different ways in which professionals and volunteers worked. They also explored the needs of local families and identified problems in the services which might require attention at the fieldworker or management level. This educational project was approved by the Joint Care Planning Team and the necessary finances were obtained from Joint Funding.

Each study group was based on a neighbourhood which coincided as far as possible with the local administrative service unit. Members were drawn from people working within that neighbourhood and representation from the health, social work, education, day care and voluntary sector of the pre-school services was carefully balanced. A University tutor with experience in group work led each group.

At the end of the project a report of the six groups' findings and recommen-dations was submitted to the senior officers of each of the relevant services and to the Joint Care Planning Team. Perhaps because they arose from small groups of fieldworkers with an intimate knowledge of their neighbourhood, many of these recommendations were immediately relevant to the local services. For instance one group suggested that waiting areas in their health centre and ante-natal clinics should be made more comfortable and suitable for families and young children. In view of the rapid changes in health visitors and social work staff in some neigh-bourhoods it was suggested that regular lists of these staff in post would be helpful for line managers and fieldworkers. Other suggestions included the pro-duction of an inter-agency manual which would list staffing structures, areas of responsibility of the different workers and would give outlines of the procedures adopted within each agency. Members of the groups felt that it would be helpful to have an identifiable 'contact' person in each agency through whom queries and information could be channelled; and that the geographical area for which field-workers were responsible could be made more explicit, perhaps with the introduction of an area map. It is encouraging that at the end of this project the field-workers found it so useful that they set up their own groups (called 'Educare' groups) to continue the work in different parts of the county.

CONCLUSIONS

The health of families is an important focus around which the statutory and voluntary agencies should come together. Yet the evidence reviewed concerning the problems of inter-agency work suggests that something more than exhortation is needed. Attention has to be given to organisational problems and to the training of all those who work in the family services, whether professionals or non-professionals.

The practical examples used to illustrate ways around these difficulties have depended on an unusual degree of commitment among the projects' members. This, more than any other factor, provided the necessary catalysing energy to innovate and to bring together people who usually worked apart. Indeed the history of many of the schemes suggested the importance of actively seeking out these hot-points o commitment and encouraging them to become catalysts for change in the family services.

If positive motivation is so essential for collaboration, certain important questions must follow. How, for instance, is such motivation created? How does it develop? What sustains it? For the selection, training and support of those workin in the family care agencies, answers to these questions must be found.

For the policymakers there is another question. Would such unusual degrees of motivation be needed if the organisational and professional barriers to inter-agency collaboration were removed?

ACKNOWLEDGEMENTS

Thanks are due to the Child Poverty Action Group and the DHSS respectively for sponsoring and funding the study 'Ways of Reaching the Consumer in the Antenatal and Pre-School Child Health Services'; and to Ioanna Burnell, Lynne Harrison, Jenn Whitfield and all the members of the Department of Community Health, Bristol University, for their assistance and support.

DISCUSSION

Everyone agrees that there is an overwhelming need for inter-agency co-operation that the obstacles and difficulties are great and that the reasons lie in all the three areas, administrative arrangements, professionalism which leads to failure i trust, and in the transfer of information; and in a lack or weakness of motivation to identify and tackle together the real needs of the clients. Exhortation to dro the barriers and to work together on the job will never of itself solve the problems. Sue Dowling's plea for starting from the 'bottom up' was well received. Involvement in dialogue of the chief officers of the various services was also necessary and probably a person should be designated to be responsible for liaison and collaboration. Co-operation is not always good within a single department. As in so many of the discussions, training of professionals was seen as anti-collaborationist and some sharing of training as well as interchange of agency workers was suggested. To protect standards, professionalism must be maintained while at the same time the creation of negative stereotypes between professional groups must be overcome. The doctor is handicapped by the awe of the mysterious elements perceived in his work by his patients and indeed by his co-workers in other professions. More care was needed in the choice of language which could impede communication.

Health education newly defined and the spread of information ought to help.

Administrative arrangements had so far failed to take full account of the change from the negative illness view of a health service to the more positive approach in which medicine is seen as only one, albeit an important element. The causes of ill-health and human under-functioning had to be observed in the form of social and other stresses, if prevention was to be effective. Occupational health services could well be extended, and workplaces, such as firms and factories, already used by health visitors for some antenatal care, should be more widely included in the health visitors' province for health information as well as service.

Sue Dowling's plea was applauded for wider formation of local groups in the community to identify local needs and to find ways of fulfilling them. The key is to be found in motivation.

CHAPTER 15

A Family Perspective in Policies for the Under Fives?

ELSA DICKS

INTRODUCTION

Family policy means to me a framework of policies directed at the well-being of all families. That parents and children are more together during the years before school ought to make family policy both essential and possible. In fact, the central policies in education, health and social services which provide for the under fives have tended to fail in this respect. They are a ragbag of fragments, each originally devised for a different purpose. They do not combine in any sensible framework, nor do they meet the needs of all families.

Local implementation of these policies is increasingly chaotic in spite of attempts at co-ordination, and central direction is diminishing. Whereas the 1976 Priorities Document (DHSS 1976c) devoted a section to the need for support for families with children and preventive work with under fives, Care in Action (DHSS 1981c) the current guidelines, makes no mention of the needs of all families with children. The widening gulf between national and local government suggests that the situation will deteriorate further.

Why do policies fail families with under fives, what is the effect of failure on families, and what are possible ways of countering this failure and giving to policies a family perspective?

REASONS FOR POLICIES FAILING FAMILIES

There are deep reasons why policies fail to meet family needs:

1. the aims of the services overall are different and are not expressed in terms of outcomes desired for the whole family.
2. There are conflicting policies and
3. difficulties in the co-ordination of policies.

1. OUTCOMES (Curtis 1980)

Education policies certainly have not been written in terms of a family service, but have focused more on the child, and in particular on the development of children's cognitive skills.

125

Although education does not aim to provide for the whole family, DES (1978b) has recently noted that it will begin to involve parents and in some areas day care is provided where full-time places and collaboration with social services combine to extend the nursery schools' day. Health services are responsible for the prevention and cure of illness in the individual, and although the rationale of social services provision may be to keep the family unit together (by avoiding care proceedings) it is actually directed, in day nurseries, to the safety and well-being of the child. Voluntary organisations have a wide range of aims. Each sector has a quite different fundamental purpose so that there is no consensus on basic questions about what the services for the under fives are intended to achieve.

2. CONFLICTING POLICIES

Existing policies for the under fives in all the sectors specifically concerned, as well as in others act against one another and against the interests of families.

The Health Sector

Health service re-organisation provides a startling example of how policies conflict and may undermine even the statutory health care surveillance for all families with under fives and for the families with children who are handicapped or have other special needs. Re-organisation abolishes the Area Health Authorities and replaces them officially on 1 April 1982 with more numerous District Authorities. Re-organisation does not continue the requirement to make appointments of specialists in Community Medicine (Child Health) or Nurses (Child Health). The community child health services, which are able to concentrate in an unique way on prevention and to deal with a total child population, unlike GP's and paediatricians who deal with the sick, may begin to disappear. And the statutory requirement that health authorities advise local education authorities and social service departments on strategy to ensure the health of children will be difficult to carry out as there will now be several Districts trying to effect liaison. The spirit and purpose of the Warnock Report, embodied in the 1981 Education Act, which suggests more co-ordination to help children with special needs, will be difficult to carry forward.

The Education Sector

Plans for nursery education and for primary or secondary education are not integrated (CPRS 1978). Whilst at national level it may be the policy of a Minister to increase the levels of provision by say 2 per cent per year, opportunities for teachers to specialise in training for early childhood education and jobs are being cut. Primary schools are being used instead of special provision for under fives, as local authorities are obliged to work within financial constraints.

What are the implications of this for families? In one local authority 10,000 extra four year olds have been taken into primary schools this autumn. Only eighty extra staff have been taken on, and no extra nursery nurses or special facilities provided. Part-time entry or staggered entry has to cease after the first half-term. Less investment is being made in nursery education. The whole policy may, however, be reversed in 1982 when the extra rates levy imposed by central government may mean the exclusion of all four year olds from the same schools, staff redundancies and confusion. Local families will look once again to nursery schools and classes and to playgroups, some of which may by then have closed for lack of support.

Planning

In the same region the policies of the Department of the Environment, pursued by local planning departments, have allowed the construction of the largest private housing development in Europe without there being any services in education, health or social services to cater for the needs of the young families that will make up the bulk of the population.

DIFFICULTIES IN CO-ORDINATION OF POLICIES

The interests and responsibilities of the departments concerned are quite separate. One fashionable antidote is co-ordination, but this is difficult to effect and other recommendations like a central policy unit or Minister for Children have been rejected.

Deep-seated problems of co-ordination include the different planning bases of services and the operation of co-ordinating machinery locally.

Planning Bases

The Department of Education and Science has some control over the number of national and local places, but its administrators have relatively little territorial knowledge and need have no regard for the distribution of other types of provision (CPRS 1978). Their colleagues in DHSS are more concerned with the determination of needs of particular groups and localities, and therefore with the precise location of services. Health service provision is made on a regional basis and related to population number in the regions, for example expressed as beds per thousand population. Voluntary organisations, because of their varied nature and the way in which they are supported, operate on entrepreneurial principles and on the whole independently of one another. Branches are often autonomous. VOLCUF has begun to effect some joint thinking on voluntary policies in its Discussion Document, published in the local authority associations' study 'Under Fives' and in its seminars and conferences. It is difficult to see how such systems can be brought together.

Local Co-ordination

Concern for the creation of a single policy or of nationally co-ordinated policies has been submerged in the promotion of local co-ordination. Two circulars on co-ordination of services for the under fives were published in 1976 and 1978 by the Departments of Education and of Health and Social Services (DES/DHSS) have also funded a study (Bradley 1981) and a national conference in 1981. There are examples of changes in the use of resources but no local authority has radically altered all of its services as a result of co-ordination. The number of departments potentially involved and of man-hours required make the tying together of services extremely difficult (Challis 1980) as Table 1 shows. There is doubt about the effectiveness of co-ordinating committees in which time is wasted in defending existing practices and in arguing about allocation of places to handicapped children, services for whom are valuable for boosting roles and strengthening the claim on resources. The argument for co-ordination would be much stronger if it produced power to see families' needs and act upon them rather than the needs of the services themselves.

THE EFFECTS ON FAMILIES

The lack of a sensible framework of policies for the under fives and their families fails families because of the resulting:

1. low levels of provision,
2. gaps in services,
3. local deficiencies and variations
4. increasing reliance on principles of eligibility and
5. focus on the needs of children rather than of families.

Table 1: Organisations involved in Formulating Policy and Planning, Running and Delivering Day Care Services for Under Fives. (example of one Inner London Borough)

ORGANISATION (b)	RELEVANT RESPONSIBILITIES (a)	ORGANISATION	RELEVANT RESPONSIBILITIES (a)
CENTRAL GOVERNMENT (b)		Directorate of Housing and Property Services	
*Dept. of Education & Science	All aspects of nursery education service.	Directorate of Construction Services	
*Dept. of Health & Social Security	All aspects of personal social service responsibilities. Regional officers, specialist officers, administration and information services, building & cost advice (until recently — loan sanctions).	*Directorate of Finance Services	Budgets, audit etc.
		*Directorate of Management Services	Establishment, organisation.
		Corporate Planning Unit	
Dept. of the Environment	Urban programme, inner city partnerships, local government, RSG, planning and land matters.	OTHER AGENCIES	
		*Council for Community Relations	Special projects.
HEALTH SERVICE		NALGO	) Trade union matters for
Regional Health Authority		*	) professional and non profes-
Area Health Authority			) sional staff.
*Health Districts (2)	Health visitors, child health clinics, creches, district nurses, visiting medical officers.	NUPE	
		*Voluntary Organisations	Enormous range: advisory and major service providers.
		*Private Organisations	Day nurseries etc.
*General Practitioners		*Childminders	Between 400-500.
Community Health Councils		ADDITIONAL BODIES WITH INTERESTS IN UNDER FIVES PROVISION (c)	
LOCAL GOVERNMENT		Inner City Partnership	
*Inner London Education Authority	All aspects of nursery education. County Hall — advice, professional support, policy, resources, administration. Division — local planning and administration etc.	Partnership Committee	ILEA/Social Services Local Standing Committee
		Partnership Committee Officer Steering Group	Standing Committee for Co-ordination
		Under fives sub group	ILEA/LA Members Standing Committee
Greater London Council		Inner City Consultative Group	
*Directorate of Social Services	Day nurseries, playgroups and registration, registration of childminders, field social work, private & voluntary schemes, grants to organisations, training, personnel etc.	Sub group on Under Fives	
		Co-ordinating Group on Under Fives	
*Directorate of Amenity Services	Libraries, books & toys, story-telling, 1 o'clock clubs, mother & toddler clubs, playspace.	NOTES:	*Indicates those agencies most closely concerned with direct service provision. (a) Responsibilities outlined for agencies marked * only. (b) Omits Treasury and Employment etc. (c) Large, complex committees with membership of officers and/or members and/or consumers.
*Directorate of Development	Physical planning, design.		

1. LOW LEVELS OF PROVISION

Provision is at low levels because local authorities have no mandate to provide, the exception being health and even this is threatened. Social Services provide a residual service although they may support voluntary services as well. The 1980 Education Act makes it clear that education authorities are not required to provide nursery education. Nationally one child out of three (30.5 per cent) will not have had significant experience of pre-school services on reaching the age of 5, according to the Child Health and Education Study (Osborn 1979). Only 2.3 per cent will have used day nurseries, 25.8 per cent will have used nursery schools and classes, and 42.4 per cent will have had experience of group care in play-groups (Table 2). Note that it is actually the voluntary sector which provides the greatest proportion of services for the under fives and their families.

The population of under fives (6 per cent of the total) has dropped and steadied from 3,061,000 in 1976 to 2,770,990 in 1979 according to the OPCS mid-year popu-lation estimates (1971–1979). Care in Action (DHSS 1981c) anticipates a growth and an additional three to four million under fives by 1990, but demographers are concerned that the birthrate will fall as families find it harder to survive financially. There has been a small increase of provision in the statutory sector, mostly part-time places in nursery classes. Changes in attendance regulations in the autumn of 1981 meant that existing places could be used by more children in future. Non-specialist provision has increased in infant schools (Osborn 1981). In the informal sector it has also increased in playgroups and in independent child-minding (Tables 2 and 3).

In theory, a greater proportion of under fives should now be able to benefit from provision, but local authorities are finding it difficult to maintain their direct services and their support for the voluntary sector. Financial support for services through the new block grant system, which is allocated on an assessment of need derived from a calculation of an average expenditure over the whole country, may reduce levels of service even further in some authorities (Westland 1981).

Benefits of provision are only felt by families whose needs are matched by facilities. Types of service differ in what they have to offer in the way of content, hours and charges. Margaret Bone's study (1977) revealed that one out of three parents did not find the kind of care that they wanted for their children or for themselves. Some of the differences in services are being blurred in combined centres (Ferri *et al* 1981), in extended day nursery schools, and in the deployment of local education authority staff in Social Services day nurseries. These projects are scattered and are not yet policy.

2. GAPS IN SERVICES

Families with children aged 1 to 3 years find gaps in services, with very little support for themselves and little formal supervised care or education for this age group. The gaps are particularly acute for families with more than one toddler. When they need support or care, they have to seek childminders or provide for themselves on the self-help and voluntary networks which are them-selves patchy. Pressures on families today may make that all the more difficult to do. The growth in home visiting schemes, while welcome, is not enough to meet family needs. Families may then be confused, in some areas, by a sudden avail-ability of services for children aged 3 and 4. Indeed, with the pressure to take 4 year olds into infant classes there may be competition to attract families to use facilities and to enrol at school early.

130   E. Dicks
                    Table 2: Child Health and Education Study (1975)
                              Nursery/Playgroup Survey.

1. PROPORTION OF CHILDREN AGED UNDER FOUR YEARS

    MAINTAINED
        Nursery schools   35%
        Nursery classes   27%
        Day nurseries   73%

    INDEPENDENT
        Nursery schools   42%
        Playgroups   53%
        Day Nurseries   62%

    ALL   49%

2. INSTITUTIONS (PROVISIONAL FIGURES)

	INSTITUTIONS	CHILDREN ON REGISTER	CHILDREN PER INSTITUTION
	%	%	
MAINTAINED			
Nursery schools	4	8	78
Nursery classes	11	14	49
Day nurseries	3	4	48
INDEPENDENT			
Nursery schools	1	1	39
Playgroups	76	70	37
Day nurseries	4	4	36
ALL (N = 100)	16,948	686,931	

3. MAIN TYPE OF PRE-SCHOOL EXPERIENCE OF CHES FIVE YEAR OLDS PRIOR TO INFANT SCHOOL ENTRY

	%
NURSERY SCHOOLS OR CLASSES (Private and LEA)	25.8
DAY NURSERIES .. .. LA	2.3
PLAYGROUPS	42.4
NO PRE-SCHOOL EXPERIENCE	30.5
TOTAL	100.0% N = 13,135

3. LOCAL DEFICIENCIES AND VARIATIONS

   Some families choose not to use provision, but others may have no chance to do
so. They may live where local authorities have decided not to provide day
nurseries or nursery schools (CPRS 1978) or they may be prevented by geography and
the expense of transport from reaching services. Local disparities between supply
and demand may be spectacular, with waiting lists of 50 to 150 at some combined
centres, which are obviously appreciated by families. The situation is aggravated
by cuts and reductions in services, for example, 5 places per day nursery are to
go in one metropolitan area.

4. ELIGIBILITY

   Families are increasingly subject to eligibility 'tests' for provision, which is

Table 3: Pre-school Places* as a Percentage of 3-4 Year
Population: 1974/5 and 1978/9.

	ENGLAND		WALES		SCOTLAND	
	1974/5	1978/9	1974/5	1978/9	1974/5	1978/9
	%		%		%	
MAINTAINED						
Nursery schools	2	3	4	5	7	13
Nursery classes	4	8	15	16		
Day Nurseries	2	2	0	0	2	3
INDEPENDENT						
Registered premises (full-time)	2	2	1	1	0	0
Registered premises (sessional)	23	31	17	24	27	33
Places occupied by under fives in infant classes	18	18	29	34	4	7
All above	51	65	66	80	40	56
Population aged 3-4 years n in thousands =	1,428	1,149	84	71	168	137

CHANGES IN PROVISION OF PLACES*FOR UNDER FIVES FROM 1974/5 TO 1978/9

	ENGLAND	WALES	SCOTLAND
MAINTAINED			
Nursery schools	+9%	+8%	+51%
Nursery classes	+62%	-7%	
Day nurseries	+7%	+230% (from one to five centres)	+7%
INDEPENDENT			
Registered premises (full-time)	-9%	-24%	-19%
Registered premises (sessional)	+9%	+16%	+1%
Places occupied by under fives in infant classes	-18%	0%	+46.9%
POPULATION (thousands)			
aged 3-4	-20%	-16%	-19%
aged 0-4	-14%	-16%	-12%

Sources: Official statistics from DES, DHSS, Welsh Office
and Scottish Social Work Services Group.

*Places in schools are taken as the equivalent of all full-
time pupils plus half the part-time pupils.

allocated on the basis of priority criteria particularly, but not exclusively, in
the social services sector. Day nursery places and sponsored provision in voluntary nurseries and playgroups are reserved for children with priority needs. The
work being done at PSSRU, Kent, on client-based assessment of need and joint
criteria may influence the situation for the better in the long term. Although
nursery education is provided in principle on a universalist basis, in practice
since the promotion of positive discrimination in the Plowden and Educational
Priority Area Reports, it has been used to meet special needs, especially in
cities. Changes of population and financial restraint have made other demands so
that bargains may be struck between social services and education departments to
transfer names from one list to another. The DES circular 'Falling Rolls and
School places'(DES 1981) has accelerated this tendency but has also encouraged
Local Education Authorities to use spare classrooms for playgroups, drop-in
centres, etc.

Day care and education are expensive, and families' ability to pay is and will
increasingly be a factor in access to provision. Families with more than one
under-five find that it is very expensive to pay for playgroups at 60p per session
and, if the mother works, for childminders at £14 per week. Only nursery education
is free and even that is threatened as the Minister is reported to be considering
charging (Guardian 27 October 1981).

There are, on the other hand, family needs which might be expected to, but do
not result in eligibility for day care as they did in the war. Mothers with jobs
find that work alone does not automatically qualify for a day nursery place. In
1976 some 200,000 children had working mothers (CPRS 1978) but, using Osborn's and
Curtis' figures together, only about three out of four of these can have had supervised day care arrangements (Table 4). Restricted allocation of day nursery places
takes little account of housing difficulties and yet some 80,000 children a year
are born into seriously under-housed families (HMSO 1980). Allocation criteria
often stop, because of shortage of places, at children on non-accidental injury
lists and from single-parent families.

5. FOCUS ON THE NEEDS OF CHILDREN RATHER THAN FAMILIES

Statutory provision is on the whole designed for children, and single children,
and in spite of good practice in some areas it is generally not flexible enough
to cater for family needs. The family with more than one child, perhaps one in
school and another in a day nursery, has problems in holidays when hours and
arrangements do not coincide. Still some 65,000 children a year are born as third
children and 30,000 as fourth or higher orders, yet most institutional facilities
do not recognise the facts of family life and are not flexible enough to accommodate
needs of families or to take in older siblings during the holidays. Bureaucratic
thinking sees children as sole offspring, but the realities of families are different

In spite of inspired and innovative work, projects, and the persuasions of selected
authorities and workers, families have not generally been seen by policy makers to
contribute to their children's education, health or welfare. Children and families
have been considered separately. Involvement of parents and family in the development and education of their families is now accepted as an important factor. It
features strongly in writing, most recently in the report of the Rampton Committee
on the educational needs of ethnic minorities (HMSO 1981). It is, therefore
surprising that policies are not more directed to its encouragement.

Table 4: Total Numbers of pre-school day care places (social
services) 1976-1980 England (DHSS feedback)

Service	(1) 1976	(1) 1977	(2) 1978	(2) 1979	(2) 1980
LA day nurseries	26,899	27,385	27,677	28,063	28,437
LA nursery groups	3,085	2,473	3,532	3,325	2,865
childminders in LA sponsored schemes	–	–	8,502	10,162	7,378*
childminder places paid for by LA	945(?)	1,210(?)	3,339	3,192	2,933*
private day nursery places paid for by LA	1,529	1,600	1,448	1,653	1,860
independent day nurseries	26,049	24,916	23,498	21,677	22,017
childminders (full day and sessional)	82,638	86,706	86,068	85,444	99,853
independent playgroups	353,547	365,759	357,950	357,027	365,003
total population aged 0-4**	3,061,000	2,896,000	2,788,600	2,770,900	2,792,400

(1) DHSS feedback A/F76/6 Children's Day Care Facilities
(2) DHSS unpublished totals for English authorities from return SSDA503

*N.B.These figures may not be reliable since they may not be all calculated on
the same basis.
**   Data from OPCS mid year population estimates (June of each year)

    Source: Personal Social Services Research Unit, University of Kent
    DHSS Feedback Data. By courtesy of Dr. S. Curtis.

WHAT IS HAPPENING TO THE UNDER FIVES?

Examination of the official statistics*for children in local education authority
nursery schools and classes (Osborn 1981) suggests that notwithstanding cuts in
public expenditure in the latter half of 1979 there was a steady, though small,
annual growth of nursery school and nursery class places throughout the decade,
although these were substantial regional variations. (Table 5).

Table 6 shows the 99% increase in the percentages of 3-4 year olds in full-time
or part time places in maintained schools.

---

*The Sources of this information are DES Statistics of Education 1977, OPCS Popu-
lation projections No 9 and personal communications to Mr. Osborn from the DES
and the Welsh Office.

Table 5

1971		1979	
Places		Places in nursery schools	
26,000		34,700	(30 per cent increase)
in nursery classes			
46,700		108,600	(increase possibly due to the number of spare primary school places
Places in infant (i.e. non-designated) classes			
216,800		233,900	

Table 6: Percentages of Children from the Total 3-4 year-old
        population.

1971	1979
Attending nursery schools and classes	
6.1%	19.0%
Attending infant classes in primary schools	
13.4%	19.9%

The policy to increase the proportion of pupils attending part-time resulted in
an increase of a further 19 per cent in the number of pupils under age five.
Numbers of pupils in the maintained sector could be increased by 94,000 if only
rising fives i.e. children whose fifth birthday comes later in a particular term
attended full-time and younger children attended part-time in infant schools.   In
1977 87 per cent of rising 5's were in infant classes and 5 per cent were in
nursery schools and classes. Excluding rising 5's the proportions of 3 to 4's in
full-time infant classes was 8 per cent and in part-time 1 per cent, which is
equivalent to 1/3 of all under fives in local education authority provision in
infant classes. There is a need for information and research on the experience of
under-fives in non-designated classes. The new trend to amalgamate infant and
junior departments to save money needs to be noted and watched.

The declining birth-rate has done more to increase the proportion of 3 to 4's in
maintained schools than either expansion in provision or part-time attendance.
The 25 per cent reduction in the size of the 3-4 year old population from 1971-1979
resulted in a 50 per cent increase in the proportion of under-fives in local
education authority schools over and above increases in the number of places and
part-time attendance.

An up-turn in the birthrate in 1977 is expected to continue and the population of
3 to 4 year olds should increase well into the 1990s. If local authorities wish to
maintain the proportion of 3 to 4's in school they must expand provision.

WAYS TO COUNTER POLICY FAILURES?

The numerous deficiencies in policy for the under fives and their families have been amply demonstrated. A sensible framework that takes account of present and known needs is a long way off. The overall picture is depressing and points to the need for fresh thinking and for legislation which recognises the realities of family need and gives local authorities and health authorities the power to re-organise their services for the under fives. Because the prospect is dim, we should not stop asking for it.

Change may be achieved incrementally by doing things at other levels to adjust the operation of existing policies. Management policies could become more flexible, so that existing facilities are used for many more purposes and in co-operation with community and voluntary organisations, as happens in some areas; and attention might be focused and good practice translated into policies through three processes, advocacy for family policy, involvement of voluntary organisations and participation.

ADVOCACY FOR FAMILIES

Advocacy for family policies is relatively recent, comes most convincingly from the independent sector, for example the Study Commission on the Family, and may yet prove its effectiveness in actual policy outcomes. Another body, the late Children's Committee, in its publication in 1980 on 'The Needs of the Under Fives in the Family', made an important plea for family perspectives in policy making. The recommendations, which received more attention from outside government than from within it, should be strongly supported.

INVOLVEMENT OF VOLUNTARY ORGANISATIONS

If policies are to be designed for families and to serve them better, family organisations should be able to contribute to their formulation. It is true that some selected and established organisations are represented on some co-ordinating committees, but voluntary organisations and community groups, which contribute to the bulk of group care for under fives, are largely excluded from the policy-making process. Since 1978 there has been some promotion of the need to involve voluntary bodies, but there is evidence that at best this is reduced to a post-planning consultation. Voluntary organisations could do much more themselves to co-operate locally and to decide how best to represent corporate views in local authority and health authority planning.

PARTICIPATION

'Family Action' and family participation are also necessary if policies are to be changed to suit the needs of families. The power of family action was demonstrated recently when a group of parents successfully petitioned an area health authority to provide for seventy under fives in a rural area with no facilities. A family perspective in policies logically requires that families are involved in influencing management and planning. In the statutory sector this is beginning with the 1980 Education Act now requiring the appointment of parent governors. In the voluntary sector participation has been the keystone of many organisations. For example 77 per cent of playgroups have parents in the majority on their committees (PPA 1980). Participation could be extended more into the Social Services day nursery provision and into the health sector.

These processes of advocacy, involvement and participation could be very much more effective if appropriate and influential structures, particularly local structures, are used or created to channel views of family needs to policy makers. Community Health Councils and the new District Health Authorities, which could be more accessible to the community than district administrations, should certainly be used. There might also be a case for broadening the constituency for under five and representing the interests of families with young children through Family Councils or Children's Councils locally, provided that these could be given the sort of power and mandate that Community Health Councils have. (There may be, however, a danger of diluting the claims of young children for special services.)

CONCLUSION

The centralist approach to policies for the under fives has certainly run into trouble and may even have been abandoned. A total restructuring of services or a comprehensive service to meet the needs of families with young children cannot be expected and will not happen until more priority is given to the needs of all families with young children.

In the meantime, all the interested parties should come together to do some fundamental thinking about aims of the services, perhaps by means of a broad and representative forum as Linda Challis (1980) recommends.

But we should not abandon hope altogether. The process of change and the development of a family perspective can be encouraged and supported locally. Efforts need to go on to find ways to unite central and local interests in favour of the under fives. We should identify and use all possible means to ensure that this is done, that local knowledge is directed into the chambers of policy makers, and that the family is the model.

DISCUSSION

Service for the under-5's was a political issue mistakenly accorded no priority. The problem could not be allocated to any one sector because too many interests were involved — housing and the design of houses, recreation and the provision of parks, recreation grounds, safe play places, swimming poools, traffic safety and the sites and construction of roads among them. A Family Commission was necessary for representing and co-ordinating these interests as they affected a locality. There should be a framework involving voluntary organizations in planning with the social services and education departments. The voluntary organizations which had stepped into the gap could do no more than plug it. Funding remains and is likely to remain a difficulty. One suggestion was that with falling rates in primary school populations the buildings could be used for short-term low cost pre-school provision.

Clifton Robinson described a group of thirteen nursery centres open from 8.00 am until 6.30 pm for children from the age of 6 weeks and closed for only one week in the year. The origin was a marriage between the Departments of Education and Health with voluntary organizations, the parents being closely involved in the management. The centres were in beautiful settings. The cost was high but so was the benefit. This was a very worthwhile example of the bottom-up approach discussed by Sue Dowling (see p.119). If as suggested all under-5 children are at risk, potential abusing and neglectful parents seeking help should get it with outreach services available for those parents who need but do not seek it.

CHAPTER 16

The Primary School and the Family

DON VENVELL

CHILD — PARENT — TEACHER PARTNERSHIP

AGE VERSUS MATURITY

These observations are restricted to the welfare of children between 5 and 10 years
of age, for most children the period of primary school education. These arbitrary
age-based descriptions of children are less helpful to those considering the
educational needs of children and their welfare than the concept say of maturation
age. The ordinary primary school includes children aged 5 whose behaviour indicates
inadequate primary socialization and children aged 10 whose physical development
and behaviour including mastery of learning skills place them well into adolescence.
The primary school age span is effectively some 10 years, not the 5 chronological
years, and the organisational arrangements for the provision of education are
chronological-year based, though they vary throughout England. In certain variations the maturation span is considerably reduced (chronological $4\frac{1}{2}$-7, 7-11, 8-12,
9-13). Since the development of full time secondary education for all, primary
schools may be described as in the main catering for the pre-adolescent children.
Teachers in primary schools are mostly relating to young families, where parents
are considerably involved in the lives of their children.. At the secondary school
stage this active involvement tends to decrease, so that the school relates more
and more directly to the young person. The primary school works more directly with
the parents whatever their family situation and places less reliance upon supportive
agencies than does the secondary school. It is a mark of professional competence
that teachers can and do actively relate to parents in the primary school system.

This position is taken up because it is at the beginning of the primary stage
that the parent effectively hands over charge of her child to the teacher who, under
law, is expected to behave as any reasonable parent would do in the care and control
of the child. The teacher, and indeed the whole school, gains credibility in an
area and is 'given' its responsibility on the basis of an assumed understanding
with parents and with the community of parents. This understanding is regularly
renegotiated as the child moves from class to class and stage to stage in development. It is a type of partnership, even though the child must attend school and
even though the maturing professional will develop a more secure expertise in looking after children than each successive generation of parents. The school that
does not see itself in partnership with its parents identifies itself as an inadequate school. It follows that a child is likely to be unhappy in school and/or
at home if this partnership does not overtly exist or is threatened, for example in
transfer from school, or in disagreements between parents and teachers.

SCHOOL, PARENTS AND CHILDREN'S WELFARE

Most children expect to be happy at primary school; if their school experience
does reward them, their welfare or well-being is considerably secured. That to be
at school and living a school life is still considered to be good by children and
by their parents can be seen by the attendance levels recorded for ILEA primary
schools. Whatever else is happening to the family or to society, if the school wo
hard at giving them this sense of security and happiness, children will attend and
parents will bring them through fog and snow (see Table 1).

Table 1: Primary school attendance as reported to Inner
London Education Authority annually.

	%		%
1976	92.7	1979	92.3
1977	92.5	1980	91.8
1978	91.8	1981	93.2

Of course some don't go willingly or go at all. Experience and study have shown
(Williams 1974; Hersov and Berg 1980) that the causes tend to lie in the anxiety o
the child concerning a home situation (illness, birth of a sibling, parental
separation, over-dependence upon, or of, the mother) though sometimes it is also
occasioned by the school experience itself (strictness, pressure on certain
standards, bullying). But during the primary school stage, some children begin to
be absent more frequently. This phenomenon varies by regions, by sex and by
parental occupation. Almost always, without effective intervention, it persists
and worsens into the secondary school stage. The causes are complex, but include
those mentioned, with a heavier emphasis upon school attainment and the increasing
influence of peer (or other) groups. Teachers often report older primary children
associating with children in secondary schools and adopting their behaviour. It
is known that many petty, and indeed some serious, offences are committed by child
ren under the age of 10 years.

School experience is an experience of a set of situations through and by which
childrens' behaviour changes. Some of these situations are specifically set up as
opportunities for learning, and of these some are monitored closely (for example
the teaching of reading). Others occur incidentally, or accidentally, and professional observation of them may be intermittent or non-existent. Habits are
developed, and a view of self and of others becomes established through the
experience of school. On the whole there is a consensus of aims and methods prevailing in the primary education system, so that a stranger visiting schools may
expect to find similar activities and features in classrooms or halls anywhere in
England (Wall 1975; DES 1978b). That consensus is based upon an assumption about
the nature of society within which the family is held to be the essential unit. O
course, there is a professional recognition that, in certain areas and amongst
certain groups, these assumptions about society may have to be modified, and some
openness adopted. But it would be unlikely for the curriculum (including the
hidden curriculum) to be set out to challenge such a basic assumption. Indeed the
problem of transition from primary to secondary stage may well be aggravated by
the early challenging, at the secondary stage, of a number of such assumptions.
This is exemplified by comparing the experience of Christmas in a primary school a
10 plus with the experience of it in a secondary school at 11 plus. The primary
school tends to be, and be seen to be, supportive of the family and of families.
One consequence of this which gives rise to anxiety is the reluctance of the
primary school to concede that it is not able to cope with the needs of all its

children. Head Teachers, who are urged to identify those with special needs and
refer them early to supporting agencies for specialist assistance, are reluctant
to take this step. To be fair some Head Teachers would argue that this is because
of the unreliability and/or unavailability of those agencies when they do attempt
to refer. They would also claim that other agencies working with the child and
family, for example health agencies, are reluctant to share information with them.
Nontheless at the secondary stage, teachers will claim the child's problems should
have been picked up earlier. Another worrying aspect is that the school is not
seen to be as supportive as is generally claimed. In inner city areas some parents
assert, or it is asserted on their behalf, that they do not know how to talk to
schools about their children, and that schools set up arrangements for contact which
do not in fact work. Even intermediary personnel such as Education Welfare Officers,
Community Liaison Officers, and Social Workers fail to establish effective communication. Self-help groups set up by sections of the community, often involving
supplementary, even alternative, schooling arrangements develop. In these circumstances the providing local education authority and the school have somehow to stay
in touch with this situation.

WELFARE ACTIVITIES

   The school is also the medium through which certain key welfare provisions have
been made and to varying degrees still are. These include child health screening,
meals, including breakfast sometimes, clothing supplements in goods or cash, and
subsidized holidays. Despite the advances made in our society, experience in Inner
London at least confirms the continuing importance of this contribution, no less
crucial now than in the latter part of the nineteenth century, a point not generally
appreciated (Table 2).

   Perhaps as a consequence of this welfare activity and of the general involvement
of the average primary school teacher in the life of the child, there is some
pressure to give the primary school teacher greater community responsibility. One
unplanned way in which this occurs already is in the leaving of their children by
harassed or neglectful parents in the early morning as well as long after school
has closed, a burden which many teachers find difficulty in carrying. In some
inner city areas schools are opened during holidays, and meals served. The
community role is furthered by relating to the school specific community facilities,
most obviously a child health clinic. The buildings too are opened up to the
community as far as is consonant with the way primary schools operate using all
their space, displaying childrens' work and leaving up models, book displays, and
stimulating objects.

   There is growing experience that where links between personnel such as the Health
Visitor, education home visitor, school nurse, class teacher, welfare worker and
family, are established in a locality, and the school is positively developing
childrens' skills, the school is a powerful force operating to secure the welfare
and well-being of children and families in the community. In this way the disadvantaged become advantaged in their access to services. In rural areas, where access
of this kind is not available, more attention might well be paid to deprivation.
Such a pattern is expensive to produce and requires high professionalism to sustain,
but there are encouraging instances of its development. There must always come a
point however, where the interests of the children and those of their parents do
not coincide, and where the education service, though given its validity by parents
handing their children over to it, must have regard to the developing needs of
these children as they see them and of the next generation. It is too cosy a view
of education to see it as totally supportive and welfare-orientated. It must also
be, at the same time, subversive and challenging. In particular, school must
encourage autonomy of the child (King 1966; Postman and Weingarten 1969). As the

Table 2: Welfare Activities of The Inner London Education
Authority Area.

Percentages of Primary-aged children 1978/9 n = 157690	
from families of 4 children or more	
Tower Hamlets	28.3
Hackney	27.4
in one-parent families	
Lambeth	28.7
Hammersmith, Fulham, Kensington, Chelsea	28.6
who changed schools during the year	
Camden & Westminster	32.3
Tower Hamlets	29.1
requiring additional English tuition	
Tower Hamlets	14.46
Camden & Westminster	10.94
eligible*for free school meals	
Tower Hamlets	36.3
Hackney	33.5
given**clothing grant (on application)	
Tower Hamlets	54.8
Hackney	39.0
Lambeth	35.9

*Free school meals are a statutory entitlement for families on Supplementary
Benefit or Family Income supplement. ILEA scale of entitlement includes incomes up to £8 per week above Supplementary Benefit level.
**Clothing grant scheme is discretionary. ILEA uses the same entitlement scale
as for free school meals.

primary school range extends into the 10 plus area, this issue begins to emerge.
Distinguishing between the needs and expectations of the family and the needs of
the child and the next generation is a delicate and difficult task. It is no help
that at this crucial stage the child moves into the secondary sector, and the
personal relationships are broken. What could be a transition becomes a breakdown
without major efforts at prevention. The Plowden Report made this case, but it
would be wrong to suggest that the education world has accepted it.

CO-OPERATION BETWEEN AGENCIES

Over the last few years, arrangements for the notification of non-accidental
injury, including injury by neglect, have been refined. Review Committees, based
upon National Health Service areas, have produced guide lines agreed between the

Health Service, Social Services, and the Education Service, which schools and welfare officers are required to observe. These formalised arrangements in respect of children severely 'at risk' come on top of other co-operative arrangements between the agencies in respect of the needs of individual children and families. It is however unusual for there to be any concerted policy even between the local authority services themselves (e.g. education, social services and housing) except in the planning of provision especially in New Towns, and in specific small scale joint projects, such as those financed from the Inner Cities Partnership Funds.

The response to a child's education and other welfare needs may be made through an Education Welfare Service, where this exists in any strength, whose officers do make representations to colleagues in other services on the child's behalf. Priorities and powers vary across local authority and other services, for example Social Services Departments have been finding their responsibilities for the elderly and the mentally sick a conflicting pressure upon their work with children and families.

There is also the question of professional credibility. Teachers are prone to believe that they know what is right for the child, and to resent the intrusion and the consequent delay in taking what seems to them to be the necessary action, occasioned by such other professionals as educational psychologists, doctors and social workers. They claim to be able to observe the child closely, and to be able to identify symptoms of risk or need. There is, as a consequence, great pressure from them to have all support services school-related, and preferably head-teacher directed.

But there are many forms of observation and the child must been seen in the context of his whole life. Even moving school or class changes his behaviour. Any teacher's view is charged with the effects of inter-action inside the school. What is assumed to be truculence, for example, may be difficulty of hearing, or the result of poor teaching method. As a consequence other professionals will tend to accept the referral but not necessarily the diagnosis and rarely the suggested remedy!

The ideal always sought is a multi-disciplinary assessment of need, but that requires multi-disciplinary training on the job. The school doctor and nurse, for example, need to train alongside the class teacher and the social worker. Except in the extreme cases of risk, such as of non-accidental injury, this process has not begun. It is rarely present in initial training either.

Underlying all co-operation however is openness, and in areas of professional work, this can only come from a sense of professional competence and security.

HEALTH EDUCATION IN THE PRIMARY SCHOOL*

For better or worse, the family is the cradle of the child's 'health career'. The school's intervention in the development of that career provides a special instance of the problem of intervention by the State in the life and practice of the family. The assumptions that have underlain the rearing of the child, and the perceptions of himself that the family circumstances have permitted, form the raw material of experience which the young child brings into the classroom. The teacher can only intervene if able to set this experience in the context of present health knowledge. He does so in order to develop in each child an understanding of his power to influence his own health career. That intervention is potentially threatening to the bonds between parent and child, in that it may counter what the family has fostered.

---

*
A note by Clyte Hampton.

Education at primary level centres upon the child, his interests and developing abilities, so that health education naturally finds a place within this process, in so far as it is concerned with self, its realisation and potential. Within the wider context of the community, health education is envisaged as extending throughout the school system (Williams 1977). What is taught in the reception class should be taught both because it is relevant to five-year olds' interests and concerns, and because it lays the foundations for work at 10 plus and 14 plus. Health education has moved away from being crisis-orientated and dealing with venereal disease, smoking and menstruation to being promotive and comprehensive. No longer is it a set of prescriptions; no longer does it concentrate upon certain limited human activities. It is all-embracing and creative of good self-image, together with a sense of responsibility. That is why it can start at 5 plus.

If we are concerned with the next generation of parents, some emphasis must be given to providing a continuous health education programme through and beyond the school system. It has however to be admitted that, perhaps because the aims and content of health education accord closely with those of normal primary education, much health education, if given at all, will be given accidentally, or at best incidentally. To be truly effective, teachers have still to recognise that health education in primary schools needs a structure and a style, and that its introduction acknowledges and presupposes its significance over a much larger period of the child's life than that for which the primary teacher has immediate responsibilities.

DISCUSSION

The relationship between school and family occupied the major part of the discussion. Parents became involved formally through Parent-Teacher Associations. As important were informal meetings between parents and teachers and parents with one another. The forgeing of these relationships brought parents into a kind of partnership which added a dimension to the process of handing over of the child by the parent and acceptance of responsibility by the teacher. Changes in attitudes during the last two decades were leading school governors to consult with and to concede and explain to parents, although unfortunately working parents were not always available. Some doubt was raised whether anything like a real partnership yet existed with ethnic communities. School architecture with high walls and narrow gateways continued to be an obstacle. The school remains an alternative to the home in which the child gains satisfaction and feels secure, maybe for the child it is the secure place. Sufficient attention is not always paid to preparation for the transition stage when the child moves from primary to secondary and, from parental choice or other reasons, the group is split into different schools. In the primary school the ethnic mix is generally a happy one, attendance problems are rare and usually reflect home troubles. A question is how far a family support system can be brought in. The school is an agent of welfare provision for meals, clothes etc. and acts as a community. Through the education welfare system troubled families can be identified. How far can they be helped? Is there sufficient collaboration between the teachers and the social workers?

More directly connected with family relationships is the part played by the school in developing the child's autonomy. It is where independence begins and the child previously treated as part of the family unit begins to achieve a status in his own right. This process was referred to in the discussions as 'subverting the family', its origins lying within the institution but also within the peer group. A biological factor related to the onset of puberty was suggested and its possible result in vandalism discussed. How far should the school remain an authoritarian institution? Teachers in primary school are reluctant to let go of the control and move to a more democratic process, so that the dismantling apparent in the secondary school is unlikely to occur. A well-run school has little violence and help comes from encouraging and giving rein to creative energy through the arts. One difficulty arises from the organizational need for the 'age cohort', which acts as a straitjacket. The pace of education cannot be regulated in step with the individual child's needs. Has the cohort curriculum got stuck? Was enough attention being paid to preparations for the secondary school and, because of the importance of the early years in forming attitudes, to preparation for life within society? The expectation of society also affected the content of the child's learning experience, tending to be conservative. Too much insistence on educational achievement could be self-defeating and secondary schools were more concerned with careers and employment than with citizenship and parenthood. No suggestions were made about how to break through local community attitudes.

One comment, on the sparseness of research on education by practitioners, raised the question of what could be monitored in school — reading age? educational age? truancy? autonomy? Finally a reminder that school should be run for children, not for teachers or politicians.

CHAPTER 17

Child-rearing: Parental Autonomy and State Intervention

MICHAEL FREEMAN

The subject of this paper was chosen some time before the 'Alexandra' case[1]* hit the
headlines in August 1981. The issues raised in the case were not new but the
poignancy of the case enables us to sharpen our focus. At root the question is who
knows best how to rear children? Is it individual parents themselves or should
decisions be left to experts, to paediatricians, the medical profession more
generally, to social workers, to the judiciary? If it is to be professional experts
are they to apply particular standards or merely exercise their own discretion in
the individual case? And if there are to be guiding principles who is to bear the
responsibility of formulating them (Kennedy 1981a)? Nor can we ignore the child
himself. In an age when we all purport to favour children's rights his wishes and
feelings must also be considered. To what extent should children themselves decide
questions which have an impact upon their present lives and future life-styles?

There are enough issues here to fill a sizeable volume, let alone a paper. What
follows is accordingly a sketch of some of the main problems. The questions raised
have been with us since at least the beginning of the century. Before then the
father's will prevailed and that was that (Graveson and Crane 1957). Despite the
relative longevity of the problem, rarely as yet have the issues come to a court's
attention in this country, though they have arisen on many occasions in United
States litigation. A powerful lobby today advocates parental autonomy in child-
rearing. Ably led by Goldstein, Freud and Solnit (1979 a and c), it argues for
strict limitations upon state intervention in matters which intimately concern
parent-child relations. In part this paper is an examination of the viability and
appropriateness of this type of view. It looks at some of the problems adoption of
this view can, and is thought likely to, cause. The question of the preservation
of the integrity of the family from intrusion by state agencies is likely to be one
of the most important social and legal issues of the coming decade.

THE PHILOSOPHY OF MINIMUM STATE INTERVENTION

The philosophy of minimum state intervention was expressed most clearly in the
United States Supreme Court in 1944 in the case of <u>Prince v. Massachusetts</u>[2]. The
case arose out of a conflict between Jehovah's Witnesses and state authority. It
was a questionable attempt by the Commonwealth of Massachusetts to extend its child
labour legislation to prevent a child selling religious literature on the streets.
This is not the place to question what to Mr Justice Rutledge was self-evident,
viz: 'the state's authority over children's activities is broader than over like

---

*Superscript numbers refer to Notes at end of chapter.

Copyright © 1981 M. Freeman.   145
Reprinted by permission.

actions of adults'. More important is the judge's statement that: 'it is cardinal
with us that the custody, care and nurture of the child reside first in the parents
whose primary function and freedom include preparation for obligations the state
can neither supply nor hinder. And it is in recognition of this that these
decisions have respected the private realm of family life which the state cannot
enter'[3]. He conceded, though, that 'the family (was) not beyond regulation in the
public interest'. Thus, the state could require, as it has done for a very long
time, compulsory education and it could prohibit child labour, insist upon the
vaccination of children etc. He also thought that whilst parents could become
martyrs themselves, they were not free 'to make martyrs of their children before
they have reached' the age of full and legal discretion when they can make that
choice for themselves'.

Mr Justice Rutledge's judgment has been regularly cited with approval in recent
American jurisprudence. It is hardly surprisingly given a similar accolade in
Goldstein, Freud and Solnit's second monograph (1979c), Before The Best Interests
of The Child (p. *217*)*. In this is to be found the fullest statement of minimum
state intervention. 'The child's need for safety within the confines of the family
must be met by law through its recognition of family privacy as the barrier to
state intrusion upon parental autonomy in child rearing' (p. *9*). This is the
explicit theme of Before The Best Interests. The purported justification for this
position is both psychologically and philosophically grounded. Its basis is in
part the authors' notion of psychological parenthood which they developed in their
earlier Beyond The Best Interests of the Child (Goldstein *et al* 1979b; and 1979c
p. *40-47*). This requires, as spelt out there, day-to-day interaction, companion-
ship and shared experiences. But this psychological relationship requires 'the
privacy of family life under guardianship by parents who are autonomous. The
younger the child, the greater is his need for them. When family integrity is
broken or weakened by state intrusion, his needs are thwarted and his belief that
his parents are omniscient and all-powerful is shaken prematurely. The effect on
the child's developmental progress is invariably detrimental (p. *9*). It is, to
say the least, questionable whether this is so but Goldstein and his colleagues
dismiss what I consider to be, the very persuasive evidence of Rutter (1981), the
Clarkes (1976), Barbara Tizard (1977), Jerome Kagan and his collaborators (1978) as
'simplistic' (p. *200*). At the very least the breaking of ties cannot be 'invariabl
detrimental! If that were the case no state intervention into the family could be
justified and the institution of adoption would also be difficult to substantiate.

Goldstein *et al* also adduce a philosophical rationale. A policy of minimum
coercive intervention by the state accords also with their 'firm belief as citizens
in individual freedom and human dignity' (p. *12*). These notions are superficially
attractive. Unfortunately in a world of basic structural inequalities, individual
freedom can be so exercised as to undermine not only the freedom of others but also
their human dignity. The parent-child relationship is a microcosm of this
imbalance. The case of Re D[4] (the Sotos syndrome sterilisation), to be considered
later in this paper, is a paradigm example of the tension. So is the recent
'Alexandra' case (Re B)[5]. Not all who favour a non-interventionist stance belong
to the radical right, though critics and commentators often lump them all together.
The Goldstein *et al* reasoning is, however, common in neo-conservative thought and,
I believe, untenable in practice. There is, they argue, a further justification
for their policy: 'the law does not have the capacity to supervise the fragile,
complex interpersonal bonds between child and parent. As *parens patriae* the state
is too crude an instrument to become an adequate substitute for flesh and blood
parents. The legal system has neither the resources nor the sensitivity to respond
to a growing child's ever-changing needs and demands. It does not have the capacit

---

*Page numbers in italics refer to Before The Best Interests of The Child (1979c).

to deal on an individual basis with the consequences of its decision, or to act
with the deliberate speed that is required by a child's sense of time' (*p. 11-12*).
Much of this is incontrovertible, though it should be said that the processes of
the legal system could be speeded up. Current delays in wardship, for example, are
inexcusable.

Goldstein and his colleagues are not alone in formulating a philosophy of
minimum state intervention in family matters. Michael Wald[6]and Robert Mnookin[7],
two prominent American child lawyers, have also questioned the wisdom of coercive
state intervention, mainly on the ground that it does more harm than good. Radical
criminologists, such as Edwin Schur (1973) and Edwin Lemert (1976), have also
called for 'radical' or 'judicious' non-intervention, in their case in the area of
juvenile delinquency, where Schur advocates 'leaving the kids alone'. Similar
views have been expressed by the authors of <u>Justice for Children</u> (Morris *et al*
1980a) and <u>In Whose Best Interests?</u> (Taylor *et al* 1980), both published in this
country in 1980. The roots of state intervention have been traced in a number of
publications, notably by Christopher Lasch in <u>Haven In a Heartless World</u> (1977) and
Jacques Donzelot in <u>The Policing of Families</u> (1979). They show that intervention
is neither straightforwardly altruistic nor politically neutral. I agree, and have
argued elsewhere (Freeman 1981), that non-intervention is basically the policy to
pursue. As Chief Justice Burger said in the important case of <u>Parham</u> v <u>J.R.</u>[8]in
1979, 'the statist notion that governmental power should supersede parental authority in <u>all</u> cases because <u>some</u> parents abuse and neglect children is repugnant ...'
But pursuit of a policy of non-intervention must not blind us to the fact that, for
all its faults and imperfections, interference with child-rearing practices is
sometimes imperative. The alternative is to throw out the baby with the bathwater.
We are thus engaged in a line-drawing exercise.

I believe that Goldstein and his colleagues, who advocate the most restrictive
grounds for intervention of any but whose views are highly influential, have drawn
the lines in the wrong place. If we are to err it should be on the child's side.
This policy, plus an emphasis on controlling the controllers and giving parents
and children adequate and speedy remedies against mistakes, inefficiency and
maladministration, is preferable to the rather dogmatic approach of the authors of
<u>Before the Best Interests</u>. Given their psychological and philosophical premises
their conclusions are inevitable. As indicated already, I am happy neither with
their rejection of behavioural psychology nor their adoption of neo-conservative
philosophical values. I therefore devote the bulk of this paper to a critique of
their proposals. Before doing so, I consider the positive side to their case. The
issue, as already indicated, is not all black and white.

THE CASE FOR NON-INTERVENTION

At the crudest the case for non-intervention is that intervention does not work.
There is evidence that police and social work intervention, far from rehabilitating,
is actually just as likely to exacerbate delinquency. David Thorpe and his colleagues (1979) found this *à propos* social work intervention. Farrington's (1977)
conclusions are not dissimilar. He compared the self-reported delinquency scores
of 285 youths who had not been labelled as delinquent with those of 85 who had
been publicly so labelled. 'In agreement with the deviance amplification hypothesis,
the 98 publically labelled youths had very significantly higher self-reported
delinquency scores at age 18 than the ... 285 non-labelled youth'. Subsequent
examination of his data to test the plausibility of alternative explanations of his
findings led him to persist in his support of the amplifications hypothesis as it
applies to delinquents. Further support for this comes from United States data.
Thus, Gold and Williams (1969) matched 35 pairs of apprehended and unapprehended
juvenile offenders (Gold 1970). 'In 20 of the 35 comparisons, the apprehended
member of the pair subsequently committed more offences than his unapprehended

control'. Only in 10 cases, half the number, did the unapprehended control go on
to commit more offences. Klein (1974) also reports evidence supporting amplification. He compared police departments having high and low rates of juvenile
diversion (that is channelling youth away from the formal criminal justice system)
He found that recidivism rates were higher in areas whose departments engaged in
less diversion than among departments with high diversion rates.

The amplification hypothesis applies to categories of deviants other than
delinquents. Scott (1969) has shown how agencies established to rehabilitate the
blind frequently encourage their subjects to '... play the kind of deviant role
traditionally reserved for the blind'. To the extent that the client meets agency
expectations, stereotypic beliefs are actualised. Scheff's work (1966) on mental
illness comes to similar conclusions. He demonstrates how mental patients are
rewarded for playing the deviant role, that is concurring in the diagnosis, and
behaving accordingly. This process is promoted by what Balint (1957) has called
the doctor's 'apostolic function' (the idea that doctors usually have well-
developed and firmly held ideas about how people with particular illnesses should
act). The doctor's efforts are reinforced by the action of other staff and
hospital patients.

INTERVENTION AND CHILD ABUSE

To return to matters of more central concern to the family and family policy, it
is worth looking at the effects of intervention on child abuse. There is no
evidence that the increased control mechanisms of the last decade have conquered,
or are likely to conquer, violence against children. There is a research finding
(Skinner and Castle 1969) that anxious visiting by social workers of families
actually increases battering of children. A rebattering incidence of 60 per cent
in a sample of cases known to a protective agency (the N.S.P.C.C.) does not
compare favourably with the estimate of 25 to 30 per cent re-battering where there
has been no intervention. Bill Jordan's comment (1975, 1976) is worth reading:
'In the tragic cases we've all heard about, the clients were not new referrals who
hadn't been investigated quickly enough, but cases known to a department for a
considerable period'. Goldstein and his colleagues are sensitive to much the same
point: 'By intrusion', they note, 'the state may make a bad situation worse'
(p. 13). There is, of course, no guarantee that children removed from home will
not suffer similar hardship, deprivation and cruelty elsewhere. It is striking,
however, how little attention is given to cases of violence by substitute parents[9].
Compare the column inches given to the Mehmedagi[10] or the Page[11] cases with the
Frankland[12] case. There a baby of six months was killed by his prospective adopters
(parents chosen by professional social workers). It fits in well with the general
ideology associated with the 1975 Children Act (Freeman 1976) that a case like this
should be given relatively little attention[13].

STANDARDS OF PARENTAL CONDUCT

A second argument supportive of non-interventionist policies concerns the vague-
ness of the standards conventionally used against which to measure parental conduct
Vague language invites unwarranted and arbitrary interventions. Where vague
standards are used it is difficult to give parents advance warning of what is
required of them. A firmly entrenched maxim of the criminal law is *nulla poena
sine lege*. Since the consequences of falling foul of the standards in children's
protective legislation is, or can be, little short of penal, similar considerations
should apply. That is why Goldstein *et al* insist, and rightly so, that parents
should be given a fair warning, so that clear, precise standards should govern
intervention. The obvious parallel is, what H. L. A. Hart (1968) has called, 'the
doctrine of fair opportunity' in criminal law.

A cognate point is that vague standards can all too easily be employed to impose
the standards of one section of the population on another. There are different
types of parenting, as a cursory reading of the Newsons' studies (1963, 1968, 1976)
of their Nottingham cohort will demonstrate. Patterns of disciplining, for example,
are not uniform. Not only are there class differences but there are also regional
and racial differences as well. Nor do the ethnic minorities constitute a homogeneous population: what constitutes good parenting amongst the Asian communities
is very different from that found in those of West Indian origin. There will often
also be differences in attitudes of different castes and tribes and different
Caribbean islands. Critics of the practices of intervention agencies allege, sometimes with considerable justification, that these operate so as to impose middle-
class and white standards of parenting on working-class parents and on the parents
of black children.

At Risk Registers

These criticisms are directed particularly at the way in which names are placed
on child abuse or 'at risk' registers, at the way place of safety orders are
sought and made and at the attitudes adopted towards the passing of resolutions
assuming parental rights. Of the third of these examples (the s.3 resolution
procedure) the authors of Justice For Children (Morris *et al* 1980b; Sutton 1981)
have persuasively written: 'The actual mechanism by which a ... resolution is
obtained is very simple and depends very much on the quality of the individual
social workers and local authority social services department. The criteria for
obtaining a ... resolution are often subjective; they depend on the social worker's
perception of the family. This is shaped by a number of factors; the social
worker's personality and training, the structure and morale of the social services
department, and the social worker's relationship with the parent and child. There
is no objective standard by which parents can be assessed as 'bad parents'. Such
an assessment can be as much a product of a clash of personalities as of the
parents' behaviour. Social enquiry reports are often scattered with such inexact
terms as 'manipulative', 'aggressive', 'inadequate', 'schizoid' and 'infantile'.
Even in trained hands psychological concepts can be misused, and there is even
greater risk that this might happen when young and untrained social workers
prepare reports'.

Separation of Child from Mother

In the wake of the Maria Colwell scandal[14] in 1973-4 the number of place of
safety orders has rocketed. In March 1973 there were approximately 214 place of
safety orders in existence each week. By March 1977 this figure had more than
trebled to reach 759. There are grounds for believing that social workers are
over-reacting to unsubstantiated fears. Only a small proportion of the orders end
up as care orders. Some no doubt are resolved by voluntary receptions under S2 of
the Child Care Act 1980 — 'going quietly' in criminal parlance — and this gives
additional cause for concern, particularly when it is realised that months may
elapse[15]. Not only are the civil liberties considerations disturbing but such a
rupture of mother and child, particularly where the child is very young, can have
deleterious effects on the bonding process (Lynch and Roberts 1977). Not uncommon
now is the taking of babies at birth (Tredinnick and Fairburn 1980). The moral
propriety of these 'pre-emptive strikes' may be questioned (Freeman 1980): where
they are first babies the legality of the measures is also highly dubious.

The At Risk Concept

Case conferences and registers have mushroomed. But to what end is all this
activity? Solnit (1980) has written of there being too much reporting and too few
services. He claims there is an 'epidemic' of reporting. It must be questioned
whether registers are anything more than insurance policies for the social services
departments. In what way do they meet the needs of families deemed to be 'at risk'?

Solnit (1978), writing of the American experience, thought registers 'were intended mainly to safeguard the conscience and legal vulnerability of our adult society'. Few would dissent from this assessment. There is no consistent policy as to which children are placed on registers. In addition to cases of confirmed abuse, suspected abuse and sexual abuse, registers include cases of children 'at risk'. Indeed, the majority of children on registers have had their names placed there because they are thought to be 'at risk'. Being 'at risk' is not equivalent to suffering from chickenpox. It is not an objective condition but is rather a label, a social construction depending upon subjective interpretation (Freeman 1979a). This is not entirely an individual decision-making process. Each agency develops a particular clientele which it designates as a control problem. As Freidson (1967) has noted, in defining and classifying a universe which they claim needs their services, all control agencies in effect become responsible for drawing clearer lines than in fact exist either in everyday life or in the processes by which the people concerned were originally led into their services. Agencies also develop processing stereotypes, simplified images as to the moral character of the person being processed, their motives etc. Unique background characteristics are submerged in standardised background expectancies. From where do social workers get the stereotypes? In part they develop during their socialisation, both as individual members of the community and as social workers. The media help to create 'folk devils'. But stereotypes are also learnt 'on the job'. Blumberg (1969) writing of lawyers, though his remarks may be generalised, sees stereotypes as generated and used as a response to the demands of bureaucratic organisations on its personnel to appear efficient, process a large volume of cases, reduce uncertainty and ambiguity in disposition and promote a smooth flow through the system. In a sense placing children's names on registers is a way social workers tackle their own problems, a point developed by Pearson (1973) in his provocative but highly rewarding article 'Social work as the privatised solution of public ills'.

It very much depends upon how one interprets (Freeman 1979b) the phenomenon of child abuse as to which children are thought to be 'at risk'. If one adopts the dominant medical interpretation (Helfer and Kempe 1976), a psychopathological model of child abuse emerges and one looks to particular, though it must be confessed, heterogeneous traits (Gelles 1973) in parents and caretakers which are assumed to be causally linked to child abuse. It is common for medical definitions of deviance to be adopted even where, as here, there is no reliable evidence that biological variables cause the deviant behaviour in question or that medical treatment is in any way efficacious. If one works within this paradigm, prediction becomes the key. Useful predictive studies have been carried out (Lynch 1976) but screening is fraught with ethical and methodological problems. Light (1974) has shown a possible 85 per cent rate of error.

Socio-economic Stress

Social and environmental explanations of child abuse are also now common, notably in social work literature[16]. Writers refer to 'multi-faceted deprivations of poverty' (Gil 1975), such as bad housing, poor education, which lead to stress which is expressed in physical force against children. For example, in 1976 one and a half million households lived in homes officially considered unfit for human habitation or lacking the most basic amenities[17]. Are all these children potentially at risk? Should their names be included on registers? The last government accepted that families with young children should be transferred out of the 'stressful conditions' of tower block life. It has nevertheless been estimated that some 300,000 children live in flats above the second floor[18]. Should all their names be registered as 'at risk' of some form of abuse?

But if interpretation (i) would require the children of (say) immature parents to be registered and interpretation (ii) would, *inter alia*, insist that all children living in bad housing conditions go on to the register, what can we say of

interpretation (iii)? This sees abuse as taking place (Gil 1975; Freeman 1979b p.
31) in any cultural setting where a stratified relationship exists, where the
victim is treated as an inferior, lacks personality and integrity, is not accorded
respect and rights. If this interpretation is right (and it must be at least part
of the explanation), then all children are at risk of abuse and registers should
contain the names of the whole child population. I remember one Director of Social
Services who had the honesty and integrity to place his own children on the 'at
risk' register because he accepted the force and logic of this argument. As
B.A.S.W. pointed out in 1978 in The Central Child Abuse Register, registers could
easily 'drift into an overburdened and increasingly long list of children about
whom professionals are concerned'.

We do not know enough about how names find their way on to registers, but the
problem is linked to case conferences. Where a case conference is called, the
child's name is invariably placed on the register. Otherwise there is no consistent policy. The result is that certain idiosyncratic policies are pursued. Geach
(1980) described a housing welfare officer in one London borough 'who placed
countless children on the register as his interpretation of 'at risk' included
children who lived in council accommodation which was not kept up to his standards
of cleanliness by the parents'. It is easy for social workers to take their
concept of the problem for the problem itself. Once a family is labelled in a
particular way, subsequent actions are often interpreted to fit those labels. If
an 'accident' occurs to a child 'at risk', the chances of parents successfully
defending care proceedings (or for that matter a criminal prosecution) are not
auspicious. As an American sociologist noted, (Lofland 1969), 'the present evil
of current character must be related to past evil that can be discovered in
biography'. Nor should it be thought that 'accident' is a real and objective
condition which exists independently of man's consciousness. What constitutes an
accident is a product of a large number of situational contingencies (Freeman 1979a).
Amidst all the glib talk of non-accidental injury, a real understanding involves
not just the parents nor even their victim children (Freeman 1977) but also the
officials, medical personnel, police, social workers and their response patterns
in terms of their definition of the situation (Berger and Luckmann 1967). This
intervening defining process is not neutral and one factor which plays an important
part is the stereotype to which reference has already been made.

Some of this could be more readily forgiven had the 'safety first' policy been
successful. The reports of inquiries make depressing reading: the communication
problems have changed little in the eight years since Colwell. It is no surprise
to learn that abuse registers are scarcely used. In Devon the Director of Social
Services (Hamson 1981) has recently written of 'minimal' use by fieldworkers:
'Our own experience', he writes, 'is a minute number of referrals are made each
year — never more than five'. The situation in Newcastle is similar. In Wandsworth
52 inquiries were made in 1980 (Fry 1981). Case conference practice is hardly more
successful, with conflicts between agencies still rife (Geach 1981). The ostensible
reason for case conferences is to protect children but, as the Director of Social
Services for Essex recently noted, 'co-operation/co-ordination ... is in danger of
becoming the reason for (their) existence'. He doubted whether 'such activity
improves services to the clients' (Hallett and Stevenson 1980; Geach 1981).

EMOTIONAL ABUSE

I have deliberately concentrated on the problematic nature of intervention in an
area which justifies intervention more than most. If these problems exist in
relation to violence against children, how much greater are they in areas where
the abuse itself is more difficult to define, for example in emotional abuse? A
recent D.H.S.S.[19]Circular on Child Abuse Registers has proposed to extend the
existing system to include 'children who suffer severe mental or emotional abuse'

which should of course, be a basis for social work intervention in some cases. But
what is 'emotional abuse'? What evidence is to be required to substantiate such
damage? I put this in legal terms but part of the problem is that we are dealing
with an administrative act, not a judicial finding.

The danger is that intervention will be grounded on vague concepts such as
'proper parental love' or 'inadequate parental affection'. As Michael Wald (1976)
has argued, language like this (and it is commonly found in social welfare literature) 'invites unwarranted or arbitrary intervention. It could be applied to
parents who travel a great deal, leaving their children with housekeepers, or who
send them to boarding school to get rid of them, or who are generally undemonstra-
tive people'. Another critic insists that 'emotional neglect' is hardly 'suscept-
ible to legally acceptable proof'. He too emphasises the difficulty of separating
prejudices regarding lifestyles from it (Krause 1977). In fact, the D.H.S.S.
Circular wisely concentrates on damage to the child. But is this the way that
social workers and others concerned with the problem will see it? It is all too
easy for agencies to concentrate on, and seek out, parental behaviour. And this
would bring us back to the problems we have just considered.

Child neglect is another problem with a standard like 'emotional abuse'. We do
not know enough about child development to be able to evaluate its long-term consequences. Nor do we know whether a child will suffer less emotional trauma when
he is removed from a home where he has been suffering emotional deprivation. The
removal itself may be damaging, the new home or homes as bad or worse or equally
bad in other ways. Intervention becomes easier to justify where there is evidence
of actual harm, demonstrated by, for example, the child's anxiety, depression or
extreme aggression. The D.H.S.S. Circular makes no such proviso. It should be
added that the coupling of actual harm in the way just suggested would not necessarily act as sufficient protection. Goldstein *et al* properly point out that
'observed behaviour is not enough for assessing a child's mental state. What
appears to be similar behaviour, whether as a symptom of illness or a sign of
health, may for different reasons be a response to a wide range of different and
even opposite psychic factors. And the same deep-seated emotional disturbance may
lead to the most diverse manifestations of a child's behaviour' (*p. 75-76*). It is
relatively easy to relate a child's physical injury to his parents' action. It is
a considerably more complex process to link emotional damage with actions that may
be called emotional abuse.

THE IMPORTANCE OF INTERVENTION AND THE LIMITATIONS OF
THE 'BEFORE THE BEST INTERESTS' THESIS

In thus casting doubt on the wisdom of state intervention in the family I have
gone along with the general tenor of the thought expressed in Before The Best
Interests. We are all engaged in a line-drawing exercise. Not even Goldstein and
his colleagues, whose position is the most extreme of all, believe in a total
laissez-faire policy. They accept without question compulsory immunisation programmes, the state's insistence on the education of children and they seem happy
with limitations on child labour. These limitations upon parental freedom are all
questionable. But Goldstein *et al*, natural conservatives that they are, accept
these long-standing examples of the *status quo* as unproblematic, though clearly
they are not. It is disappointing that they do not grasp the nettle of compulsory
education laws, given widespread current dissatisfaction with the education
system[20].

THE GROUNDS FOR INTERVENTION

The principles underlying the grounds for intervention which Goldstein and his colleagues stipulate need a close and critical examination. I find their grounds arbitrarily narrow and unacceptably rigid. Nor, as the examples already given demonstrate, are the authors necessarily consistent in the logic they employ. If their principles were to be accepted, the children would suffer, the usual effect of putting parents first. Much of the rest of this chapter is devoted to a critique of the grounds in Before The Best Interests. My endeavour is to resurrect children's rights, for which Goldstein and his colleagues do not care, and which are totally eclipsed in their monograph.

First, I summarise the grounds for state intervention which Goldstein *et al* support. The first ground (p. 31) is that a parent has requested that the state place a child. This ground would exist if separated parents failed to arrive at a custody decision themselves or if either or both requested a voluntary termination of their parental rights. A consequence of this is that court intervention would not be permitted where parents were in agreement as to a child's disposal, even when the court sensed or was convinced that the placement chosen by the parents was unsuitable. This limitation on a court's powers is reminiscent of the authors' arguments about leaving decisions about access to the custodial parent (Goldstein *et al* 1979d) and is difficult to accept.

Secondly, Goldstein *et al* envisage that where familial bonds (psychological parentage) exists between long-term non-parental caretakers and children, a long-term caretaker might seek to become the legal parent or at any rate might refuse to relinquish the child to his parents or to a state agency. In such a situation, state intervention would be justifiable. 'Under this ground', they argue, 'the time for intervention is when both the child and caretaker have turned to and accepted one another' (p. 41). Although, we are told, 'the complex process of forming psychological parent-child relationships is not beyond description (and they give one), its timetable cannot be set precisely' (p. 42). Despite this, they argue that 'parental rights must rest on objective data which are readily obtainable with the minimum of intrusion' (p. 45). To this end they put forward statutory periods (12 months for a child up to 3 years at the time of placement and 24 months for a child of 3 years plus at the time of placement) which, they stress, are 'time with (caretakers), not time away from (parents)' (p. 48). They see these time spans coupled with the caretaker's wish to continue custody as reliable indicators for granting legal recognition to the new relationship and terminating the legal relationship between the children, absent parents and state agencies. To this they make one exception, that of older children, of more than 3 years at the time of placement and in continuous parents' care for 3 years at the time of placement. When the separation from parents was not because they inflicted or attempted to inflict serious bodily injury nor because they were convicted of a serious sexual offence against the child concerned and if the parents were still the psychological parents, the child would first be the subject of a 'special hearing' designed to determine psychological parenthood and 'whether (the child's) return to (the) parents would be the least detrimental alternative'. They add: 'in the event that such evidence is inconclusive, the child's relationship to his longtime caretakers should be given legal recognition' (p. 48).

Where termination takes place the authors of Before The Best Interests see adoption as the best solution; failing this, they believe in what they call 'care with tenure' (p. 49). Care with tenure is not spelt out: in conception it appears close to our, as yet unimplemented, notion of custodianship[21]. I am not happy with 'care with tenure', partly because it is so imprecise (to what rights and duties does it give rise?) but also on policy grounds (Freeman 1976). All in all the process of divestment of parental rights looks ominously like the sort of administrative process with which we associate an assumption of parental rights. If anything the protection, the 'due process', accorded parents is weaker than that in operation under s.3 procedure. I find it strange also that the reason why a child is in care should count for absolutely nothing. There is surely a difference between a child voluntarily placed with foster parents and one taken from parents because of abuse or neglect. It is also notable that, even with older children, their wishes and feelings are imputed rather than sought out, an issue discussed later.

A third ground for intervention is 'the death or disappearance of both parents, the only parent or the custodial parent — when coupled with their failure to make provision for their child's custody and care'. This is 'designed to provide the state with the authority to discover and to safeguard children for whom no day-to-day care arrangements have been made by parents who die, disappear, are imprisoned or hospitalised' (p. 59). Our statutes deal with abandonment[22], and voluntary reception into care under s.2 of the Child Care Act 1980 deals with hospitalisation and similar emergencies. Where the Goldstein et al standard is new is in authorising intervention only if the absent parent failed to make provision for the care of the child. Further intervention would only be allowed if the parent substitute's actions brought him within another of the grounds for intervention.

The fourth ground is more controversial, viz: conviction of a sexual offence (p. 62) against the child (or acquittal by reason of insanity). The ground is controversial because the authors insist on conviction of the parent in a criminal court as a pre-requisite to any intervention. There are any number of objections to this. The trend in the treatment of sexual abuse within the family is to see it as a social problem concerned with family dysfunction. There is a move away from penal responses (Giarretto 1976). It is recognised that the criminal law is a clumsy instrument. Yet Goldstein and his colleagues seem to want to return to punitive responses. Looked at from the perspective of the child, what does the proposed standard achieve? First, it will allow most sexual abuse to continue. As Appleton (1980) asks, 'what of the teenager who does not want to put her parent behind bars?' Secondly, if intervention must await a conviction there will be inevitable delays in taking measures to protect children. Who gains from this? Thirdly, the narrowness of the test will mean that protective measures will be impossible where a conviction is not obtained because of a technicality or where sexual offences are committed by, for example, the mother's boyfriend. Fourthly, although Goldstein et al are aware that harm done by the inquiry may be more than that caused by not intruding (p. 64), they are prepared to subject children to an involvement in the criminal process which is not attuned to their needs and which is likely to perpetrate greater harm to them than any juvenile court placement process. It is difficult to see, as Katz[23] also notes, how authors who express concern for family integrity and protection of the family from invasion of its privacy can possibly want to encourage the continued use of the criminal law and its processes to tackle incest and allied offences.

The fifth ground for intervention is 'serious bodily injury inflicted by parents upon their child, an attempt to inflict such injury or the repeated failure of parents to prevent their child from suffering such injury' (p. 72). They define serious bodily injury narrowly. The ground is intended 'to provide protection to children who are brutally kicked, beaten or attacked by their parents. It is meant to safeguard children whose parents may have attempted to injure them, for example by starvation, poisoning or strangling ... It is designed to safeguard children from parents who prove to be incapable of preventing their child from repeatedly suffering serious bodily injury or being exposed to such harm' (p. 72). Besharov[2] has rightly complained of the way Goldstein and his colleagues construct rigid one dimensional rules, as in this example. For, whilst they would limit intervention to 'serious' injuries, thus ruling out of court a whole range of conduct deleterious to children, they have no doubt that when serious bodily harm has been inflicted, parental rights should always be permanently terminated. 'Parental maltreatment', they claim, 'leaves psychological scars which endure long beyond any physical healing and preclude a child from regaining the feeling of being safe, wanted and cared for in his parents' presence — the very emotions on which his further

development advances need to be based' (p. 73). They believe that battered children should always be adopted, an inflexible position difficult to understand.
Parents who batter their children can be helped to become adequate caretakers
(Lynch 1975; Lynch and Ounsted 1976; Cohn and Miller 1977). Children returned to
parents who have battered them do not develop differently from those placed in
foster homes or, for that matter, from working-class children brought up by their
own parents in comparable environments (Elmer 1977).

But, if the consequences of battering are to be so drastic, why do so many forms
of conduct fall short, on Goldstein *et al's* test, of warranting intervention at all?
It seems strange that a parent who beats his child should risk losing him but one
who chains his child to a bed or locks him in a cupboard or insists on dressing
him in female clothes should be immune from state intervention (Wald 1980). Two
further points should be made. Although Goldstein and his colleagues specify in
some detail what is meant by 'serious' bodily injury they leave themselves open to
a criticism they make of existing standards, *viz:* that they are vague. For, what
is a 'serious' injury? This surely depends upon values. What is a 'brutal' assault?
Is the parent's motive relevant? Take the case of R v Derriviere in 1969[25]. A West
Indian father whipped his 12 year old son to punish him for coming home late. He
was convicted of an assault occasioning actual bodily harm. He claimed that he
was using a method of chastisement common among parents of his background. The
court held that immigrant parents must conform to English standards (whatever they
are (Newson and Newson 1963, 1968, 1976)) in the correction of their children.
Goldstein *et al* would, I think, have intervened here. But would they intervene in
the case cited by Wald in his critique of Before The Best Interests? His example
is of a child 'physically disciplined by a parent using a paddle in a manner sufficient to leave bruise marks and to cause the child pain in walking, but where it
cannot be shown that the parent was attempting to cause more severe injuries'
(Wald 1980). It would seem not. How easy then would it be to lay down standards
relating to corporal punishment, to give parents the 'fair warning' that is thought
so essential?

The second point is the reluctance of Goldstein and his colleagues to intervene
in cases of less than serious injury which may lead to danger signs not being
picked up. Minor injuries often forewarn of more dangerous traumas (Bourne and
Newberger 1979). It is a vicious circle for, as suggested earlier, intervention
can cause an amplification of the deviance.

The sixth ground for intervention hinges on failure to take medical care and is
the most controversial. Goldstein *et al* argue that intervention can be justified
where there is a 'refusal by parents to authorize medical care when (1) medical
experts agree that treatment is non-experimental and appropriate for the child,
and (2) denial of that treatment would result in death, and (3) the anticipated
result of treatment is what society would want for every child — a chance for
normal healthy growth or a life worth living' (p. 91). They define adequate
medical care in as narrow a way as possible: the child must be faced by death, not,
for example, blindness; there must be medical consensus in the type of intervention
and on the fact that it is therapeutic; and, dealing specifically but not exclusively with 'defective newborns', the child must have a chance to live 'a normal
life or a life worth living'.

This ground raises profound social, legal, medical and ethical issues. What,
for example, is non-experimental treatment? Is a procedure experimental because it
is not orthodox?[26] Suppose a child, or better still an adolescent, would like to
take the risk of being cured by treatment which is still at the experimental stage?
What is a 'life worth living'? Whose decision should matters of life and death be?
Goldstein and his colleagues insist that 'when death is not a likely consequence
of exercising a medical choice, there would be no justification for governmental
intrusion. Where the question involves not a life-or-death choice but a preference

156 M. Freeman

for one style of life over another, the law must restrain courts and doctors from coercively imposing their personal preferences in the form of medical care upon non consenting parents and their children' (p. 92) (Goldstein 1977). There is surely a distinction, which they do not acknowledge, between giving parents some autonomy and allowing courts to review the decisions made by parents.

Goldstein et al are critical of the Connecticut case of Hart v Brown[27]. The case arose out of a decision by parents to save an 8 year old daughter's life by a kidney transplant from her healthy twin sister. Acting on medical advice, the parents consented to surgery. The hospital would not operate without a court review. The court upheld parental choice though, as Goldstein et al write, 'not their autonomy to decide' (p. 107). They are concerned that neither doctors nor judges are trained or in any other way qualified to impose their values about what is right for children or families in such situations. But this is surely not the point. In cases so fraught with emotion as an isograft kidney transplant there is a strong case for an objective review of the decision. Nor is it necessary for a judge or a doctor, merely to impose his own prejudices and views. There ought to be guiding standards, acceptable to the community as a whole. It may be difficult to decide upon these — abortion decisions are still fraught with controversy (Sumner 1981) but this should not discourage us from trying to formulate principles

One final ground for state intervention is a child's need for legal assistance. This intervention would depend on a 'request by parents who are unable to obtain legal assistance for their children, an adjudication of any ground for modifying or terminating parent-child relationships, or an emergency placement pending adjudication' (p. 111). Once again children get little say as legal battles are polarised between their parents and the state[28].

FOUR CASE STUDIES

Four case studies, two from each side of the Atlantic, test out and show the problems with the thesis presented in Before The Best Interests.

1. CONSENT FOR STERILISATION (Re D)

Goldstein et al make only a passing reference to the issue of sterilisation of a child as a result of a parental decision. 'It may be', they write in a note, 'that parental consent to surgery for the irreversible sterilisation of a child ought not to be sufficient to authorize the operation without court review (p. 257). There follows a reference to A.L. v G.R.H.[29], an Indiana decision similar to Re D, (discussed below) and a discussion of Stump v Sparkman[30] which, for what it is worth, gets the decision wrong! If Goldstein et al think A.L. v G.R.H. right, their view of this case seems inconsistent with their general arguments. Let us, therefore, examine Re D, the well-known English sterilisation case decided in 1976.

In Re D[31] an application was made via wardship proceedings by an educational psychologist employed by a local authority to prevent the sterilisation of an 11 year old girl suffering from Sotos Syndrome. It should be stressed that it was a chance intervention: other similar sterilisations had taken place. The proposed operation had the consent of the girl's widowed mother. The girl was precocious in development and presented behaviour problems which suggested that she might become pregnant in the near future. There was medical evidence that any child she might have could be abnormal. Reliance on the view that parents — and in this case medical experts too — know best would have deprived the girl 'of a basic human right, namely the right of a woman to reproduce'. Heilbron J. held that 'if performed on a woman for non-therapeutic reasons and without her consent, (it would be) a violation of such right'. The proposed sterilisation was stopped. Re D

exposes the limitations of the Goldstein *et al* approach. Their grounds for intervention are based on parental failures to meet particular standards. But the
mother in Re D was not neglecting or inflicting injury on her daughter — or at
least this is not how she saw it. If anything, she was trying to protect her
daughter from dangers she thought she would lack the maturity to fend off. Bernard
Dickens expresses this particulary well[32]. He comments: Before The Best Interests'
tests seem to lack the fine tuning required to deal with the situation presented
by Re D, since they are directed primarily at decisions to remove children entirely
from parental custody and control. Further, they are concerned with parents whose
treatment of their children falls short of legislated or judicially set minimum
standards of care. They seem not to address parents whose well-meaning and con-
scientious initiatives are misguided or insensitive in ways denying children future
rights. The tests set by Before The Best Interests are illustrated by failure to
come up to the standards and do not consider deviations from norms of child-rearing
by, for instance, over-protectiveness. They do not deal with causing harm to children by violating or pre-empting their human rights, such as their rights of reproduction. In a sense the problem can be generalised by noting that the Before
guidelines are too clear-cut, too rigid, too polarised. Just as there are adults
on the one hand and children on the other, so there are 'black' decisions and
'white' decisions. There is no understanding of grey areas, any more than there
appears to be of the rights or wishes of adolescents.

2. COMMITTAL TO MENTAL HOSPITAL (Parham v J.R.)

The problem in Re D (and A.L. v G.R.H.) can be seen in another context in the
important recent United States Supreme Court case of Parham v J.R.[33] The case
revolved about children committed to mental hospitals by their parents or legal
guardians without adequate procedural protections. The court concluded that a
parent or guardian might effect an admission to a mental hospital. It states that
'precedents permitted the parents to retain a substantial, if not the dominant,
role in the decision, absent a finding of neglect or abuse'[33]. It favoured the
'traditional presumption that the parents act in the best interests of the child'.
Nevertheless, it recognised that the risk of error involved was sufficiently high
to require a pre-admission inquiry by a neutral factfinder. It thought, however,
that the admitting psychiatrist constituted an adequately neutral and independent
decision-maker. The opinion was given shortly before the publication of Before
The Best Interests. One commentator (Watson 1980a) thinks it regrettable that that
book was not available to the Court. An earlier article of Joseph Goldstein's
(1977) was, and was, along with other psychologic literature, influential in the
decision. But the decision departs from the Before The Best Interests position to
a considerable degree. It recognises, as after Planned Parenthood v Danforth[34]it
had to do, that children had interests in liberty from detention and treatment.
It accepted as well that adolescents, capable of admitting themselves, also had
the legal power to leave a mental hospital.

The decision in Parham v J.R., something of a compromise, recognises the state's
interest in avoiding unnecessary and destructive interventions. 'The State in
performing its voluntarily assumed mission also has a significant interest in not
imposing unnecessary procedural obstacles that may discourage the mentally ill or
their families from seeking needed psychiatric assistance. The *parens patriae*
interest in helping parents care for the mental health of their children cannot be
fulfilled if the parents are un-willing to take advantage of the opportunities
because the admission process is too onerous, too embarrassing or too conten-
tious'[35]. Indeed, as an author in the Harvard Law Review noted 'the Court allowed
minors to be institutionalised with fewer procedural safeguards than it has required for the termination of welfare benefits'[36]. Watson (1980b), Before The Best
Interests' most loyal supporter, would have preferred the court to have defined
the admission process 'solely as a therapeutic contact between family and doctor'.

He argues that 'to conceptualise automatically hospital admission as a danger to the child's welfare ... runs counter to the Court's preferences for parental privacy'. He is concerned that protection of parental decision-making, rather than children's liberty interests, should have been 'the opening question in Parham'. The dangers inherent in this approach are profound. Szasz (1977) in an authoritative article has depicted them[37]. Analogies with tonsillectomies, appendectomies and other similar medical procedures, to which the court in Parham drew attention, are not apposite. For, as Watson (1980c) concedes, 'the child's medical symptoms (of mental illness) may stem from parental problems ... and the child may serve as the scapegoat and a symbolic focus for intrafamily conflicts. This sort of admission', he continues, 'differs from hospitalisation for other medical purposes because it presents the question under what circumstances the state should intervene into family psychological or social difficulties that hinder the development of the child'.

3. CONSENT FOR LIFE-ENHANCING SURGERY IN A MONGOL (Re: Phillip B.)

A third case which highlights the shortcomings in the Goldstein *et al* approach is the sad saga of Phillip Becker (Re: Phillip B)[38]. The decision, faithful to the letter and I fear the spirit of Goldstein and his colleagues, has led one commentator to ask poignantly: 'what happened to the best interests of the child?'[39]. Perhaps they will be buried with Phillip Becker. Like the notorious case of Alexandra, Phillip Becker was a mongol. At the time of the litigation in 1979 he was 11. He was mentally retarded with an I.Q. of slightly under 60. He was capable of developing social and communication skills and could go some way towards looking after himself. He went to school, was a Boy Scout and, it was predicted, would be able to function in a sheltered workshop when (or if) he grew up. He also had a congenital heart defect which in a normal child would have been correctable by standard surgery with a 5 to 10 per cent chance of dying during operation. A Down's Syndrome child has a risk of post-operative complications. Without surgery he would progressively deteriorate. With surgery he would develop into a healthy adult with a reasonable capacity for enjoyment of life.

The Santa Clara County Juvenile Probation Department filed a petition to have him declared a dependent of the court so that he might receive the cardiac surgery to which his parents refused their consent. The action was dismissed by a judge who ruled that there was no clear and convincing evidence to sustain the petition. The Court of Appeals affirmed the dismissal and the United States Supreme Court denied *certiorari*, thereby sanctioning a common law doctrine permitting parents to refuse non-emergency medical treatment to their unemancipated children. The parents' opposition to surgery was based on three grounds: since Phillip's life was not a 'life worth living', he should not have his life prolonged by surgery; he would outlive them if surgery were performed and they would be unable to supervise his placement and care; and concern because the operation was too risky and Phillip might die[40].

It is difficult to see what legitimate claim Phillip's parents had to have their view heard, let alone accepted. Phillip had never lived at home with his parents: he had always been in residential care. His parents visited him about every two months. The home where he lived thought the operation should be performed. This case was just the sort of decision which ought to have been taken on the basis of an objective review: in fact it was taken by endorsing parental preferences where their interests should have counted for little. It is remarkable that in deciding as the courts did they were ignoring uncontradicted medical testimony to the effect that without the operation death could result in the near future; indeed, that surgery to repair the defect could only be performed within a short time if Phillip were to have any worthwhile existence. Re: Phillip B encapsulates the Before The Best Interests philosophy, with its use of the expression 'life worth

living' and the dominance given to parental autonomy in decision-making. The case
shows once again the inflexible and over-narrow grounds for intervention prescribed
by Goldstein and his colleagues.

4. CONSENT FOR LIFE-SAVING SURGERY IN A MONGOL (Re B)

The final example concerns another Down's Syndrome child, raising the issue, as
yet unconsidered in this chapter, of 'defective newborns'. The facts of Re 'B'
(the 'Alexandra' case) are relatively straightforward (The Times August 8 1981).
Alexandra was born on July 28 1981. She suffered from Down's Syndrome, complicated
by an intestinal blockage which would be fatal without operation. The parents took
the view that it would be kinder to let her die. They, therefore, refused to
consent to the operation. The doctors made contact with the local authority, the
London Borough of Hammersmith and Fulham whose Director of Social Services had
personal experience of having a Down's Syndrome child. The Borough made the child
a ward of court and asked Ewbank J. to give them care and control and to authorise
them to allow the operation to be carried out. The judge made the necessary orders.
When the child was transferred from the hospital where she was born to another
hospital for the operation, the surgeon declined to operate on being informed that
the parents objected. The local authority, accordingly, returned to the judge.
He, after hearing the parents, refused his consent. The local authority appealed
to the Court of Appeal. Inquiries showed that other surgeons were prepared to
perform the operation. It was reckoned that, if the operation proved successful,
the child would have a life expectancy of 20 to 30 years. The Court of Appeal, in
Templeman L. J.'s words, saw the question for the Court as: 'was it in the best
interests of the child that she should be allowed to die or that the operation
should be performed? ... Was the child's life going to be so demonstrably awful
that it should be condemned to die; or was the kind of life so imponderable that
it would be wrong to condemn her to die?' He held that 'it was wrong that the
child's life should be terminated because, in addition to being a mongol, she had
another disability. Accordingly, the court's duty was to decide that the child
should be allowed to live'. Dunn L. J. thought 'Alexandra should be 'put in the
same position as any other mongol child'. The Court of Appeal thought Ewbank J.'s
error was that he had been influenced by the views of the parents, instead of
deciding what was in the best interests of the child.

The Goldstein, Freud and Solnit view on this case is clear. The quote (p. 97)
from Duff to the effect that: 'families know their values, priorities and resources
better than anyone else. Presumably they, with the doctor, can make the better
choices as a private affair. Certainly, they, more than anyone else, must live
with the consequences ...' Duff and Campbell (1973), are of the same mind as
Goldstein and colleagues: 'We also acknowledge', they write 'that there are limits
of support that society can or will give to assist handicapped persons and their
families'. This, unfortunately, is true. Goldstein et al, accordingly, insist,
with considerable justification, that in the case of children who receive medical
treatment rejected by their parents, 'the state must take upon itself the burden
of providing the special, financial, physical and psychological resources essential
to making real the value it prefers for the child it 'saves' (p. 97).' This, of
course, may involve finding foster or adoptive parents: at the least it involves
fully financing special care requirements.

This argument, that if the state is going to step in and override the parents'
decision it must be prepared to shoulder the cost, has been much in evidence in
Britain in the aftermath of Re 'B'. Thus, estimates of how much the care of
Alexandra is going to cost the local authority have been given considerable atten-
tion in the press. The case has sparked off considerable controversy. The British
Paediatric Association (The Times, August 19, 1981) immediately re-affirmed an

existing line that parents must ultimately decide whether a severely handicapped
baby is to be treated. An organisation (Prospect) has been formed to promote the
rights of parents to make the decision when they want their severely handicapped
newborn babies to be allowed to die (The Times, September 14, 1981). Claire
Tomalin in The Times (September, 1981) has referred to the decision in Re 'B' as
'the cruel folly'. 'Those who call for legal intervention in preference to the
quickly reached private decisions made between parents and trusted doctors seem to
me', she wrote 'to lack understanding of the moral capacities of ordinary people'.
She calls for parents to be able to make their decisions 'privately and peacefully
and with people whose goodwill (they) can trust'.

The Goldstein *et al* view is thus not without support. The fault with their
thesis and the more generalised line of argument pursued in the wake of Re 'B' and
the prosecution of Dr Arthur, who was acquitted of manslaughter, is that withholding
medical assistance so that the child dies or being burdened with the care of the
child are not true alternatives. There is a third option, the termination of the
parental relationship and with it parental rights, powers and duties. As
Robertson (1975) has written: 'while parental discretion to terminate the parental
relationship may be justified, it does not follow that parents should also have
the right to decide whether the child lives or dies. Clearly, discretion to
terminate a relationship of dependency does not mandate that one has the power to
impose death on the terminated party'[41].

PROBLEMS AND PRINCIPLES

There are both procedural and substantive problems at issue. Goldstein and his
colleagues for obvious reasons concentrate on the procedural. Within outer and
narrow limits they leave the decision to the parents and expect them to get some
assistance from doctors. But neither parents nor doctors are disinterested parties
and they cannot accordingly be impartial. Each has a committed personal interest
in the decision. Both, but particularly the parents, are emotionally involved.
These are not the actors to take a rational decision. This is why I believe that
outside intervention is important and that courts are, to pinch a phrase coined by
Goldstein, Freud and Solnit, (*p. 53*), the least detrimental alternative. I do not
look to the courts for 'palm-tree' or, what Weber (1954) called, 'Khadi justice'
(Blumberg 1969). Like Ian Kennedy (1981b) I believe that a code of principles
should develop and prefer their development and testing in real human cases in
courts to legislation 'in the cold' by Parliament (Freeman 1973). The clearer the
principles become the fewer cases will be referred to courts.

The formulation of these principles constitutes the substantive issue. First, it
may be worthwhile to attempt to classify the different types of case that may
arise. One useful typology has been constructed by Ruddick (1978a). There are, at
one extreme, children who have no life possibilities at all. Karen Quinlan[44],
though not a child, came into this category. It may even be argued that she had no
'life' to which she could be said to have a right (Kennedy 1976; Kohl 1978).
Alexandra, of course, had life possibilities.

Secondly, there will be children who, even with treatment, have no life possibilities acceptable to their parents or to parent substitutes, so that they will be
institutionalised. This to me is the most difficult case. Ruddick (1978b) can
accept the decision of parents in such circumstances to refuse surgery. He writes:
'Parents of spina bifida infants ... may in their initial disappointment, resentment
and guilt too quickly assume that (1) no acceptable individual parent substitute
can be found and that (2) institutional life is unacceptable. But if', he
continues, 'after suitable counseling and reflection, they refuse surgery for their
infant, they do not violate our parent principle, even if death ensues'. Ruddick's
(1978c) 'parent principle' is too narrow. In his words 'it only requires that
(parents) give serious thought to the future in the rearing of children'. It
adopts as a value the view that no life is better than life in an institution.

Whilst it is difficult to compare and measure the two options, intuitively I feel bound to disagree with his preference.

The third type of case is very close to Re 'B'. This concerns children who, if treated, have independent life possibilities but none that the parents can accept, even though there are willing foster parents who can bring the child to accept the limitations.

A fourth type of case concerns children with no independent life possibilities acceptable to both parent and child without treatment, but with some life possibilities with standard medical treatment. Examples are children with cleft palates and tumours[43].

Our concern here is with the third type of case. Ruddick's typology is useful though his reasoning is not attractive. A useful distinction, made by Angela Holder (1977), is between treatment which can cure the condition for which it is performed and that which cannot. She argues: 'It seems to be legally mandatory for treatment to be instituted if it can cure the condition for which it is performed. If a Down's baby has an intestinal obstruction or ... an infant has a fistula, either one of which can be cured by relatively simple surgical procedures and if those procedures would clearly be performed by court order if necessary on an otherwise normal newborn, then it is arguable that treatment is legally required.

'On the other hand, neurosurgery for a paralyzed newborn is by no means 'ordinary care', since normal babies do not require it. Second, the condition for which surgery might be performed is not curable, and thus the operation may be regarded as both futile and one that would subject the baby to more pain than he would have felt if left alone. Third, if the child survives he may well have sufficient self-awareness to suffer the agonies of knowing his limitations and to be tormented by them. Thus, it may be possible to justify as good medical practice a determination that a child whose condition is incurable should not be subjected to surgery for that condition solely to keep him alive'. Dickens (1979) amplifies this: 'the mongoloid child with bowel obstruction may be in the same position as a normal child refused a necessary blood transfusion by parents who are Jehovah's Witnesses; the medical care in issue will restore normal function to the part of the child's body for which it is indicated, and cannot lawfully be withheld'.

These highly persuasive arguments are not offered as a definitive blueprint but they open up a path for principled rather than *ad hoc* decision-making, keeping discretion to a minimum. A school of juristic thought, associated primarily with Dworkin (1977a), requires of judges that they search out the 'right answer' by considering all the relevant principles. Although critical[44]of much of his thesis, I believe that he has much to offer us in the 'hard cases' and that decisions relating to defective newborns should be (Dworkin says 'are') 'generated by principle' (Dworkin 1977b), that litigants (and in our case subjects of litigation) are 'entitled' to the judge's 'best judgment about what their rights are' (Dworkin 1977c). Dworkin admits that different judges can come to different conclusions 'because a constitutional theory requires judgments about complex issues of institutional fit, as well as judgments about political and moral philosophy' (Dworkin 1977d). He insists that judges must rely not on their own political views but on their beliefs in 'the soundness of those convictions' (Dworkin 1977e). These decisions are too important to be left to judges acting alone and what is required is informed and interdisciplinary debate as well as mutual respect between the professionals involved. Principles can only evolve in this way.

A CONCLUDING COMMENT

In this paper I have examined the pros and cons of state intervention in the

family. Much has been omitted. Elsewhere (Freeman 1981) I have traced the ways
in which state intervention developed and the reasons why it did. I accept that
what has happened in the twentieth century is that the liberal state has provided
itself with a system of indirect controls which preserves the appearance, even
some of the reality, of private initiative within an over-arching structure of
professional supervision. As Lasch (1980) has written, the therapeutic apparatus
leaves the family 'always 'justified' in theory and always suspect in practice'.
Although I do not think that Goldstein and his colleagues would agree with the
language used, their thesis is an attempt to guard against further intrusion by
the liberal state into the family. My position, as expressed in this paper, is to
suggest that there are considerable problems in leaving the family alone. Victory
for the family often means defeat for the children. It is, as I have indicated, a
line-drawing exercise. Goldstein and his colleagues have erred in drawing the
line too close to the parents' interests and too far from the children's. But the
picture is not all black and white. Goldstein *et al* seem to think in polar
positions (you are, for example, either an adult or a child): I hope I do not. I
recognise that intervention has its problems but I do not ignore its benefits.
Intervention must be properly controlled. This requires an activist, committed
judiciary capable of forging principles with the collaboration of other disciplines
involved. The recent decision in A v Liverpool City Council[45]does not offer us
much hope that they will be prepared to tackle these problems as vigorously as
they should. One detects a *laissez-faire* attitude in our judges as well: this is
the world of 'social administration', not law, said Lord Scarman in another recent
case [46]. Perhaps cases like Re D and Re 'B' offer hope for the future. I would
like to think so. I cannot help thinking, however, that they, laden with emotion
as they are, represent the exceptions rather than the rule. The judiciary must be
prepared to control the controllers if intervention is ever to be acceptable.
This, it may be thought, leads inevitably to one of the most commonly posed
questions of all: *quis custodiet ipsos custodes?* An answer to that thorny question
is well beyond the scope of this chapter.

DISCUSSION

Michael Freeman applied a logical legal mind to the vexed question of non-
intervention as opposed to intervention into family life by experts, so-called
but also so regarded by the 'public' and employed as such by the courts. Is it
ever possible to know with certainty what are the best interests of any child or,
indeed, of any family? Studies of cases that went wrong lend little support to the
idea that best interests and the best ways of promoting them can be reliably
ascertained. Some cases do go right. Experts are as much moved by gut-feelings
as anyone else and as between different breeds of workers and between them and
their clients much occasion for feelings exists. A true reconciliation between
the black and white of law and the colour of human interactions is likely always
to elude success. When intervention is balanced against non-intervention, those
involved in the caring professions who are given the tasks of helping other
people to solve their problems are unlikely to resign their responsibilities.
Right as well as rights exist on both sides.

NOTES ON CHAPTER 17

1. (1981) 1WLR 1421: leader in The Times, August 10, 1981. A second case was
   reported in The Daily Telegraph, May 26, 1982.
2. (1944) 321 US 158
3. idem 166
4. 1976 Fam. 185.
5. The Times, August 8, 1981.

6. See 27 Stanford Law Review 985 (1975); 28 Stanford Law Review 623 (1976); and 78 Michigan Law Review 645 (1980).
7. 43 Harvard Education Review 599 (1973).
8. (1979) 442 US 584.
9. Note the case of Richard Clark, badly injured by foster parents, which does not feature in Martin (1978). See his Chapter 9.
10. London Borough of Southwark, June 1981, given wide press coverage June 11. See also M. D. A. Freeman (1981) 145 JP 440.
11. Essex CC, March 1981.
12. The Times, September 24, 1981. Child killed by prospective adopters.
13. The Children Act 1975 is better characterised as a substitute parents' charter than a children's charter.
14. Field-Fisher Report, DHSS 1974. East Sussex CC also commissioned an enquiry (Children At Risk, 1975).
15. See Re Cullimore, The Times, March 24, 1976.
16. A good example is J. Garbarino's research. See Child Development 1976, 47:178.
17. Housing Policy (1977) Technical Vol. III, Cmnd 6851 HMSO London.
18. A towering problem for children Community Care, January 1979, no 246:8.
19. LASSL (80) 4.
20. See R. White and D. Brocklington (1978) In and Out of School, RKP, R. White (1980) Absent with Cause, RKP and the writings of John Holt, Ivan Illitch and Paolo Freire.
21. See Children Act 1975 s. 33; M. D. A. Freeman (1976) Custodianship — new concept, new problems 6 Family Law 57; Custodianship and Wardship 7 Family Law 116.
22. Children and Young Persons Act 1933 s. 1; Child Care Act 1980 s. 3.
23. (1981) 45 Albany Law Review 525, 529.
24. (1981) 34 Vanderbilt Law Review 481.
25. (1969) 53 Cr. App. Rep. 637.
26. See the Green case (1979) 393 N.E. 2d 836 and the Hofbauer case discussed on pp. 250-252 in Before the Best Interests of the Child.
27. (1972) 289 A. 2d 386.
28. There are additional grounds in Goldstein et al (1979) Appendix II. Note that the language of the grounds is not necessarily congruent with that in the main text of the book.
29. (1975) 325 NE 2d 501.
30. (1978) 98 S. Ct. 1099.
31. (1976) Fam. 185.
32. B. Dickens 1981 The modern function and limits of parental rights 97 LQR 462.
33. (1979) 442 US 584, 604.
34. (1976) 428 US 52.
35. (1979) 442 US 584, 605.
36. (1979) 93 Harvard Law Review 1: 97-99.
37. See also G. Koocher (1976).
38. (1979) 156 Cal. Rptr. 48, Cert. denied, (1980) S. Ct. 1597.
39. Donna Mitchell's (1980) In re Phillip B.: What happened to the best interests of the child? 12 Toledo LR 151. The case is also discussed by W. C. Moeller (1980) Marquette L. R. 511.
40. Mitchell op. cit. p. 167.
41. See also P. Foot, 1977, Euthanasia, Philosophy and Public Affairs 6: 85.
42. (1976) 355 A. 2d 647. See also the informative symposium in (1977) 30 Rutgers Law Review 243-328.
43. The two American cases Re Sampson (1972) 278 NE 2d 918 and Re Seiferth (1955) 127 NE 2d 820 are commonly quoted.
44. See Lord Lloyd and co-editor M. D. A. Freeman, (1979) Introduction to Jurisprudence 4th ed. Stevens p. 841. Similar views are expressed by R. Sartorius (1975) See Individual Conduct and Social Norms, Dickenson Pub. Co. and generally B. Hoffmaster (1982) Understanding Judicial Discretion, Law and Philosophy 1: 21-55.

45. (1981) 2 All E.R. 385 and see M. D. A. Freeman (1981) Is care without wardship
    wardship without care? 145 JP 733.
46. Lewisham LBC v Lewisham Juvenile Court (1979) 2 WLR 513, 538.

CHAPTER 18

Does Britain Need a Family Policy?

MALCOLM WICKS*

INTRODUCTION

Scientific and popular interest in the family is not new. Yet it is only relatively recently that the family in Britain has taken the stage as a public issue and become the concern of political parties and governments. Even in 1970 for example Margaret Wynn could note that 'no political party in the UK had identified itself with the social and economic interest of the family' and one comparative study classed Britain among those countries which have no explicit family policy (Kamerman and Kahn 1978).

During the 1970s, however, there was an almost unseemly haste on the part of politicians to claim the family as their own. Mrs Thatcher at the 1977 Conservative Conference declared that 'We are the party of the family'; Mr Dennis Healey called his 1978 Budget a 'family budget'; and Mr Patrick Jenkin has suggested that we need 'to bring the well-being of families into the spotlight of our affairs'. In addition, two independent bodies with a focus on the family and family policy have been set up: the Family Forum and the Study Commission on the Family. This interest is matched abroad, not only within countries (see below) but also internationally: the EEC, OECD, UN and ILO have all undertaken work on the theme of family policy in the last few years.

A FAMILY POLICY?

The prime purpose of this paper is to explore the nature, feasibility and desirability of a family policy in Britain. However before considering these questions it is important to note briefly the context in which the issue of 'family policy' is being discussed in Britain (Craven *et al* 1981). There are, in fact, a number of demographic, social and economic factors that are important.

CHANGING FAMILY PATTERNS

In Chapter 2, Lesley Rimmer analyses how family patterns in Britain are changing.

---

*This paper is largely based on Sections of 'Family Issues and Public Policy' prepared by Edward Craven (of the Civil Service College) and Lesley Rimmer and Malcolm Wicks (of the Study Commission on the Family).

Here we need simply note the evidence of increasing marital breakdown; higher
divorce rates and larger numbers of one-parent families. In addition the roles of
women and men, in relation to the family and work, are changing. All these trends
have heightened public interest in 'the family' and, more specifically, raise a
range of policy questions in fields such as social security and taxation.

PUBLIC EXPENDITURE

Government expenditure as a percentage of GNP rose from 37.8 per cent in 1955 to
55.2 per cent in 1975 and fell back to 49.3 per cent in 1978. Within this, total
social welfare expenditure increased most rapidly, and expenditure on the five main
social services now makes up over 50 per cent of total spending. With needs in
many areas increasing at a time when governments have often been concerned to
reduce public spending, this has led to governmental interest in what families can
do for themselves in areas as diverse as the under-fives and the care of elderly
people.

FAMILY POVERTY

Family poverty was 'rediscovered' in the mid 1960s, and the Child Poverty Action
Group provided cogent monitoring of the disadvantaged treatment of families with
children and the extent of family poverty within an affluent society. Much concern
about the situation of families was focussed in the mid 1970s around the introduction of the Child Benefit Scheme. Those who were concerned about the financial
position of families added their voice to the demands for a family policy.

THE FAMILY AND THE MACHINERY OF GOVERNMENT

Throughout the 1970s there was also concern about the fragmentation and overlap
of policy — epitomised by the poverty trap — which culminated in a CPRS (1975)
report on the Joint Approach to Social Policy. The report called for better co-
ordination of services, a greater need to deal with people 'in the round', and a
greater appreciation of the overall impact of policies on particular groupings, of
which the family is a key example.

DOES BRITAIN NEED A FAMILY POLICY?

Before considering this question directly, it is important to sound a cautious
note. 'Family Policy' has, on occasions, been an instrument in the service of the
very worst totalitarian regime (as in Nazi Germany) or has been a means of overriding individual interest in pursuit of national objectives. For example, in
Eastern Europe women have been portrayed as primarily 'mothers' or 'workers',
depending on the state of the economy or the level of the birth rate. Social
policies have been adjusted according to the objectives of the day.

These cautions suggest that ideas about family policy have to be thought through
carefully. Certainly a focus on the family unit will not produce a cosy consensus
on social policy. Neither is it possible to look elsewhere in Europe for a ready-
made family policy that can be applied in Britain. Some specific ideas may well
be worth considering, as we discuss later, but within Europe 'family policy', which
is a more common concept than in Britain, varies greatly and draws its inspiration
from different sources.

In their review of 'Family Policy in Fourteen Countries', Kamerman and Kahn
(1978) have highlighted some of those differences. In France the interest in

family policy which emerged in the second world war has always been pro-natalist
and heavily weighted towards the financial support and encouragement of families
with children. Recently, for example, the post-natal allowance for families with
a third or subsequent child has been doubled in value to around £1,250 per child
and is now paid as a lump sum rather than over a two-year period.

In Sweden, the emphasis on family policy which emerged in the 1930s was also the
result of fears about a dwindling population, but the protection of illegitimate
children, and by extension their mothers, and the move towards sexual equality have
also been important themes.

Within countries the emphases of family policy have changed over time: in Sweden
concern about illegitimate children in the 1980s, gave way to debates about
'fairness' and freedom of choice in the 1960s, and to concern with low paid workers
and larger families in the 1970s. And the treatment of women, which was so important a part of policy in the 1970s is now giving way to the treatment of 'parents'.
It is also difficult to delineate the boundary between family policy and social
policy generally. Family policy is therefore a difficult concept or, at least, one
that is open to different interpretation. Nevertheless, 'family policy' might have
relevance for Britain in three forms. First, a future development might see
different political parties and organisations putting forward their own 'family
policies'. This would enable the electorate to evaluate more clearly than they can
now how different policy ideas affect their own families. This would be a useful
way of political parties firming-up their proposed interest in the family, but
there are some major barriers standing in the way, for as Frank Field (1980) has
argued:

'British politics have divided on class lines ever since the early 1920s with
the result that it is immensely difficult for issues which are not class issues
to find a place on the political agenda. Class issues relate to the vertical
distribution of income. Those who are concerned about families wish to promote
a debate on the horizontal distribution of income — an issue which cuts across
classes but which divides along age lines.'

Field also notes that:

'No-one should underestimate the forces of class politics in Britain or the
difficulties of raising new issues which cut across traditional class boundaries.

It may well be that the political parties will only be nudged into effective
action when they are convinced that there is a significant constituency of public
interest in family policy matters. This leads to the second form that family
policy might take in Britain.

Family policy could be developed by alliances of different interest around
specific and very tangible issues. This might lead to the emergence of a family
lobby or movement in Britain. Child benefit provides the best current example of
such an alliance: with Conservative back benchers, Conservative women and the
churches joining forces with CPAG, other pressure groups and the Labour party in
favour of substantial increases in the level of benefit. Similarly the recently
formed Maternity Alliance with a wide membership campaigns for policies to reduce
the infant mortality rate.

More ambitiously the Family Forum has been established to bring together those
voluntary organisations with an interest in family life and while it is a forum for
discussion, it also aims to influence policy-makers and provide a voice for
families in British politics. However, as has been argued elsewhere 'if the Family
Forum is to develop into some kind of pressure group or 'movement' for all families
in Britain, it will risk losing the support of traditional voluntary bodies who shy

168   M. Wicks

away from 'political action' (Wicks 1981). Nevertheless, if the Family Forum can
avoid these obvious obstacles in its path and concentrate on building alliances
around certain specific issues, and avoid all subjects on which different groups
adopt radically different positions, it just might develop into a force to exert
pressure on both political parties and government policy-makers.

                        A FAMILY PERSPECTIVE

   Alongside the partisan advocacy of distinctive family policies, or alliances
around specific family issues, there is a need for the development of a family
perspective in the policy process, namely taking fully into account family units
in the planning, monitoring and evaluation of policy. And it is in this sense that
the term is most useful and has the widest applicability.

   What would such a family pespective involve and how could it be achieved? There
are three aspects: a sensitivity to changing family patterns and relationships; a
full recognition of family roles and functions; and the monitoring and evaluation
of the effects of public policy on families.

FAMILY PATTERNS IN BRITAIN

   First, a family perspective within the policy process should be based on a sound
understanding of changing family patterns in Britain. Many of the assumptions
about family life made by government, as well as by industry, advertising agencies
and other bodies, are based on a model of a fairly standard family consisting of
two parents, married to one another(!) and two or three dependent children. In fact
only 35 per cent of households in Britain are of this kind, and about one in eight
children are being brought up currently in one-parent families. More than one in
three marriages in 1980 involved remarriages for one or both partners, so that increasing divorce and remarriage must lead to more varied family patterns: parents
living apart, and more and more children with step-parents, step-siblings, or
'step-grandparents'. While such diversity should not be exaggerated, for most
children are still being brought up in fairly traditional families, the number who
are not is growing and significant changes are taking place which have important
implications for policy-makers.

   The argument is not that policy-makers are in complete ignorance of changing
family patterns, but there is a sense in which certain policies are merely
adjusted in the light of significant trends, rather than thoroughly reappraised
and, where necessary, recast. For example, today the supplementary benefits system
represents the major source of funds for some 336,000 one-parent families, or 35
per cent of the total, and yet this benefit system was created for quite different
purposes. Certainly many would doubt whether a cash allowance scheme, based mainly
on principles developed in the 1940s and designed to support the elderly and the
longer-term unemployed, is adequate to cope with the needs of a major 1970s
phenomenon, the one-parent family.

   Another traditional assumption about family life assumes that the male is the
major and probably the only breadwinner. Much of our taxation and social security
policies are based on the assumption contained in the Beveridge Report (1942) that
'all women by marriage acquire a new economic and social status, risks and rights
different from those of the unmarried. On marriage a women gains a legal right to
maintenance by her husband as a first line of defence against risks which fall
directly on the solitary woman'.

   This assumption looks increasingly outmoded today when 56 per cent of all married
women are in paid employment, albeit a high proportion of them in part-time jobs,

when on average the earnings of working wives account for a quarter of family income and when, were it not for wives' earnings, the number of families in poverty
would increase three or fourfold. Facts of this kind have particular implications
for taxation policy which have been highlighted by the publication of the Green
Paper on the taxation of husband and wife (Inland Revenue 1980).

FAMILY FUNCTION

The second feature of any family perspective in policy-making involves a better
understanding by government of family functions and roles and the need for a better
partnership between family and state. Moss and Sharpe (1980) have argued for an
awareness of how 'different kinds of family actually function in society, so that
they can attempt to predict the likely responses of different kinds of families —
their mediating role — to proposed variations in policy, before these are implemented'. In education, child development and health, a better understanding on the
part of government as to how families affect the development of children could
lead to more sensitive 'family' policies; a better relationship between parents and
teachers, doctors, health visitors and other professionals; and a better mesh
between family needs and service provision. Certainly within education, a growing
body of research over the last two decades has shown the important effect of the
home and parental aspirations on attainment. The importance of parents in their
child's education was highlighted in 1967 by the Plowden Report (1967). Evidence
from the surveys conducted for the Plowden Committee:

'... pointed to the influence upon education performance of parental attitudes.
It follows that one of the essentials for educational advance is a closer
partnership between the two parties to every child's education.'

And more recently the Taylor Report (1980) emphasises that:

'... every parent has a right to expect a school's teachers to recognise his
status in the education of his child by the practical arrangements they make to
communicate with him and the spirit in which they accept his interest ... we
wish to produce a structure within which every parent will have a role in
supporting the school and increasing its effectiveness.'

EVALUATION

A third way of achieving a family perspective in British policy-making is through
monitoring and evaluation. The new interest in family and policy questions is in
part due to a belief that policies fail to be formed on the basis of a realistic
evaluation of how they will affect families of different kinds in practice. All
too often, it is argued, policies fail to relate specific issues and objectives to
other policies, do not then respond to critical questions of implementation and are
not firmly based on actual family circumstances and needs. More specifically, many
policies relate to the needs of individuals and may therefore fail to relate
adequately to the family as a unit.

These kinds of anxieties about the interface between families and policy have
become recognised by leading politicians in recent years. The former Secretary of
State for Social Services, Mr Jenkin (1978), has noted, while in opposition:

'What we need is to make sure that existing institutions bring the family into
much sharper focus as they develop their policies.'

In similar vein, Mr Callaghan (1978), the Prime Minister, stated that:

'I don't believe that the Government has done enough, hardly started to consider as a whole the impact of its policies on the family when we take our decisions in Cabinet and in government.'

Evaluating the effects of policy on families is necessary at different stages in the policy process. First, it is important at the early stages of policy development when different options are being considered. Second, it is important at the stage when policies are being finalised and are processed in Parliament. At this stage, a point developed later, the idea of a 'family impact statement' is useful. Finally, once implemented, it is important to develop some monitoring and evaluation to look at the implementation of policy in practice. Such evaluation may well lead to policy adaptation and will feed into more fundamental reappraisals of policy when these take place.

Evaluating Policy Options

A family perspective in policy would involve a sensitivity to changing family patterns and relationships with the family and an appreciation of family roles and functions in areas like education, health and care. These perspectives would be important at the earlier stages of the policy process, when problems and issues are being assessed and when different policy options are being evaluated. An option that is favoured on grounds of administrative convenience may well be ruled out when viewed from a family perspective. At the very least, policy-makers would be more likely to make clear their assumptions about the family and test them against objective evidence.

Evaluating Policy Proposals

This stage in the policy process is an internal one, when civil servants and Ministers move towards a decision on a particular issue. The next stage involves a more public debate when the policy is announced — often involving the need for new legislation. A family perspective is critical at this stage and the concept of 'family impact statements' is relevant here.

The hope for family impact statements is that they would lead to policies which are more in tune with contemporary family life, which take more account of family functions and which meet family needs and aspirations. This is inevitably idealistic but impact statements would encourage a family focus in policy-making. In the preliminary stages of policy-making civil servants, aware of the need to produce an impact statement, would be more likely than now to take into account family considerations. And, during the Parliamentary consideration of new legislation, MPs would consider specific policy changes in the context of the impact statement, as would interest groups and the media. Impact statements should also stimulate public debate. As the Family Impact Seminar observed in their recommendations to the White House Conference (1980 p. 18).

'The primary element that a family impact approach should borrow from environmental impact is the heightened public consciousness it created; in this case, heightened public consciousness about the effects of public policies on families.

It follows that these family impact statements should be published and they might well appear at the beginning of a Parliamentary Bill alongside the statements, which are already required, on financial implications and civil service manpower.

There has been little detailed thinking in this country as to the content of an impact statement. Naturally the content would vary from one policy measure to the next. There are, as some American academics have noted, some difficult problems involved, but we believe that a useful start could be quickly made and, indeed, for some measures a statement could be a relatively short document. The kind of factor to be considered in a family impact statement might include:

a) the impact of the proposed policy on <u>different</u> family units (including one-
parent and dual-worker families)

b) assumptions made about family life, including male and female roles

c) the association between the new policy and existing related policies and the
likely overall impact of related policies on families

d) the rights and responsibilities of families

e) intelligibility of new policy — access, complexity, etc.

f) policy goals — how these will be achieved: monitoring and evaluation.

Evaluating Policy Effects

Following the introduction of a new policy, the monitoring and evaluation of its
effects should also involve a family perspective. This is what might be termed
'family impact analysis' and it would essentially involve testing out whether the
intentions of the policy, as expressed in the earlier impact statement, had been
realised, whether there had been any unintended consequences and what families
themselves think of the policy.

MECHANISMS

For the development of a 'family perspective' in policy-making, three possible
elements have been discussed: sensitivity to changing family patterns; an appreciation of family functions and roles; and the need for monitoring and evaluation of
'family impact'. With the exception of the impact statement, a 'family perspective'
could become no more than a fragile bubble full of good intentions and high hopes,
soon to disappear in the real world of policy and politics.

This therefore suggests a need for something more substantive. But what exactly?
An often voiced 'solution' is the appointment of a Minister for the Family or even
the establishment of a Ministry for the Family. Such a Minister/Ministry would
bring together the range of policies and services that affect families, would
ensure that harmful overlaps were ended and would bring policies more into line
with family needs.

In practice we would reject the proposal. It is unlikely that any 'Minister for
the Family' would have a separate Department. It is more likely that such a title
would go to an existing DHSS Minister, and even if such a Department were created
the difficulties would be immense. As a German commentator has noted:

'Family policy tends to be as diffuse as its object, the family. In other words,
because the family constitutes itself as the private integration of the almost
total range of public influences, virtually all family policy problems are
genuine problems of other branches of policy. A family ministry, then, can be
considered a governmental department for everything — or nothing.' (Niedhardt
1978a).

In Germany the family ministry has responsibility for legislative initiatives
only in child allowances. Decisions in cabinet are taken on a majority vote and
this ensures that the Minister of Family Affairs exerts some influence:

'But it is evident that the family ministry, lacking the prerogative to prepare
and propose such decisions in almost any substantial field, is very weak within
the give-and-take processes of competing departments.

Family policy interests, therefore, do not seem to be very well represented — if they are not precisely parallel with the interests of other fields of policy.' (Niedhardt 1978b).

For Britain, both David Ennals and Patrick Jenkin have argued against a separate Family Ministry which is unlikely to occur despite the advocacy of some pundits from time to time. This does not rule out the occasional necessity of giving a Minister responsibility for a particular family policy issue, especially where it cuts across departmental boundaries. This kind of proposal was made by the authors of 'Marriage Matters', a Consultative document by the Working Party on Marriage Guidance (Home Office 1979). They noted that 'specific responsibility (for marital work) is not vested anywhere' and that four central government departments were involved, as well as three other central agencies. They argued that 'with this multiple division of responsibility, there is a need for a centre to co-ordinate and stimulate' and proposed that such responsibility should rest with a Minister.

A FAMILY POLICY REVIEW

Family impact statements might be a valuable part of the evaluation of policy from a family perspective but the process of evaluation and monitoring should be continuous. This could be achieved through the publication of an annual 'family policy review'. The CPRS has made a valuable contribution to the debate with their recent publication 'People and their Families' (1980), and either the CPRS or a body outside government could take on the task of reporting annually on the changes which have affected families over the year. The Study Commission on the Family has decided itself to produce, as a pilot exercise, such a review. It will look at changing family patterns and their implications for policy-makers, and at the impact of policy changes on families.

A FAMILY COUNCIL?

A possible new mechanism for bringing about better 'family policies' might be the establishment of a 'family council' which would maintain a watching-brief on policy developments and which might consider proposed policy changes at an early stage. Its membership might combine representatives of voluntary bodies and family organisations, as well as family members with a direct knowledge of the issues and problems at stake. Such a council might be a purely voluntary organisation, and would be one possible way ahead for the Family Forum, or it might be a statutory body with powers and rights vested in it by Parliament. A 'Family Commission' has been proposed by Barbara Rodgers (1980) and Muriel Brown (1980). In the Netherlands a 'Family Council' exists which is a non-governmental, independent foundation, although fully state-aided. With an aim to serve the interests of the family, and with five ministries having an advisory member on the board, it has a double task: to be an advisory council for the government, and to be a national umbrella organisation for other private organisations which work in the field of the family.

A CABINET COMMITTEE?

Some, arguing the importance of the family, might call for a special Cabinet committee to consider family and policy questions. Such a committee might, for example, consider family impact statements prior to their publication and would help to co-ordinate policy across Whitehall. While Prime Minister, Mr Callaghan (1978) considered the idea of a Ministerial committee on the family. Whether or not such a committee is necessary, it would be important for existing Cabinet committees to consider family questions more rigorously in their deliberations and for this to be a focus within a more general 'joint approach to social policy'.

CONCLUSION

A number of factors have led to a growing interest in the concept of 'family policy'. While such a concept can lead to no easy consensus on social policy questions, the idea of a 'family perspective' in policy-making is important. It should involve a sensitivity to changing family patterns; an understanding of how families function in areas like education, health and child care, and monitoring and evaluation of the impact of public policies on families. Such a 'family perspective' will only occur if some new mechanisms are introduced both within Whitehall and outside it, and the idea of 'family impact statements' deserves particular attention.

DISCUSSION

Political parties claim to have an interest in the welfare of families, but so far this has not led to any positive steps which could be included in an election manifesto. There is no direct relationship between government and the family. The question of giving some structure to this relationship was discussed from two main standpoints, what sort of structure and what sort of policy, both of which would result from and encourage 'thinking family'. Matters have been brought to a head by a number of developments including the changing pattern of families with the increase in divorce and single parenthood, the dependency within the Welfare State of family income on benefits, and a new interest in the rights of children and the clamour of the feminist voice, claiming that the family is oppressive to women. As in all family problems, basic difficulties stem from absence of a definition, although it is the existence of dependent members, young, handicapped or old, which causes the concern. We are all members of families, nevertheless narrowing the concept to the presence of dependents could help focus on special needs. The suggestion of a Minister for the Family was not supported. Other possibilities were a Cabinet Committee to discuss the family, a special Family Council or a Family Policy Review Committee. The two most favoured ideas were for an Ombudsman with special responsibility and the preparation of Family Impact Statements. The recent Norwegian Ombudsman's functions are described in the Appendix. The Ombudsman should be able to initiate as well as to comment. His independence should ensure his freedom from political ideologies and his perspective on what are the best interests of children. The 'Family Impact Statement' would be attached to all Bills coming before Parliament in the same way as the statement of financial implications. It should go to all interested parties. The Government should be more open and should state what influenced them when they took the final decision. A widening to a 'Social Policy Impact Statement' had some support since the solution of such problems as equal opportunities and the eradication of poverty have direct relevance to the family and its dependents. The evaluation of the impact of policy decisions on the family could not be once and for all. Monitoring and a regular family policy review would be essential and while policy would be central, administration would be local where lay the detailed knowledge of need. Data on the effects of unemployment on the family, now lacking, should be collected and studied.

CHAPTER 19

Family Policy Targets

PETER BOTTOMLEY

The functions and behaviours of families in addition to their circumstances have been studied throughout the ages. The development of a family perspective on social and economic policy has been less explicit although some other countries gave more attention to the contents of policy before many people in Britain re-developed the subject.

Family policy or policies for families can be seen as bringing the family life cycle into social and economic policy. A cursory glance through the charts and table of Social Trends illustrates differences between families as well as changes over time for families of all kinds. The work of Margaret Wynn (1970) in Family Policy over ten years ago focused attention on family incomes, putting forward the case for a more explicit, realistic and functional allocation or redistribution of resources during the years when children are dependent.

More recently, Sheila Kamerman and Alfred Kahn produced the study, Family Policy — Government and Families in Fourteen Countries (1978). They divided countries into those that had explicit and comprehensive family policy, others with family policy as a field and finally, a group of countries, including the United Kingdom and the United States, where family policy was seen as implicit and reluctant. I recommend the introductory chapter, Families and the Idea of Family Policy, and the concluding chapter, Family Policy as Field and Perspective. The concluding paragraphs to each are:

'Clearly, family policy is in the middle of many societal contradictions. Yet it should be obvious that if the family is a central institution in all our societies it will be viewed as a critical agent both for those who seek change and those who strive to avoid it.'

'... political and cultural diversity thus far have precluded explicit family policy and is behind much current hesitancy. The issue here, as everywhere, will be whether the possible payoff in decreased policy sprawl and coherent public goals will be worth the risk. The decision remains, for this subject as for others, in the realm of politics. Scholars and analysts may define and make proposals about 'quantity, quality, and equality' — and for whom. But government leaders and citizens must clarify, through the political process, just what it is that people want and how much they want it.'

In the United States in 1980, government, families and others tried to answer

that last question. The report of the White House Conference on Families showed
that three-fourths of the delegates agreed on three-fourths of the recommendations.
The topics and issues were considered under four headings: Families and Economic
Well-being; Families: Challenges and Responsibilities; Families and Human Needs;
Families and Major Institutions.

Families and Economic Well-Being   Families and Human Needs

1. Economic Pressures   12. Education
2. Families and the Workplace   13. Health
3. Tax Policies   14. Housing
4. Income Security   15. Child Care
5. Status of Homemakers   16. Handicapping Conditions

Families: Challenges and   Families and Major Institutions
Responsibilities

6. Preparation for Marriage and   17. Government
   Family Life   18. Media
7. Specific Supports for Families   19. Community Institutions
8. Parents and Children   20. Law
9. Family Violence
10. Substance Abuse
11. Ageing and Families

    In the United Kingdom, a succession of Reports such as those on Primary Education,
Child Health and Juvenile Crime have demonstrated the effect of how families behave as well as the differences between them in influencing or affecting avoidable
disadvantage, distress and handicap. I want to argue that explicit discussion of
family policy targets will bridge the gap between analysis and action in addition
to increasing the awareness, competence and confidence of families and individuals
within families. National and local discussion of targets is valuable in itself.
It also has the advantage of bridging the gap between people and the political
process and can be used as a way of integrating the concerns of those who would
otherwise be seen as separate and too often with conflicting interests and opinions.

    It is not easy to separate discussion of the target from the means of working
towards it. In practice, much of the value of putting each subject on the agenda
comes from consideration of what can be done by whom for themselves or for others.
I look at this field with the aim of helping people achieve the outcome that they
desire for themselves rather than from the point of view of a social engineer.

    Start with conception. Whether or not we believe that every conception should be
planned or wanted, is it desirable or possible to reduce the number of pregnancies
which the mother wants to be ended in abortion? Leaving aside the other issue of
what the law should be, is it desirable to halve the number of abortion requests
over a ten year period? If it is, what action is needed by those concerned and
others around them? Discussion on this issue may lead to more desirable outcomes
as seen by those directly involved as more relevant than action which leaves a
choice between trying to get a legal or an illegal operation.

    Let us move on to ante-natal care. Fit for the Future, the Report of the Commit-
tee on Child Health Services (Court 1976), emphasises the period of the child's
life during which growth is most rapid, the risk of death is greatest and the
foundations of subsequent development are laid. It is pointed out that the well-
being of the child is almost inseparable from that of the mother. Chapter Eight

on the unborn and newborn baby includes the following:

'Many of the changes which have transformed the lives of women and greatly
reduced the mortality and morbidity related to childbirth have been gradual and
cumulative'.

'The reticence and ignorance about reproductive matters which marked the attitude
of sections of society, often the most influential, in the past has quite recently
given way to the positive advocacy of 'sex education' as part of health education.
We have a particular concern over family planning, termination of pregnancy and
sexual attitudes because of our knowledge of the vulnerability of illegitimate
and unwanted children to a variety of medical, educational and social troubles
and of the special demands imposed on services by them.'

'While we would emphasise the need for young people — particularly those whose
experience of family life has been unhappy — to be prepared for parenthood, we
recognise the difficulties in recommending more 'education for parenthood' in any
formal sense. There are problems in determining how information and advice should
be presented to ensure that it is helpful and educative without necessarily being
prescriptive, and in deciding how far it is justifiable to promulgate a particular
set of values and attitudes about what constitutes good parenting.'

'In view of the importance of the subject we would like to see further study of
this aspect of pre-natal care aimed at providing those involved with clearer
guidance both on what advice parents need during the ante-natal period and how
best to give it to them.'

How many of our schools arrange for discussions between staff and parents about
education for parenthood? Insofar as this affects school children, is the shared
responsibility one that is talked about between those involved? The National
Association of Youth Clubs recently did a survey on older teenagers' knowledge of
reproduction. It showed appalling ignorance. It would be easy to carry out
locally a survey of what people think they know and then to set local targets for
improvements in straightforward knowledge (even if it is more difficult to assess
attitudes). The opening chapter to Fit for the Future indicates other areas where
assessment of incidence of avoidable problems can lead on to discussion and action
for improvement. As an illustrative example, who beside specialists has considered
what would be necessary to reduce infant mortality rates in each region of the
United Kingdom so that the gap between the United Kingdom and Sweden or Japan was
halved during the next ten years?

There are many other areas of interest where it would be valuable to consider
what would be necessary to reverse or reinforce undesirable or desirable trends
without condemning all or any of those affected. What would be likely to halve the
number of children under the age of sixteen involved in their parents' divorces?
The number has doubled in ten years. Is that necessary or irreversible? The number
of children of compulsory school age in the care of local authorities in England
and Wales nearly doubled in the fifteen years up to 1976. This was presumably
unintended both by the authorities and by the families concerned. What would be
needed to reduce this total?

In 1977, a young male between the ages of fourteen and sixteen had nearly a one
per cent chance of being convicted or cautioned for a serious offence. Family
action or inaction is a prime determinant of juvenile crime. In how many areas is
there a focus or a local forum which brings together the ambitions of families to
avoid this with the professionals who have to cope with the young offender? In how
many areas is there any sharing of the knowledge of the Juvenile Bureau of the
police, the social workers and others so that family confidence and awareness of
their positive influence can be raised or helped to be more effective? How many

Education Authorities publish their truancy or unexplained absence rates in a way
that involves parents rather than creating headlines from which people dissociate
themselves? A community desire to halve truancy rates over a specified number of
years, involving both schools and parents, is likely to be much more effective than
hiding the problem which is a breeding ground for less effective education and for
higher crime.

In housing, is there even one local authority which knows or publicises the chance
of a young married couple getting a council home or a home at the time of family
formation in the private sector whether owner occupied or rented? Not all these
areas of concern necessarily require more public resources — more accurately, the
transfer of resources from people in one set of circumstances to people in other
circumstances.

I believe that the conscious discussion of how best to match people's needs with
resources can be combined with a renewed consciousness of family responsibilities.
Helping ourselves to fulfill family responsibilities clearly is associated with the
resources needed and desired. Almost any rational analysis of the individual and
family economic life cycle shows that we are, whether consciously or not, transferring resources from one period of our lives to another. The area where this has
happened 'worst' is in financial support for those when they have dependent children
A family policy target twenty-five years ago would have been to preserve, or
preferably to increase, the level of child income support for families. In practice
because of lack of attention, average earnings and the value of retirement pensions
have increased dramatically while the real level of child income support has fallen.

If it were agreed that Child Benefit should be at least at the level of the short-
term National Insurance Benefits for children, we could promote the target of
achieving that logical and desirable end within say five years.

I have aimed to open the field with illustrative examples. The value of pursuing
the idea of family policy targets is to promote discussion and to improve family
and individual well-being through more appropriate and explicit social and economic
policy. Those policies continue with or without the family perspective. Family
Forum, an association of voluntary organisations concerned with families, provides
one way of bringing together those concerned with family well-being. Activity at
local and national level is needed to carry out discussion of family policy as well
as providing the range of knowledge and points of view which are needed for both
the discussion and the achievement of family policy targets.

                    DISCUSSION

If Family Policy is to receive serious consideration, it must enter political
consciousness. It should not enter, and there should be no need for it to enter,
the party political arena. Targets must be set which promote the well-being of
families and aid them in carrying out their job. In setting the targets consumer
needs must be explored and respected, 'we' should not do this for 'them', but
rather local groups should form to include families and those who help them. Not
only disadvantaged but all families are involved. Public awareness and acceptance
that what families do matters should lead to the questions, how do families function
and with what? Government action to provide resources in cash, which is the main
problem, would need some re-distribution of tax and benefits, most advantageously
if reviewed with a 'life cycle' perspective. On the other hand, since supply
creates demand, families should try to reduce their demands. For example, the
provision of an abortion service has led to its profligate use. In education, non-
attendance needs study: although only a small proportion in primary education (10
per cent) children aged 14 to 15 years are seriously involved. The guide lines
on sex education are out of date and these too should be reviewed. Much is known

about good practice, information needing to be spread more widely. Local radio
could assist. On specific problems alliances could usefully form. Besides increasing public awareness, more discussion should be promoted among politicians.
For Trades Unions, who deal with people rather than families, family policy is not
yet important. Families have little power and the caring professions a low status.
These attitudes must be changed.

CHAPTER 20

The Final Session

ALFRED WHITE FRANKLIN

If a geriatrician were managing this symposium, the family needs would be reviewed a little differently, but not all that differently. However, we see ourselves in competition for both personnel and cash with other groups. We press for the family, knowing that our sights have to be on the second generation in order to advance and to break into relevant cycles, if we believe that they exist. We have now to prepare a generation of unstressed mothers-to-be by helping the grandmothers-to-be. Palliation soon, yes, but real progress not until then.

Let us begin by accepting the need for some plan for the care of babies during their dependency period. The usual arrangement is generally known as a family, but the structure of the family is variable. In any dependent child containing group there have to be adults with responsibility for providing the care. This responsibility, because of the difficulties in its discharge, needs to be a commitment. Sir Edmund Leach recognises this in his paper but points out that the group, adult and child, cannot function effectively except in a context of some kind of society. Society provides what we now call a network, kindred and neighbours or appointees of the state in the person of social workers, foster parents, school teachers and so on.

Lesley Rimmer showed that the group has a dynamic rather than a static existence. Those private systems in contact with the group consisting of relatives, friends and neighbours and the professional public systems who have caring and, in a good sense, interfering functions, as well as the policy makers, must recognise and accept the variety of forms taken by the group. Each must be accorded its own reality and normality even although we do not all support some of the forms with unqualified approval.

Dr Kellmer Pringle and Dr Franklin looked briefly at what the baby needs from its caregivers so that it has the best chance to develop into a mature adult, able ultimately to take a responsible place in our society. In the context of our discussion, what is most important is the ability to be a parent of the next generation. Both the authors stressed the critical importance of the early days, weeks, months and years, because by the age of 5 years much of the future personality and patterns of behaviour of the new individual has been established.

The discharge of the caring responsibility stresses the adults in the group both by duties imposed and activities inhibited. Both careers and pleasure have to be adapted. Some of the adults who have had difficult or bad experiences in their own early life can be recognised as vulnerable. Although to be vulnerable is not

FM - M

necessarily to fail, and we would like to know what makes the difference between
failure and success, the vulnerability can lead to failure in child rearing, which
is the ultimate test and of greater importance to society than the intelligence
quotient or a good score on the social adjustment scale.

The symposium addressed itself to the adverse environmental stresses which appear
to be dangerous for the vulnerable as amply shown in studies of abusing and neglect
ing families. The need for the support of the network is greater, although unfortunately many vulnerable people reject support preferring isolation. The
presence of handicap makes caring more difficult but, equally, it motivates the
majority of adults towards extra caring effort. Nevertheless the modern paediatric
policy, especially with immature newborn and deformed babies, needs assessment to
establish how far current methods are increasing the numbers of survivors with
handicaps.

Ethnic complexity and different cultural patterns produce their own problems and
their own different needs which must be fulfilled. Prejudice takes many forms —
not only between indigenous and immigrant populations but also between different
immigrant groups. Tension exists between integration by the adoption of indigenous
attitudes and habits and the segregation and boundary formation implicit in the
survival of the culture, something which may be necessary for the maintenance of
both individual and group self-esteem.

Muriel Brown reported on the complex studies of cycles of deprivation, how they
arise and how transmitted. From her remarks and from the ensuing discussion the
environment seemed the important cause of stress but in the end problems and their
solution were transformed into the need for cash, raising fiscal issues on a grand
scale. Nevertheless the importance of changed attitudes was agreed while the
question of how to change them remained unanswered.

The supply and allocation of housing came into question as of critical importance
to the success of family life. The discussion did not clearly distinguish between
those families with intrinsic problems such as alcohol, drug addiction, mental
handicap, distorted personalities and those who created problems by habits and
practices dissonant from the society surrounding them. Perhaps this lack of
differentiation simply reflects the view that the problems are intertwined. Again
cash presented itself as a major solution. Much deprivation stemmed from the
lowest standard of housing and the ugliness of the surroundings. A true priority
for the success of family life would be to bring both houses and their surroundings
to an acceptable standard. The conflict was recognised between the social exploration through the global appreciation of each family and its difficulties and needs
and the business of housing, managed as a commercial undertaking. The provident
landlord had somehow simultaneously to be the caring landlord, a combination more
easily accomplished by Housing Associations than Housing Departments.

The question, how can true co-operation be achieved between housing, health,
social work and tax and benefit led us on to fiscal policy and the whole question
of collaboration and what that implies. This would have to be at government
departmental as well as at local level. Joan Cooper and Sue Dowling addressed
themselves to the problems of collaboration, and Peter Moss and Jonathan Bradshaw
to the fiscal complexities and how they might be resolved.

Elsa Dicks and Don Venvell agreed with the need for priority to be given to the
younger age groups where so much of the future school success or failure of the
child was influenced. Parents should be better informed and should play a greater
part in the school system. Society should rethink what it regarded as the function
of education. Examination success certainly affected the later career but what
more could be done to help the child in the development of its personality?

Much was seen as needing change. Where can change begin to ensure that resources of money and personnel are used to the best advantage in reducing the environmental stresses on the family group? Is it from the grass roots, the factory floor where well motivated and caring people can organise themselves into valuable and effective cross-professional groups with non-professional involvement? or do we look to ministerially executed changes of policy, of attitudes and of priorities?

With this synopsis in mind no attempt was made in the final session to agree specific resolutions. What we hoped we had accomplished was an exchange of perspectives about the way the family and its stresses and difficulties looked. The experience of working on a particular problem develops an expertise of great value but it is often at the price of narrowing the field of vision. Leisurely contact between the possessors of different varieties of expertise is rarely possible: where it happens both information and stimulus can set minds re-thinking practise. This was what we wanted to do and we agreed that an attempt should be made to spread to a wider public audience an interchange of fact and concept within what had had of necessity to be a small circle.

The essential needs that permeated the discussion were, indeed, for the spread of information and for true co-operation born of mutual respect and trust between those whose work deeply affects the success or failure of family life. Health, housing, education, terms of employment, wages, taxes and benefits, all of which depend heavily on policy decisions by governments were represented. The importance of the legal aspects of child and parent rights is recognised. The case for non-intervention by the State into family life was strongly made by stressing the failures of intervention in practice and the illogicalities of its theoretical basis. Unfortunately in the end some families like some people do require protection against themselves. Ethics achieve an honourable mention but not religion or spiritual health. The family members should help by identifying their own problems, sharing in the knowledge that is available about family life and its importance to the healthy development of children, and should play their part in the policy-making process. Feedback about the effectiveness of policies was vital.

Sue Dowling's 'bottom-up' approach was welcomed. The realisation of community begins as a local affair, interested parties coming together for the common good. Seen from the bottom, more money was needed to reinforce the family's ability to discharge its responsibility, most help going to those most in need. The status of child rearing must be enhanced since so much of the future depends upon its success. Clifton Robinson, on behalf of ethnic minorities, wanted a parity of esteem, a fairer distribution of resources and a wider educational process. Ethnic variety should be treasured rather than distrusted. At least for the present, minority groups should enjoy favourable positive discrimination. As regards housing, Valerie Karn showed how prejudice, inflexibility and failure to consider different cultural needs disadvantaged allocation to minority groups who were perceived as 'atypical'.

Many of those who discuss social problems tend to have high hopes of education and in this the symposium proved no exception. The school curriculum should be reviewed. Human development should be a compulsory subject, a balance being struck between instruction, the absorption of knowledge, and personal development with preparation for socialising in the wider community and the taking on of adult responsibilities. A shared basic training should help to develop co-operative attitudes between the various workers who have responsibility in family social welfare. The legal profession needs a better understanding of child development and of the effects on the children of broken family life which should be more closely observed and studied. For the sake of the children, even without a Child's Bill of Rights, such knowledge might lead to more energetic efforts at reconciliation.

The discussants' instructions warned them not to advocate increased spending but rather to suggest what changes could be made within present financial limits. Changes would, therefore, have to come from new attitudes and agreements about priorities. Adequate child benefit and adequate family income must be accepted by society as basic necessities for the growth and development of children, which means a thorough review and reconstruction of the whole apparatus of tax and benefit.

The moral of all this seems to be that as a society we need to become more concerned about the stresses placed upon the adults who have responsibility for caring for dependent children. These are obviously and undeniably the citizens of the future who will, in their turn, care for the ensuing generation, and this remains true however we define the family and whatever we feel about its structure. From the child's point of view there is little doubt about what the family has to do, about its functions in providing love, acceptance, security and a degree of discipline as well as satisfying physical needs. Assisting children to grow into responsible citizens and well-motivated parents in their turn is a function that parents share with school. However, a satisfying environment is a pre-requisite for self-discipline. Later, for the adolescent, the tension has to be resolved between his acceptance of some control and discipline within the family and his overpowering wish to be free. Encouragement and opportunity for the over 16s should replace the present critical trend towards rejection and punishment.

The will to improve on present arrangements can only start at the local level. Feeling and opinion must change. The theme was constantly repeated that the status of caring for children by their families must be raised. As to methods, District Health Authorities might appoint someone to be responsible for matters that concern children and their families. At the national level, it will be for academics to think out in larger terms what society as a whole can do to foster this process.

The idea of a Minister for the Family was thought to be impractical since so many Departments of State were involved. The idea of a Ministry was not even discussed. More favourably viewed were a Commissioner for Child Welfare with an advisory panel and the recognition that Family Impact Statements should accompany all Parliamentary Bills. An Ombudsman could be effective but only if he had the power to initiate discussions.

We must acknowledge the fact of deprivation and the serious effects that it has on dependent children whose parents are trying against odds to give them proper care. How much more difficult is it for those parents who begin their parenthood disadvantaged by their own bad experiences in earlier life and rendered through a distrust of authority inaccessible to outside help. There must be a sincere commitment to tackle deprivation and to limit its effects.

Unfortunately, the solutions to most of the environmental problems have become not so much political as party political. Ideas are more easily cherished than people. It is more attractive to embrace a political ideology than the members of a deprived family struggling for existence. A first step is to give priority to the family.

On the Bill Relating to a Children's Ombudsman in Norway*

INTRODUCTION

In February 1981 the Norwegian Storting adopted an Act on a Children's Ombudsman. In the Bill containing the proposal for the new act, the Government outlined the following background and reason for the Bill:

Children are an important as well as a weak and vulnerable social group. Good intentions, plans and regulations are not enough to safeguard the interests and needs of children. What we have learned from the UN Children's Year is not least an affirmation of that. The wishes and requirements of children have a fairly low degree of penetration. When confronted with groups of strong organizations and spokesmen, children often lose out when important decisions are taken, particularly when children's and adults' interests clash.

The Ministry's Bill for the establishment of the post of a Children's Ombudsman is in the main based on the views expressed in the Report of the Committee dealing with legislation relating to children (NOU 1977:35, The Act Relating to Children and Parents).

THE OMBUDSMAN'S TASKS

The Ombudsman will not have the final authority, but will initially act as an independent body looking after the interests of children.

The Ombudsman's duty is to further children's interests in relation to the authorities and private individuals and institutions, and to follow the development of the quality of childhood.

The Ombudsman is to ensure that the rules and regulations in force for the benefit of children are obeyed in practice. The Ombudsman may also suggest new regulations. As a permanent hearings instance, and on his own initiative, the Ombudsman may assess the effects of various reports and plans on the quality of childhood.

---

*This paper comes through the courtesy of Judge Helge Rostad of the Supreme Court of Oslo.

The Ombudsman shall also make sure that the authorities provide satisfactory information on the rights and needs of children. Everyone shall be entitled to turn
to the Ombudsman — children, individual adults, organizations, public bodies etc.

The Ombudsman will not relieve the public administration of its responsibility to
safeguard the rights and interests of children. The Ombudsman may bring pressure
to bear in order to get that responsibility attended to more efficiently.

THE CHILDREN'S OMBUDSMAN IS NOT A SINGLE EVENT

New measures are under preparation for the improvement of children's position in
a number of matters. An Act Relating to Children and Parents has recently been
adopted. (See Proposition to Odelsting No. 62, 1979/80). The Ministry of Social
Affairs is working to strengthen the Juvenile Welfare Boards etc. and counter
cruelty to and neglect of children.

A new Bill on Urban and Regional Planning will contain provisions for better
protection of children's interests in all planning and development. During the
Children's Year, the work of finding accident spots along roads they used on the
way to school included schoolchildren throughout the country and the material is
being used in traffic safety work throughout the country. Municipalities preparing
plans to improve the quality of childhood are now given State grants.

A report will be made on the quality and working environment of schools. The
Ministry of Consumer Affairs and Government Administration is following up the
Report to the Storting on the Quality of Childhood. This implies co-operation with
those municipalities interested in developing new measures for children and in
ensuring that children's needs and interests are given more attention in the munic:
pality's planning and other activities.

The Norwegian Cultural Council has set up a separate sub-committee for cultural
questions concerning children and is planning to publish a journal for children.
The Consumer Council has paid special attention to 'children in their capacity as
consumers'.

The establishment of the Children's Ombudsman is only one of several reforms intended to improve the quality of the childhood in our society.

WHY DO WE NEED AN OMBUDSMAN FOR CHILDREN?

In the Bill, the Ministry gave the following reasons for the need for a Children
Ombudsman:

Children cannot safeguard their own interests by taking part in political activities, through professional bodies etc. Children, moreover, lack the means of
assessing plans and decisions available to adults and cannot foresee how things wi
affect them.

Professional and industrial bodies play an important part in decision-making in
our society and are frequently consulted in advance. Proposals are often amended
so as to become acceptable to those who have been consulted. Children as a rule
lack such means of influencing events.

Children's requirements often conflict with other social considerations. In
urban planning matters, for instance, children's need for playgrounds may clash
with the need for a site for building purposes. When the authorities make their
decisions, the well-organized demands of the developers reach the decision-makers
while children's need to play is ignored.

Children are also in a much weaker position in securing their legal rights, or making formal protests against plans made, compared with adults.

Children's inability to use political means to attain their goals deprives them of a method of changing their factual and legal position if that position does not protect their interests adequately. Children without the vote cannot react by helping to replace a party or an individual candidate.

Many parents have made a major effort to improve the quality of childhood. Among other things they have campaigned to preserve children's playgrounds, to make roads used by children on their way to school safer, to provide more kindergartens and better schools. But parents also lack unifying and effective organizations with the main task of formulating demands for a more child and family oriented policy on the part of the authorities.

The public bodies looking after children's interests are generally weak and do not usually have the legal authority to intervene against plans or decisions conflicting with the interests of children. Despite some strengthening of the position of children, the Ministry considered it important to intensify the efforts of the Administration on children's affairs.

The Ministry found a definite need for a strong independent body with the duty of safeguarding children's social interests in the wider sense, both in relation to the authorities and to private individuals and institutions.

The Ministry came to the conclusion that a Children's Ombudsman would be the most effective solution. An Ombudsman will have greater authority and penetration than a council or a committee. The Ombudsman will also have far greater opportunity to follow through the plans and reports prepared by the authorities and by private and public institutions. An Ombudsman will be able to react far more quickly than a council or a committee which will only have a limited number of meetings during the year.

The Ministry, furthermore, considered it imperative that the Children's Ombudsman will be a visible institution for children and others requiring the Ombudsman's help.

NOT ONLY THE CHILDREN HAVE THEIR OMBUDSMAN

Over the last few years a number of underprivileged groups have obtained better legal protection and have improved their situation through the establishment of various Ombudsman posts and councils. 'The man in the street' now has the Civil Ombudsman's protection against arbitrariness in public administration. Equal rights are now being protected by the Equal Opportunities Commissioner and the Equal Opportunities Council. The consumers' interests are being looked after by the Consumer Council and the Consumer Ombudsman. However, all along, these groups have had the opportunity to further their interests politically and through the legal machinery, in addition to the protection they have had through the respective Ombudsman offices. Children have none of this.

THE OMBUDSMAN'S COUNCIL

A council will be set up in affiliation with the Ombudsman's office. The Council will assist the Ombudsman in his work, by discussing the more fundamental aspects of his activities.

The Ombudsman will also be able to draw on the expertise of the various Council members outside Council meetings.

THE OMBUDSMAN'S SECRETARIAT

A small secretariat to assist the Ombudsman will be established, consisting of a Deputy Ombudsman, one officer and a clerk, with an office in Oslo.

The establishment of the Children's Ombudsman is scheduled to take place on 11 August 1981.

BILL RELATING TO A CHILDREN'S OMBUDSMAN

1   (Object)

The object of this Act is to help further the interests of children in society.

2   (Children's Ombudsman)

The King shall appoint a Children's Ombudsman for a four-year term of office.

The King shall appoint a Council to act as an advisory body for the Children's Ombudsman.

3   (The Duties of the Ombudsman)

It shall be the duty of the Ombudsman to further the interests of children in relation to the public and private authorities and to follow developments in respect of the quality of the childhood.

In particular the Ombudsman shall

a) of his own accord or as a hearings instance safeguard children's connection with planning and reporting in all fields;

b) make sure that the laws protecting children's interests are obeyed;

c) suggest measures to strengthen the legal protection of children;

d) propose measures to solve or prevent conflicts between children and society;

e) make sure that sufficient information is given to public and private authorities about children's rights and the measures they require.

The Ombudsman may work on his own initiative or at the request of others. The Children's Ombudsman decides himself whether a communication is sufficiently important to deal with.

4   (Access to Institutions and the Obligation to Give Information, etc.)

The Ombudsman shall have free access to all public and private institutions for children.

The Authorities and public and private institutions for children shall, irrespective of any pledge of secrecy, give the Ombudsman the information required to carry out the Ombudsman's task pursuant to this Act. Information required to execute the Ombudsman's duties under Section 3, second sub-section, litra b, may, irrespective of any pledge of secrecy, also be demanded from others. If information is demanded under this sub-section, the submission of records and other documents may be required.

The provisions of Section 204 (1) and Sections 205-209 of The Civil Disputes Act similarly apply to the Ombudsman's right to demand information. Any dispute arising from the application of these provisions is brought before the County or City Courts, who will decide on the matter.

5 (Statements of the Ombudsman)

The Ombudsman is entitled to make statements on matters within his field. It is the Ombudsman who decides to whom his statements are to be addressed.

6 (Instructions for the Ombudsman and the Council)

The King lays down the general instructions on the organizational pattern and the procedural policies of the Ombudsman and the Council. Otherwise, the Ombudsman and the Council shall perform their duties independently.

7 (Entry into Force, etc.)

This Act also applies to Svalbard.

This Act enters into force from the time fixed by the King.

References

Agar, M. (1980). *The Professional Stranger*. Academic Press, N.Y.

Ahrons, C. (1981). The binuclear family: an emerging lifestyle for post divorce families. In W. Dumon & C. de Paepe (Eds.), *XIX International Seminar on Divorce and Re-marriage*.

Appleton, P. (1980). Growing up with Goldstein, Freud and Solnit. *Texas Law Review*, 58:1343.

Ashley, P. (1983). *Money, Deprivation and the Poor*. Heinemann, London.

Baird, Sir D. (1980). Environment and reproduction. *British Journal of Obstetrics and Gynaecology*, 87:1057-67.

Balint, M. (1957). *The Doctor, His Patient and His Illness*. International Universities Press, N.Y.

Bandman, E. L. and Bandman, B. (1978). (Eds.), *Bioethics and Human Rights*. Little Brown, Boston, Mass.

Banting, K. (1979). *Poverty, Politics and Policy*. Macmillan, London.

Batley, R. (1982). The politics of administrative allocation. In R. Forrest, J. Henderson and P. Williams (Eds.), *Urban Political Economy and Social Theory*. Gower Press, Aldershot.

Benson, J. K. (1977). Orgnisations: a dialectical view. *Administrative Science Quarterly*, 22:1-22.

Berger, P. and Luckmann, T. (1967). *The Social Construction of Reality*. Doubleday, N.Y.

Berthoud, R. (1983). Who suffers social disadvantage? In M. Brown (Ed.), *Some Structural Factors in Deprivation*. Heinemann, London.

Beveridge, Sir W. (1942). *Social Insurance and Allied Services*. Cmnd 6404. HMSO, London. Para. 108.

Blaxter, M. (1981). *The Health of Children: a Review of Research on the Place of Health in Cycles of Disadvantage*. Heinemann, London.

Blumberg, A. (1969). The practice of law as a confidence game. In V. Aubert (Ed.) *Sociology of Law*. Penguin, Harmondsworth.

Bone, M. (1977). *Pre-school Children and the Need for Day-care*. HMSO, SS 1031, London.

Bourne, R. and Newberger, E. (1979). *Critical Perspectives on Child Abuse*. Lexington Books, Lexington, Ma.

Bradley, M. (1981). *Co-ordination of Services for Children Under Five*. S. Katherine's College, Liverpool.

Bradshaw, J. (1980a). *Equity and Family Incomes*. Occasional paper no. 5. Study Commission on the Family, London.

Bradshaw, J. (1980). Child benefits, Is CPAG policy right? *Poverty*, 45.

Bradshaw, J. and Piauchaud, D. (1980). *Child Support in the European Community*. Bedford Square Press, London.

Briault, E. and Smith, R. (1980). Falling Rolls in Secondary Schools. NFER, Windsor, p. 52.

Brown, G. W., Ehrolchain, M. N. and Harris, T. (1975). Social class and psychiatric disturbance among women in an urban population. *Sociology*, 9:225-254.

Brown, G. W. and Harris, T. (1978). *Social Origins of Depression*. Tavistock Publications, London.

Brown, M. (1980). The family and social policy. T. G. Barritt (Ed.) *Family Life*. Papers from a National Children's Home Conference 24 Oct. 1978. Cited in P. Moss, and D. Sharpe (1980) cit. p.152.

Brown, M. (1983). (Ed.). *Some Structural Factors in Deprivation*. Heinemann, London.

Brown, M. and Madge, N. (1982). *Despite the Welfare State*: a Report on the SSRC/DHSS Programme of Research into Transmitted Deprivation. Heinemann, London.

Bruce, N. (1980). *Teamwork for Preventive Care*. Research Studies Press, Wiley, Chichester.

Bullowa, M. (1979). (Ed.) *Before Speech: The Beginning of Inter-personal Communication*. Cambridge U.P.

Burnell, I. and Wadsworth, J. (1981). Personal communication.

Butler, N., Dowling, S. and Osborn, A. (1982). *Britain's Five Year Olds*. Routledge & Kegan Paul, London.

Butler, N., Gill, R., Pomeroy, D. and Fewtrell, J. (1978). *Handicapped Children — their Homes and Life Styles*. Dept. of Child Health, U. of Bristol.

Callaghan, J. (1978). Speech at Women's Labour Conference, Southport, May 14.

Cartwright, A. (1979). *The Dignity of Labour?* Tavistock Publications, London.

Challis, L. (1980). *The Great Under Fives Muddle: Options for Day Care Policy* (ISBN 86197 026 8). University of Bath.

Chamberlain, R. and Chamberlain, G. (1975). (Eds.) *British Births*. Heinemann, London.

Cicourel, A. (1968). *The Social Organization of Juvenile Justice*. Wiley, N.Y.

Clarke, A. M. and Clarke, A. C. B. (1976). *Early Experience: Myth and Evidence*. Open Books, Shepton Mallet, Som.

Coffield, F., Robinson, P. and Sarsby, J. (1981). *A Cycle of Deprivation? A Case Study of Four Families*. Heinemann, London.

Cohn, A., and Miller, M. K. (1977). Evaluating new modes of treatment for child abusers and neglectors. *Child Abuse and Neglect*, 1:453.

Commonwealth Health Ministers. (1981). *Health and the Family*. 1980 Conference, Commonwealth Secretariat.

Community Relations Commission. (1978). Evidence to the Royal Commission on the Distribution of Income and Wealth. Lower Incomes Report No. 6. Cmnd 7175. H.M.S.O., London. p. 94.

Cooke, R. (1980). Head start program 1965. *Courrier*, 30:337.

Coote, A. and Hewitt, P. (1980). The stance of Britain's major parties and interest groups. In P. Moss & N. Fonda (Eds.). *Work and the Family*. Temple Smith, London.

Court, S. D. M. (1976). *Fit for the Future*. Cmnd 6684. H.M.S.O., London.

Coussin, J. and Coote, A. (1981). *Families in the Firing Line*. C.P.A.G., London.

C.P.R.S. (1975). *A Joint Framework for Social Policy*. Central Policy Review Staff. H.M.S.O., London.

C.P.R.S. (1978). *Services for Young Children with Working Mothers*. Central Policy Review Staff. H.M.S.O., London.

C.P.R.S. (1980). *People and Their Families*. Central Policy Review Staff. H.M.S.O., London.

Craven, E., Rimmer, L. and Wicks, M. (1982). *Family Issues and Public Policy*. Study Commission on the Family, London.

C.S.O. (1979). *Social Trends*, Central Statistical Office, 10, Table 6.10 (ref. to 1977) & *Hansard*, written answers, 12 Dec. 1979.

Curtis, S. (1980). A client-based approach for the prediction of need for the pre-
school services among children living in the community. *Personal Social
Services Research Unit*, University of Kent.
Dalton, M. (1959). *Men Who Manage*. Wiley, N.Y.
Daniel, W. W. (1980). *Maternity Rights*. p. 51., London.
Davidson, K. and Mocroft, I. (1981). *Volunteers in Primary Health Care*. The
Volunteer Centre, Berkhamsted.
Davie, R., Butler, N. and Goldstein, H. (1972). *From Birth to Seven*. N.C.B.,
Longman, London.
D.E.S. (1978a). *Progress in Education:* A report on recent initiatives. H.M.S.O.,
London.
D.E.S. (1978b). *Primary Education in England:* a survey by H.M. Inspectors of
Schools. H.M.S.O., London.
D.E.S. (1981). *Falling Rolls and Surplus Places*. Circular 81/no 577.
D.E.S./D.H.S.S. (1976 & 1978). *Co-ordination of Services for the Under Fives*.
LASSL (76) 5/S21/47/05 & LASSL (78) 1/HN (78) 5/S47/24/d3.
Deutsch, H. (1945). *The Psychology of Women* Vol. 2. Grune & Stratton, N.Y.
D.H.S.S. (1976a). *Prevention and Health: Everybody's Business*. A Re-assessment of
Public & Personal Health. H.M.S.O. London.
D.H.S.S. (1976b). *Joint Care Planning: Health & Local Authorities*. H.C. (76)
18/LAC (76) 6.
D.H.S.S. (1976c). *Priorities for Health and Personal Social Services*. H.M.S.O.,
London.
D.H.S.S. (1978). *Collaboration in Community Care:* A discussion document. H.M.S.O.,
London.
D.H.S.S. (1981a). *Social Security Statistics 1980*. H.M.S.O., London. Table 34. 89.
D.H.S.S. (1981b). *The Primary Health Care Team*. Joint working group of the Standing
Medical Advisory Committee & the Standing Nursing & Midwifery Advisory
Committee. H.M.S.O., London.
D.H.S.S. (1981c). *Care in Action*. H.M.S.O., London.
Dickens, B. (1979). *Medico-Legal Aspects of Family Law*. Butterworth, Sevenoaks,
Kent. p. 105.
Dobash, R. E. and Dobash, R. (1980). *Violence against Wives*. Open Books, London.
Dobbing, J. and Smart, J. L. (1973). Early undernutrition, brain development and
behaviour. In S. A. Barnett (Ed.) *Ethology and Development*. Clinics in
Developmental Medicine No. 47. Heinemann, London. Chapter 2, pp. 16-36.
Donajgrodzki, A. P. (1977). (Ed.) *Social Control in Nineteenth Century Britain*.
Croom Helm, London.
Donzelot, J. (1979). *The Policing of Families*. Random House, N.Y.
Douglas, J. D. (1970). *Deviance and Respectability*. Basic Books, N.Y.
Douglas, J. W. B. (1975). Early hospital admissions and later disturbances of
behaviour and learning. *Developmental Medicine and Child Neurology*, 17:456-480.
Douglas, J. W. B. and Blomfield, J. M. (1958). *Children Under Five*. George Allen
& Unwin, London.
Dowling, S. (1982). *Reaching the Consumer in the Antenatal and Pre-school Child
Health Services*. Report of a D.H.S.S./C.P.A.G. Study. C.P.A.G., London.
Duff, R. S. and Campbell, A. G. (1973). Moral and ethical dilemmas in the special
care nursery. *New England Journal of Medicine*, 289:890-4.
Dunnell, K. (1979a). *Family Formation 1976*. H.M.S.O./O.P.C.S. (SS1080). London,
p. 36.
Dunnell, K. (1979b). Ibid., p. 17.
Dworkin, R. (1977a). *Taking Rights Seriously*. Duckworth, London.
Dworkin, R. (1977b). Ibid., p. 97.
Dworkin, R. (1977c). Ibid., p. 104.
Dworkin, R. (1977d). Ibid., p. 117.
Dworkin, R. (1977e). Ibid., p. 124.
Elmer, E. (1977). *Fragile Families, Troubled Children: the Aftermath of Infant
Trauma*. U. of Pittsburgh Press.

194   References

Engels, F. (1940). *The Origin of the Family, Private Property and the State*. Lawrence & Wishart, London. English translation of ed. 4, Moscow 1934.

Essen, J. and Wedge, P. (1982). *Continuities in Childhood Disadvantage*. Heineman, London.

European Commission. (1977). *The Perception of Poverty in Europe*. European Commission.

Faragher, A. (1981). The need for protection from violence for 'battered wives'. *D.H.S.S. Seminar on Violence in the Family*. U. of Kent, unpublished.

Farrington, D. P. (1977). The effects of public labelling. *British Journal of Criminology*, 17:112.

Ferri, E. (1976a). *Growing Up in a One Parent Family*. N.F.E.R., Windsor. p. 33-34.

Ferri, E. (1976b). Ibid., p. 36-37.

Ferri, E., Birchall, D., Gingell, V. and Gipps, C. (1981). *Combined Nursery Centres*. National Children's Bureau, London.

Field, F. (1980). *Fair Shares for Families: the Need for a Family Impact Statement*. Study Commission on the family, London.

Finer, Sir M. (1974). *Report of the Committee on One-Parent Families*. Cmnd 5629. H.M.S.O., London.

Fogelman, E. (1976). *Britain's Sixteen Year olds*. National Children's Bureau, London. Table 7.1.

Franklin, A. W. (1982). Mother-infant interaction. In J. Bonner (Ed.). *Recent Advances in Obstetrics and Gynaecology*. Churchill Livingstone, Edinburgh, London & N.Y.

Freeman, M.D.A. (1973). Standards of adjudication, judicial law-making and prospective over-ruling. *Current Legal Problems*, 26:166, 178-9.

Freeman, M. D. A. (1976). *The Children Act 1975*. Sweet & Maxwell, London.

Freeman, M. D. A. (1977). What do we know of the causes to child abuse? *Family Law*, 7:182.

Freeman, M. D. A. (1979a). Child Welfare: law and control. In M. Partington and J. Jowell (Eds.). *Welfare Law and Policy*. Frances Pinter, London. p. 223.

Freeman, M. D. A. (1979b). *Violence in the Home — A Socio-Legal Study*. Saxon House, Aldershot.

Freeman, M. D. A. (1980). Removing babies at birth: a questionable practice. *Family Law*, 10:131.

Freeman, M. D. A. (1981). The state, law and the family in the eighties. *Kingston Law Review*, 11:129.

Freidson, E. (1967). Disability as social deviance. *Social Problems*, 14:493-500.

Fry, A. (1981). Slipshod use of NAI Registers by Councils. *Community Care*, no.373:2.

Fuller, R. and Stevenson, O. (1983). *Policies, Programmes and Disadvantage*. Heinemann, London.

Garcia, J. (in press). Women's views of antenatal care. In M. Enkin and I. Chalmers (Eds.). *Effectiveness & Efficiency in Antenatal Care*. Spastics International Medical Publications. Heinemann, London.

Geach, H. (1980). Child abuse registers — a major threat to civil liberties. In Morris *et al.* (1980a).

Geach, H. (1981). Case Conferences — time for a change. *Community care*, no.375: 16-17.

Gelles, R. (1973). Child abuse as psycho-pathology: a sociological critique and reformulation. *American Journal of Orthopsychiatry*, 43:611.

Ghodsian, M. and Essen, J. (1980). The children of immigrants: social and home circumstances. *New Community*, 3 no.3.

Giarretto, H. (1976). Humanistic treatment of father-daughter incest. In R. Helfer and C. H. Kempe (Eds.). *Child Abuse and Neglect*. Ballinger, Cambridge, Mass. pp. 143-158.

Gil, D. (1975). Unraveling child abuse. *American Journal of Orthopsychiatry*, 45: 346, 352.

Gill, O. (1977). *Luke Street, Housing Policy, Conflict and the Creation of a Delinquent Area*. Macmillan, London. p. 28-29.

Gluckman, M. (1966). *Essays on the Ritual of Social Relations*. U. of Manchester Press, Manchester.

Gold, M. (1970). *Delinquent Behaviour in an American City*. Brooks, Cole, Monterey, Ca.

Gold, M. and Williams, K. (1969). National study of aftermath of apprehension. *Prospectus — a Journal of Law Reform*, 3:3.

Goldberg, E. M. (1978). *Social Work since Seebohm*. National Institute for Social Work, London.

Goldstein, J. (1977). Medical care for the child at risk. *Yale Law Journal*, 86:645.

Goldstein, J., Freud, A. and Solnit, A. J. (1979a). *Beyond the Best Interests of the Child*. Revised ed., Free Press, N.Y.

Goldstein, J., Freud, A. and Solnit, A. J. (1979b). Ibid., p. 17-20.

Goldstein, J., Freud, A. and Solnit, A. J. (1979d). Ibid., p. 38.

Goldstein, J., Freud, A. and Solnit, A. J. (1979c). *Before the Best Interests of the Child*. Free Press, N.Y.

Goldthorpe, J. H. (1980). *Social Mobility and Class Structure in Modern Britain*. Clarendon Press, Oxford.

Goody, E. N. and Groothues, C. M. (1977). The quest for education: West Africans in London. In J. L. Watson (Ed.). *Between Two Cultures*. Blackwell, Oxford.

Graham, P. J. (1977). *Epidemiological Approaches in Child Psychiatry*. Academic Press, London.

Graveson, R. and Crane, F. R. (1957). (Eds.). *A Century of Family Law 1857-1957*. Sweet & Maxwell, London.

Hadley, R. and McGrath, M. (1980). *Going Local*. Neighbourhood Social Services. N.C.V.O., Bedford Square Press, London.

Hagberg, B., Hagberg, G., Lewerth, A. and Lindberg, U. (1981). Mild mental retardation in Swedish School children. *Acta Paediatrica Scandinavica*, 70:445-452.

Haggerty, R. J. (1980). Life stress, illness and social supports. *Developmental Medicine & Child Neurology*, 22:391.

Hall, F. and Pawlby, S. J. (1981). Continuity and discontinuity in the behaviour of British working-class mothers and their first-born children. *International Journal of Behavioural Development*, 4:13-36.

Hall, F., Pawlby, S. J. and Wolkind, S. N. (1979). Early life experiences and later mothering behaviour: a study of mothers and their 20-week old babies. In D. Schaffer and J. Dunn. *The First Year of Life*. Wiley, London.

Hallett, C. and Stevenson, O. (1980). *Child Abuse, Aspects of Interprofessional Co-operation*. George Allen & Unwin, London.

Halsey, A. H. and Heath, A. F. (1980). *Origins and Destinations*. Clarendon Press, Oxford.

Hamson, J.(1981)Abuse registers scarcely used. *Community Care*, no. 352:2.

Hart, H. L. A. (1968). *Punishment and Responsibility*. Oxford U. Press.

Hart, Judith. (1965). Paper to *the Association of Social Workers* (Scottish group), November 28.

Hastings, J. (1909) (Ed.) *Dictionary of the Bible*. T. & T. Clark, Edinburgh.

Hatch, S. (1980). *Outside the State, Voluntary Organizations in Three English Towns*. Croom Helm, London.

Helfer, R. and Kempe, C. H. (1976). *Child Abuse and Neglect*. Ballinger, Cambridge, Mass.

Hersov, L. and Berg, I. (1980). (Eds.) *Out of School: Modern Perspectives in Truancy and School Refusal*. Wiley, Chichester.

Heyderbrand, W. (1977). Organisational contradictions in public bureaucracies. *Sociological Quarterly*, 18:1.

H.M.S.O. (1980). *National Dwelling and Housing Survey 1978*. H.M.S.O. London.

H.M.S.O. (1981). *West Indian Children in Schools*. Cmnd 8273. H.M.S.O. London.

Hoffman, L. W. (1974). Effects of maternal employment on the child — a review of the research. *Developmental Psychology*, 10:204-228.

Hoffman, L. W. (1979). Maternal employment 1979. *American Psychologist*, 34:849-865.

Holder, A. R. (1977). *Legal Issues in Pediatrics and Adolescent Medicine*. Wiley, Chichester. p. 114.

Holman, R. (1973). *Trading in Children*. Routledge & Kegan Paul, London.

Home Office. (1979). *Marriage Matters: a consultative document by the Working Party on Marriage Guidance*. H.M.S.O., London.

Hotaling, G. T. and Straus, M. A. (1980). (Eds.). *The Social Causes of Husband-wife Violence*. U. of Minnesota, Minneapolis.

Hughes, M., Mayall, B., Moss, P., Perry, J., Petrie, P. and Pinkerton, G. (1980). *Nurseries Now*. Penguin Books, Harmondsworth.

Hunter, D. J. (1980). *Coping with Uncertainty, Policy and Politics in the National Health Service*. Research Studies Press, Wiley, Chichester.

Illsley, R. (1955). Social class selection and class differences in relation to stillbirths and infant deaths. *British medical Journal*, 2:1520-1524.

Ineichen, B. (1983). Council housing and disadvantage: the allocation of council housing and its relation to social stratification. In M. Brown. (1983).

Inland Revenue. (1981). *The Taxation of Husband and Wife*. Cmnd 8093. H.M.S.O., London.

Jackson, S. (1979). *Innovation and Good Practice in Pre-school Provision: A Feasibility Study*. S.S.R.C., London.

Jay, P. (1979). *Report to the Committee of Enquiry into Mental Handicap and nursing care*. Cmnd 7468. H.M.S.O., London.

Jenkin, P. (1978). Speech to Conservative Political Centre one-day Conference on the 'Future of Welfare in Britain' 28 January.

Jobling, M. (1973). Children of working mothers. *Highlight no.2*. N.C.B., London.

Jordan, B. (1975). 'Is a client a fellow citizen?' *Social Work Today*, 6:471-475.

Jordan, B. (1976). *Freedom and the Welfare State*. Routledge & Kegan Paul, London.

Kagan, J., Kearsley, R. and Zelazo, P. (1978). *Infancy: its Place in Human Development*. Harvard U.P.

Kamerman, S. (1980). Managing work and family life: a comparative policy overview. In P. Moss & N. Fonda (Eds.). *Work and Family*. Temple Smith, London.

Kamerman, S. B. and Kahn, A. J. (1978). *Family Policy — Government and Families in Fourteen Countries*. Columbia U.P., N.Y.

Kempe, R. S. and Kempe, C. H. (1978). *Child Abuse*. Fontana/Open Books, London.

Kennedy, I. (1976). The Karen Quinlan case: problems and proposals. *Journal of medical Ethics*, 2:3.

Kennedy, I. (1981a). *Unmasking Medicine*. Allen & Unwin, London.

Kennedy, I. (1981b). Where doctors and the law can meet. *The Times*, September 8.

Khan, V. S. (1979). (Ed.). *Minority Families in Britain*. Macmillan, London.

Kilbrandon, Lord. (1964). *Report on Children and Young Persons in Scotland*. Cmnd 2306. H.M.S.O., Edinburgh.

King, E. J. (1966). *Education and Social Change*. Pergamon, Oxford & London.

Klein, M. W. (1974). Labeling, deterrence and recidivism: a study of police dispositions of juvenile offenders. *Social Problems*, 22:292.

Kohl, M. (1978). Karen Quinlan: human rights and wrongful killing. In E. L. Bandman and B. Brandman. (1978). p. 121.

Kolvin, I., Miller, F. J. W., Garside, R. F. and Theron, S. (1981). Three generational study of the transmission of deprivation. Interim Report to the *DHSS/SSRC Joint Working Party on Transmitted Deprivation*.

Koocher, G. D. (1976). *Children's Rights and the Mental Health Professions*. Wiley, N.Y.

Krause, H. D. (1977). *Family Law in a Nutshell*. West Pub., St. Paul Minn. p. 436.

Kushlick, A. (1968). Social problems of mental subnormality. In E. Miller (Ed.). *Foundations of Child Psychiatry*. Pergamon, Oxford & London.

Lasch, C. (1977). *Haven in a Heartless World*. Basic Books, N.Y.

Lasch, C. (1980). Life in the therapeutic state. *New York Review of Books*, 27:24.

Lazar, F., Hubbel, V. R. *et al*. (1977). The persistence of pre-school effects. *National Collaborative Study*, (14853), Community Service Laboratory, Cornell U., Ithaca, N.Y.

Lambert, L. (1978). Living in one parent families: school leavers and their future. *Concern*, no.29, p. 26.

Lambert, L. and Streather, J. (1980). *Children in Changing Families*. N.C.B. Macmillan, London. p. 56.

Leat, D., Smolka, G. and Unell, J. (1981). *Voluntary and Statutory Collaboration*. N.C.V.O. London.

Lemert, E. (1976). Choice and change in the Juvenile Court. *British Journal of Law and Soc.*, 3:59-75.

Light, R. J. (1974). Abused and neglected children in America: a study of alternative policies. *Harvard Educational Review Report*, 43:556-598.

Lindley, R. M., Whitley, J. D. and Elias, D. P. (1981). Review of the economy and employment. *Manpower Research Group*. Warwick U.

Lister, R. (1981). *Social priorities in taxation*. C.P.A.G., London.

Lofland, J. (1969). *Deviance and Identity*. Prentice Hall, Hemel Hempstead, Herts. p. 150.

Loizos, P. (1978). Some Mediterranean examples. In J. P. Martin (Ed.). *Violence and the Family*, p. 183-196.

London Health Planning Consortium (1981). *Report of a Study Group on Primary Health Care in Inner London*. D.H.S.S., London.

Longford, Lord (1964). *Crime — A Challenge to us All*. Transport House, London.

Lynch, M. (1975). Family unit in a child's psychiatric hospital. *British medical Journal*, 2:127.

Lynch, M. (1976). Child abuse — the critical path. *Journal of Maternal and Child Health*, 1:26.

Lynch, M. and Ounsted, C. (1976). Residential therapy — a place of safety. In R. Helfer & C. H. Kempe. (1976). p. 206.

Lynch, M. and Roberts, J. (1977). Predicting child abuse: signs of bonding failure in a maternity hospital. *British medical Journal*, 1:624.

Madge, N. (1982). *Families at Risk*. Heinemann, London.

Martin, J. P. (1978). (Ed.). *Violence and the Family*. Wiley, Chichester.

Matza, D. (1967). The disreputable poor. In R. Bendix & S. M. Lipset (Eds.). *Class, Status and Power*. Routledge & Kegan Paul, London.

Mayall, B. and Petrie, P. (1977). *Mother, Minder and Child*. N.F.E.R., Slough.

Mayall, B. and Petrie, P. (In press). *Report on a study of day-care for children under 2*. Thomas Coram Research Unit, London.

Morgan, L. H. (1964). *Ancient Society*. Harvard U.P., Cambridge.

Moroney, R. M. (1976). *The Family and the State*. Longman, London.

Morris, A., Gillet, H., Geach, H. and Szwed, E. (1980a). *Justice for Children*. Macmillan, London.

Morris, A., Gillett, H., Geach, H. and Szwed, E. (1980b). Ibid., p. 112-113.

Mortimore, J. and Blackstone, T. (1982). *Disadvantage and Education*. Heinemann, London.

Moss, P. (1980). Parents at work. In P. Moss & N. Fondo (Eds.). *Work and the Family*, Temple Smith, London.

Moss, P. (In press). Community care of young children. In A. Walker (Ed.). *The Meaning and Development of Community Care*. Martin Robertson, Oxford.

Moss, P. and Sharpe, D. (1980). Family policy in Britain. In M. Brown & S. Baldwin (Eds.). *The Yearbook of Social Policy in Britain 1979*. Routledge & Kegan Paul, London. pp. 137-157.

Murie, A. (1982). *Housing, Inequality and Deprivation*. Heinemann, London.

McLennan, J. F. (1970). *Primitive Marriage: An Inquiry into the Origin of the Form of Capture in Marriage Ceremonies*. U. of Chicago Press.

National Council for one parent families (N.C.O.P.F.). (1980). *Annual Report 1979-80*, p. 14.

Newson, J. and Newson, E. (1963). *Patterns of Infant Care*. Allen & Unwin, London.

Newson, J. and Newson, E. (1968). *Four Years Old in an Urban Community*. Allen & Unwin, London.

Newson, J. and Newson, E. (1976). *Seven Years Old in the Home Environment*. Allen & Unwin, London.

FM - N

Niedhardt, F. (1978a). The Federal Republic of Germany. In S. B. Kamerman & A. J. Kahn. op. cit. pp. 217-238.

Niedhardt, F. (1978b). ibid. p. 225.

Niner, P. (1980). *Transfer Policies: A Case Study in Harlow*. Research Memorandum 79, Centre for Urban and Regional Studies, U. of Birmingham. p. 12.

Norton, A. and Rogers, S. (1977). *Collaboration Between Health Authorities and Local Authorities* Interim Report. Institute of local government studies, U. of Birmingham.

Olsen, K. and Olsen, M. (1967). Role expectations and perceptions for social workers in medical settings. *Social Work*, 12:70.

O.P.C.S. (1980a). *Marriage and Divorce Statistics 1978*. H.M.S.O., London. Table 3.1

O.P.C.S. (1980b) Loc. cit., Table 4.1.

O.P.C.S. (1980c). Loc. cit., Table 3.7. O.P.C.S., (1980d). Loc. cit., Table 4.1.

O.P.C.S. (1981a). *Population Trends 24*. H.M.S.O., London. Table 5.

O.P.C.S. (1981b). Monitor FM2 81/2, Divorces 1979.

Osborn, A. F. (1979). *Sources of Variation in the Uptake of Pre-School Provision*. Dept. of Child Health Research Unit, U. of Bristol.

Osborn, A. F. (1981). Under fives in schools in England and Wales. *Educational Research*, 23: no.2.

Outer Circle Policy Unit (1978). *A New Perspective on the National Health Service*. Outer Circle Policy Unit.

Owens, P. (1981). Ph. D. Dissertation, Cambridge.

Page, R. and Clark, G. A. (1977). (Ed.). *Who Cares?* National Children's Bureau, London.

Pahl, R. E. (1975). *Whose City?* Penguin, Harmondsworth.

Parker, J. and Dugmore, K. (1976). *Colour and the Allocation of GLC Housing*. Research Report 21, G.L.C., London.

Parker, S. (1981). The law, courts and police intervention in marital violence. D.H.S.S. Seminar on *Violence in the family*. U. of Kent. (Unpublished).

Pawlby, S. J. and Hall, F. (1979). Evidence from an observational study of transmitted deprivation among women from broken homes. *Child Abuse & Neglect*, 3:844-850.

Pearson, G. (1973). Social work as the privatised solution of public ills. *British Journal of Social Work*, 3:209.

Piachaud, D. (1980). *The Cost of a Child*. C.P.A.G., London.

Piachaud, D. (1981). *Children and Poverty*. C.P.A.G., London.

Plowden, Lady. (1967). *Children and Their Primary Schools*. A Report of the Central Advisory Council for Education. H.M.S.O., London. p. 37.

Polachek, S. W. (1975). Discontinuous labour force participation and its effect on women's market earnings. In C. B. Lloyd (Ed.). *Sex Discrimination and the Division of Labour*. Columbia U. Press, N.Y.

Postman, N. and Weingarten, C. (1969). *Teaching as a Subversive Activity*. Penguin Books, Harmondsworth.

Poulton, G. and Campbell, G. (1979). *Families with Young Children*. A Hampshire based study project. Departments of Education & Sociology & Social Administration, U. of Southampton.

P.P.A. (1980a). *Facts and Figures*. Pre-School Play Groups Association.

P.P.A. (1980b). *Play Groups in the Eighties*. Pre-school Play group, Scottish and Northern Ireland Pre-school Play groups.

Prendergast, S. and Prout, A. (1980). What will I do ...? Teenage girls and the construction of motherhood. *The Sociological Review*, N.S., 28:517-535.

Quinton, D. and Rutter, M. (1976). Early hospital admissions and later disturbances of behaviour: an attempted replication of Douglas's findings. *Developmental Medicine & Child Neurology*, 18:447-459.

Quinton, D. Rutter, M. and Rowlands, O. (1976). An evaluation of an interview assessment of marriage. *Psychological Medicine*, 6:577-586.

Ranson, S., Hinings, B. and Greenwood, R. (1980). The structuring of organisational structures. *Administrative Science Quarterly*, 25:1-17.

Reid, I. (1978). *Social Class Differences in Britain*. Open Books, Shepton Mallet. Som.

Richman, N. (1976). Depression in mothers of pre-school children. *Journal of Child Psychology & Psychiatry*, 17:75-78.

Richman, N. and Graham, P. J. (1971). A behavioural screening questionnaire for use with three-year-old children. Preliminary findings. *Journal of Child Psychology & Psychiatry*, 12:5-33.

Richman, N., Stevenson, J. E. and Graham, P. J. (1975). Prevalence of behaviour problems in three-year-old children: an epidemiological study in a London borough. *Journal of Child Psychology & Psychiatry*, 16:277-287.

Rimmer, L. (1981). *Families in Focus*. Study Commission on the family, London.

Robertson, J. D. (1975). Involuntary euthanasia of defective newborns. *Stanford Law Review*, 27:213, 263.

Rodgers, B. (1980). Strategy for change. In P. Moss & D. Sharpe (1980) loc. cit., p. 152.

Rodgers, R. (1981). *Smash and grab*. The Guardian, Sep. 22.

Rodman, H. (1973). Illegitimacy and the Carribean social structure. In I. Deutscher (Ed.) *What We Say/What We Do*. Scott, Foresman & Co., Glenview, Ill.

Rowbottom, R. and Hey, A. (1978). Collaboration between health and social services. In E. Jaques (Ed.). *Health Services*. Heinemann, London.

Ruddick, W. (1978a). Parents, children and medical decisions. In E. L. Bandman & B. Bandman (1978). q.v. p. 165.

Ruddick, W. (1978b). Ibid., p. 169.

Ruddick, W. (1978c). Ibid., p. 168.

Rutter, M. (1981). *Maternal Deprivation Re-assessed*. ed. 2. Penguin Books, Harmondsworth.

Rutter, M. and Quinton, D. (In press). *Childhood Experiences and Parenting Behaviour*. Heinemann, London.

Salaman, G. (1978). Towards a sociology of organisational structure. *Sociological Review*, 26:3.

Satyamurti, C. (1981). *Occupational Survival*. Blackwell, Oxford.

Schaffer, H. R. and Schaffer, E. B. (1968). *Child care and the family*. Occasional papers in Social Administration No.25. G. Bell & Sons, London.

Schatzman, L. and Strauss, A. (1973). *Field Research*. Prentice Hall, Englewood Cliffs.

Scheff, T. J. (1966). *Being Mentally Ill: A Sociological Theory*. Aldine Publishing Co., Hawthorne, N.Y.

Schorr, A. (1980). *'... thy father and thy mother'*. Dept. of Health and Human Services, Washington, D.C.

Schur, E. (1973). *Radical Non-Intervention: Rethinking the Delinquency Problem*. Prentice Hall, Hemel Hempstead, Herts.

Scott, R. A. (1969). *The Making of Blind Men*. Russell Sage Foundation, N.Y.

Seebohm, Lord (1968). *Report of the Committee on Local Authority and Allied Personal Social Services*. Cmnd 3703. H.M.S.O., London.

Skinner, A. and Castle, R. (1969). *78 Battered Children: A Retrospective Study*. N.S.P.C.C., London.

Smith, D. (1977). *Racial Disadvantage in Britain*. Penguin, Harmondsworth.

Smith, D. (1981). *Unemployment and Racial Minorities*. Policy Studies Institute, London.

Solnit, A. J. (1978). Child abuse: the problem. In J. Eekelaar & S. Katz (Eds.). *Family Violence*. Butterworth, Sevenoaks, Kent. pp. 243, 246.

Solnit, A. J. (1980). Too much reporting, too little service: roots and prevention of child abuse. In G. Gerbner, C. J. Ross and E. Zigler (Eds.). *Child Abuse, An Agenda for action*. O.U.P., N.Y. and Oxford. pp. 135-146.

Spence, J. C. (1946). *The Purpose of the Family*. The Convocation Lecture National Children's Home, London. p. 33.

Stevenson, O. and Parsloe, P. (1978). *Social Service Teams*. H.M.S.O., London.

Stockwell & Vauxhall Neighbourhood Council. (1979). *Mawbey Brough, A Health Centre for the Community?* Published by the Council, 157 South Lambeth Rd., London, S.W.8.

Sumner, L. W. (1981). *Abortion and Moral Theory*. Princeton U. Press.
Supplementary Benefits Commission. (1978). Evidence to the Royal Commission on the Distribution of Income & Wealth, Report No. 6. Lower Incomes. Cmnd 7175. H.M.S.O., London.
Supplementary Benefits Commission. (1980). *Annual Report for 1979*. Cmnd 8033. H.M.S.O., London.
Sutton, A. (1981). Science in Court. In M. King (Ed.) *Childhood, Welfare and Justice*. Batsford, London. pp. 45-104.
Szasz, T. (1977). The child as involuntary mental patient: the threat of child therapy to the child's dignity, privacy and self-esteem. *San Diego Law Review*, 14:1005.
Taylor, L., Lacey, R. and Bracken, D. (1980). *In Whose Best Interests?* Cobden Trust/Mind, London.
Taylor, T. (1980). *A new partnership for our schools*. H.M.S.O., London. p. 43.
Thatcher, M. (1977). Speech to Conservative Party Conference, Blackpool.
Thorpe, D. (1979). The making of a deliquent. *Community Care*, no. 261, p. 18-19.
Tizard, B. (1977). *Adoption: A Second Chance*. Open Books, Shepton Mallet, Som.
Tonge, W. L., Lunn, J. E., Greathead, M., McLaren, S. and Bosanko, C. (1982). Generations of 'problem families' in Sheffield. In N. Madge (Ed.) *Families at Risk*. Heinemann, London.
Townsend, P. (1979). *Poverty in the United Kingdom*. Penguin, Harmondsworth. p. 505.
Townsend, P. (1980). Social Planning and the Treasury. In N. Bosanquet & P. Townsend (Eds.). *Labour and Equality*. Heinemann, London.
Triseliotis, J. and Russell, J. (1983). *A Retrospective Study of Late Adoptions and of Children Growing Up in Residential Establishments*. Heinemann, London.
Tredinnick, A. and Fairburn, A. (1980). Left holding the baby. *Community Care*, no. 310:22-25.
U.S.H.P. (1979). *Rethinking Community Medicine*. A report of a study group. Unit for the Study of Health Policy Report.
Valentine, C. (1968). *Culture and Poverty*. U. of Chicago Press.
Wald, M. (1976). State intervention on behalf of 'neglected' children: a search for idealistic standards. In M. Rosenheim (Ed.). *Pursuing Justice for the Child*. U. of Chicago Press. pp. 246, 261.
Wald, M. (1980). Thinking about public policy toward abuse and neglect of children. *Michigan Law Review*, 78:645, 665-666.
Wall, W. D. (1975). *Constructive Education for Children*. Harrap, London.
Wallston, B. (1973). The effects of maternal employment on children. *Journal of Child Psychology & Psychiatry*, 14:81-83.
Watson, A. (1980a). Children, families and courts: Before the Best Interests of the Child and Parham v J.R. *Virginia Law Review*, 66:653.
Watson, A. (1980b). Ibid., p. 672.
Watson, A. (1980c). Ibid., p. 676.
Watson, J. L. (1977). *Between Two Cultures*. Blackwell, Oxford.
Webb, A. L. and Hobdell, M. (1980). Co-ordination and teamwork in the health and personal social services. In S. Lonsdale, A. Webb and T. L. Briggs (Eds.). *Teamwork in the Personal Health Services & Health Care*. Croom Helm, London.
Weber, M. (1954). *On Law in Economy and Society*. Harvard U. Press.
Westland, P. (1981). Day Care provision for the under fives. *Municipal Review*, no. 615 (June), p. 51.
White House Conference on Families. (1980). *Listening to America's Families*. Action for the 80s.
Wicks, M. (1981). Changing family patterns and deprivation in the inner city. Unpublished paper prepared for the *Inner Cities Research Seminar*, Sunningdale, April 1981.
Wicks, M. (1982). A family cause? Voluntary bodies, pressure groups and politics. British Family Research Committee. *Families in Britain*. Routledge & Kegan Paul, London.
Williams, P. (1974). (Ed.). *Behaviour Problems in School: a Source Book of Readings*. U. of London Press.

Williams, T. (1977). *All About Me and Think Well*. Schools Council Health Education (Project 5-13). Nelson, Sunbury-on-Thames.

Wilson, E. (1978). *Women and the Welfare State*. Tavistock Press, London.

Wistow, G. and Webb, A. (1980). *Patients First: One Step Backwards for Collaboration?* Loughborough U.

Wolff, P. H. (1965). The development of attention in young infants. *Annals of the New York Academy of Sciences*, 118:815-830.

Wolkind, S. N. (1977). Women who have been 'in care' — psychological and social status during pregnancy. *Journal of Psychology & Psychiatry*, 18:179-182.

Wolkind, S. N. (1979). The Family Research Unit study of child development: I. The setting up of the study. *Child Abuse & Neglect*, 3:819-823.

Wolkind, S., Hall, F. and Kruk, S. (1979). A longitudinal study of child development in single parent families. Final Report *DHSS/SSRC Joint Working Party on Transmitted Deprivation*.

Wolkind, S. N., Hall, F. and Pawlby, S. J. (1977). Individual differences in mothering behaviour: a combined epidemiological and observational approach. In P. J. Graham (1977).

Wolkind, S. N., Kruk, S. and Chaves, L. P. (1976). Childhood separation experiences and psycho-social status in primiparous women: preliminary findings. *British Journal of Psychiatry*, 128:391-396.

Wolkind, S. N. and Rutter, M. (1973). Children who have been 'in care' — an epidemiological study. *Journal of Child Psychology and Psychiatry*, 14:97-105.

Wolkind, S. N. and Zajicek, E. (1981). *Pregnancy: A Psychological and Social Study*. Academic Press, London.

Wynn, M. (1970). *Family Policy*. Penguin, Harmondsworth.

Zajicek, E. and Wolkind, S. N. (1978). Emotional difficulties during and after the first pregnancy in a sample of married women. *Journal of Medical Psychology*, 51:379-385.

Zimmerman, D. H. (1971). The practicalities of rule use. In J. D. Douglas (Ed.). *Understanding Everyday Life*. Routledge and Kegan Paul, London.

INDEX